"This book should be required reading for every current and aspiring politician."

PAUL TAYLOR, executive director, Foodshare Toronto

"An interesting and timely book on what basic income can mean to so many people—a leap from the realm of necessity into the realm of freedom. Jamie Swift and Elaine Power vividly capture the struggles and dreams of the precious working class in Canada, allowing people with experiences of poverty and aspirations for self-betterment to speak for themselves and make themselves heard."

MOHAMMAD FERDOSI, co-author, *Southern Ontario's Basic Income Experience*

"Anyone interested in social justice should read this book. Swift and Power trace the emergence of the idea of a basic income in Canada and globally. They focus on how the Ontario pilot made a real change in the lives of those who participated. Using the words of participants, they tell a story of hope. Some see the cost of a basic income as out of reach. However, reading this book will convince you it would be money well spent!"

WAYNE LEWCHUK, co-author, *Southern Ontario's Basic Income Experience*

"For forty long years, Ayn Rand–blessed politicos have preached that 'the greatest good' belongs to those who achieve the 'greatest gain' (even if by theft or fraud), so 'labour pools' and 'capital flows'— 'efficiently.' But the COVID-19 pandemic—like the Great Depression nearly a century ago—has proven the free market a hoax. There's no way for democratic societies to achieve 'Freedom, Security, Justice,' unless citizens demand that governments return *renminbi* (the people's money) to the people, in part by providing a basic income."

GEORGE ELLIOTT CLARKE, E.J. Pratt Professor of Canadian Literature, University of Toronto

"In this timely contribution, Swift and Power make a powerful case for basic income as a transformative poverty reduction strategy with the potential to reinforce a welfare state apparatus eroded by decades of neoliberal policies. The authors use the personal narratives of former OBIP participants to illustrate in vivid detail how basic income can change the lives of those who receive it for the better."

TOM MCDOWELL, department of politics and public administration, Ryerson University

"The COVID-19 pandemic has surely taught us that we need societal resilience. This book adds to the growing body of evidence that only a basic income as an anchor of a new income distribution system would provide us with that resilience."

GUY STANDING, author of *Basic Income: And How We Can Make It Happen*

"In the not-too-distant future, Canadians will look back and try to remember how we made possible a guarantee that everyone would have an income sufficient to live a modest life with dignity. This wonderful book captures the stories of the tireless activists and real basic income experts—those who tried to survive with the broken social systems of the past. It documents the opportunities lost when Ontario cancelled its prescient basic income guarantee experiment, but it also captures the hope and optimism that will ultimately prevail."

EVELYN FORGET, author of *Basic Income for Canadians: From the COVID-19 Emergency to Financial Security for All*

"This urgent case study brings to life a grassroots movement whose time has come. Swift and Power write passionately from the inside, shining a vital lens on Ontario's fight for basic income."

JOHN GREYSON, queer filmmaker/activist

"In a most touching and compelling manner, the authors underscore the vital role that the Ontario Basic Income Pilot played in the lives of participants. They also identify how a guaranteed livable basic income could help address current economic, social, and health crises, as well as the massive systemic inequality laid bare by COVID-19 and the patchwork of federal, provincial, and municipal responses. In addition to challenging myths and discriminatory attitudes of critics and naysayers of various political persuasions, the authors discuss how everyone will benefit from basic income initiatives, in no small part because of the ways they provide insurance against current and future unpredictable life events."

The Honourable **KIM PATE**, C.M., Senator for Ontario

THE CASE FOR BASIC INCOME

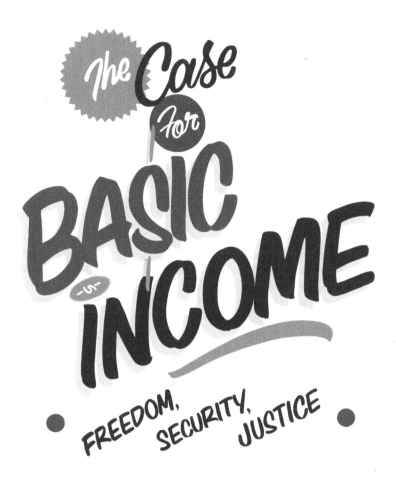

The Case for BASIC INCOME

FREEDOM, SECURITY, JUSTICE

JAMIE SWIFT &
ELAINE POWER

Foreword by
DR. DANIELLE MARTIN

BETWEEN THE LINES
TORONTO

Cataloguing in Publication information available from
Library and Archives Canada · ISBN 9781771135474

Cover design by Pascale Arpin
Back cover photograph by Pamela Cornell
Text design by DEEVE

Printed in Canada

We acknowledge for their financial support of our publishing activities: the Government of Canada; the Canada Council for the Arts; and the Government of Ontario through the Ontario Arts Council, the Ontario Book Publishers Tax Credit program, and Ontario Creates.

To the 4,000 courageous people who took a chance on the Ontario Basic Income Pilot—and whose good faith hopes were shattered when a Progressive Conservative government arbitrarily and prematurely cancelled it.

While poverty persists, there is no true freedom.

—Nelson Mandela

CONTENTS

FOREWORD
Dr. Danielle Martin

Medicine is a social science, and politics is nothing else but medicine on a large scale.

—Rudolf Virchow

At the height of the first wave of the COVID-19 pandemic, I was worried about a lot of people.

As a family doctor, I knew that the impact of the virus would be felt in different ways by different patients in my practice. An 86-year-old retired lawyer was living alone and found himself cut off from his kids, grandkids, and social circle. He knew he was at higher risk of getting seriously ill, but longed for the simple pleasure of a meal with friends or a hug from a loved one. A young woman with a history of anxiety, pregnant with her first baby, was terrified of giving birth in the hospital, knowing that people with the virus were being cared for in the same building.

But I kept thinking about that dance teacher.

I knew she owned a small business teaching ballroom dancing and how much she loved it. And I knew that when the lockdown came and her studio was closed indefinitely, this extroverted and expressive woman with a huge smile would be hanging by a thread. I called her to check in. "I'm okay," she assured me as soon as she picked up the phone. "I'm on the CERB."

At that moment, the Canada Emergency Response Benefit and the Canada Emergency Wage Subsidy were stabilizing the incomes of tens of thousands of Canadians, preventing them from losing their housing and enabling them to put food on the table. The impact on people's lives was obvious—but what may have been less obvious to some was the impact on their health.

In Canada, we pride ourselves on having designed systems of essential health services that are available to everyone. Those systems are deeply imperfect, but the uncoupling of health insurance from being employed is still a powerful force for health. At the height of the pandemic, as at all other times, Canadians could access necessary testing, physician visits, and, if necessary, hospital and even ICU care without having to worry about whether their insurance would cover it or whether they would have to take out a second mortgage to pay for their care.

But the CERB was as much an investment in health as any of those systems. More than anything we do for people in operating rooms or clinics, in chemotherapy suites or with high-tech diagnostic machines, reducing or ending poverty has always been the best investment we can make in health. Children born into low-income families start out with worse health than those born into high-income families; those differences persist throughout their lives and then are passed on to their own children. From lower birth weights to higher rates of asthma, more chronic disease to shorter life expectancy, poverty makes people sick.

And as we keep learning, sometimes at great human cost, poverty is only one facet of a complex set of social dynamics that shape health. Being a woman, a racialized person, a worker in a precarious job in the gig economy, a person with a disability—these factors and others intersect with people's experiences of poverty and make it even harder to live to the fullest.

To protect people from the full blow of economic insecurity is to protect their housing, their nutritional status, their ability to fill their prescriptions for chronic disease, their sense of stability, and—through all those channels and more—their mental and physical health. The CERB was an imperfect experiment in a Basic Income, just as the Canada Child Benefit, Old Age Security, and the Guaranteed Income

Supplement have all been. And like those programs, the CERB stood like an antiviral shield between people such as that dance teacher and ill health.

In *The Case for Basic Income: Freedom, Security, Justice*, Jamie Swift and Elaine Power document the many powerful arguments in support of a Basic Income guarantee. The simplicity of its design, which appeals across the political spectrum. The humanity of releasing people from the grinding work of filling out forms, standing in line, and filling out more forms to prove their "worthiness." The uncoupling of gendered definitions of labour from the ability to feed one's family. The higher-order principles of justice and community that are shifting in the gig economy. The book also honours the narratives of so many people whose advocacy has paved the route to the ongoing conversation about BI in Canada. All those who are joining the global movement in support of "freedom from want" stand on the shoulders of the many giants whose stories are honoured in these chapters.

Neither money nor health is an end in itself. Both are building blocks for a meaningful life. As the authors point out in Chapter 8, sometimes a basic income allows people to imagine different forms of work, to engage in caregiving for children or elders, or to clear some of the mind-space previously filled with preoccupations about which bills to pay in what order. Like health, financial security is an invisible building block for the ways in which we want to participate in our communities. For many decades, that conversation sat outside much of mainstream political debate. But in a heartbeat, with the arrival of the global pandemic of 2020, something shifted. It is now hard to imagine that we can ever go back to traditional models of social assistance and income support.

My patient weathered the storm of COVID-19. She didn't have much left at the end of the month, but when the rug was pulled out from under her in the midst of a national lockdown, she didn't lose her health insurance and she didn't lose her home. Just as that health insurance had been uncoupled from her employment because of medicare, her income security had been similarly uncoupled from her employment because of a new income security program that allowed her to assure me "I'm okay." That simplicity and decency of spirit is what underpins strong social programs like medicare and, as we begin to heal from the pandemic, the Basic Income guarantee that we must now put in place for all Canadians.

Dr. Danielle Martin is a family physician in Toronto, founder of Canadian Doctors for Medicare, and an advocate for health equity and health system improvement.

ON BASIC INCOME
A poem by
George Elliott Clarke
2020

The economy's an abyss whose bottom is a grave,
And each tightrope walker wobbles as a mere wage-slave.
And those who freefall, screaming, screeching, as they go,
Clutching for handholds or toeholds, only hope to slow
Their plummet to a crashing or a smashing that'll whack
Wallet and skull, household and heart, for debt's the crack—
The airy nothing through which poor and jobless catapult—
Down, down, down, to either suicide or homicide result.

Capitalism insists each citizen's alone
To bargain with Fate and to barter blood and bone—
To work the best deal each can despite layoff
Or disease, bankruptcy or injury, and to play off
Labourer against labourer, to suffer or succeed,
As individuals, whatever shall be the collective need.
But yet a contradiction is ever starkly evident:
Businesses can't sell products to customers indigent.

No matter how rich the rich, the people own greater riches—
For our tax dollars are ours to fulfil all our wishes.
Why not weave ourselves a mass, protective web
To catch all who tumble, whether the poor or pleb,
Off the high-wire of capitalist high-jinks and low-down tricks,
The badly frayed ropes and the greasy balancing sticks.
Why not grant ourselves—because the people's money's ours—
Platforms to stand on, cushions to land on, fail-safe moors?

Time to paraphrase the bards John Lennon and Yoko Ono!
Basic Income is ours; we can have it; purely pro bono—
If we want it. We can have it if we want it—just like health care,
U.I., the baby bonus, public transit, public schools, welfare. . . .
There's no end to what we can do to improve our lives
Against all odds, if we'll stand as one against capitalist thieves.
Basic Income is the price of bottom-line social equality:
So that all can ascend—escaping Poverty's gravity.

George Elliott Clarke started as a songwriter, and he has worked with opera composers, as well as blues, gospel, folk, and rap. He was the fourth Poet Laureate of Toronto (2012–15) and the seventh Parliamentary Canadian Poet Laureate (2016–17). He has published twenty-six works of poetry since 1983, plus three books in Chinese, Italian, and Romanian. A pioneering scholar of African-Canadian literature at the University of Toronto, Clarke has taught at Duke, UBC, McGill, and Harvard. He is a seventh-generation Afro-Métis of Nova Scotia.

ACKNOWLEDGEMENTS

We wish to thank the people who participated in the Ontario Basic Income Pilot, both those whose stories are featured here and others who shared their experiences.

Big thanks to all the members of the Kingston Action Group for a Basic Income Guarantee, past and present, who provided support and inspiration. Toni Pickard, known jocularly as "Fearless Leader," merits particular mention—as do the hundreds of Basic Income activists across Canada and around the world who have taken their own inspiration from sociologist Barbara Wootton (a.k.a. Baroness Wootton of Abinger) who pointed out so memorably that "it is from the champions of the impossible rather than the slaves of the possible that evolution draws its creative force."

For kind hospitality we thank Ruth Frager and Don Wells, Ian McKay and Rob Vanderheyden, Susan Gottheil and Len Prepas, Sandra Hardy and Doug Smith, Rob Clarke and Ferne Cristall, Sonya Swift and Simon Greenland-Smith—otherwise known as "cadgees." Thank you to Kathleen Power and Janette Haase for expert transcription of audio interviews.

Thanks also to Bob Chodos and Susan Joanis for their stalwart editing. Books never take final shape without the sharp-eyed scrutiny of experienced editors. What follows owes much to Bob and Susan. And a tip of our hats to Claire Stewart and Janet Pearse, both of whom lived with this book for a good long time.

Elaine Power is supported in part by funding from the Social Sciences and Humanities Research Council.

INTRODUCTION

The good we secure for ourselves is precarious and uncertain until it is secured for all of us and incorporated into our common life.

—Jane Addams, 1892

Captain Ahab. Nurse Ratched. Darth Vader. Villains have long stalked the pages of fiction and cinema screens. Irredeemable nasties, symbolizing evil. One villain stands out, however, because he eventually saw the light. He became a good guy after seeing the error of his ways.

His creator caught the spirit of his times so successfully that both his name and that of his character became catchwords—we talk about the "Dickensian" era and someone who is being a "Scrooge." Charles Dickens hammered away at the spirit of greed during the "Hungry Forties" of the nineteenth century. The protagonist of the massively successful 1843 novella *A Christmas Carol* was, of course, Ebenezer Scrooge—"a squeezing, wrenching, grasping, scraping, clutching, covetous old sinner."

It was the heyday of unrestrained free-market individualism in England, cradle of capitalism. Dickens used a half-dozen adjectives to capture the era's zeitgeist. The "undeserving poor" were paupers without jobs, whom the state forced into prisons called "workhouses"—the conditions of which were purposely made as grim as possible since their aim was to discourage people from claiming poor relief.

In *A Christmas Carol*, a couple of do-gooder businessmen approach Mr. Scrooge, a successful entrepreneur, seeking a Christmas donation to help those paupers still "outside," resisting the workhouse. The miserly capitalist responds, "Are there no prisons? . . . And the union workhouses, are they still in operation?" When told that these institutions were still working with full vigour but many poor people would rather die than enter, Scrooge famously replies, "If they would rather die, then they'd better do so at once and decrease the surplus population."

Of course, things have changed since the Hungry Forties. Capitalism is constantly adapting over time as social movements work to dull its sharp edges. Yet there remain two constants, both amplified by the pandemic that struck the world in 2020. One is that many are excluded, left in poverty and hunger, just as they were in the 1840s. Hunger, rebranded food insecurity, persists in Canada today.

Some two centuries after the industrial revolution was transforming England, the 2020 pandemic offered a mirror and a spotlight, highlighting our society's brokenness. Around the world, COVID-19, a new disease caused by a novel coronavirus, consistently took its highest toll in poor communities. In Canada, the disease ravaged neighbourhoods where racialized people, many working in precarious jobs, are crowded into inadequate apartments.

The word *vulnerable* became common currency, particularly with respect to overcrowded and underfunded institutions housing senior citizens (who, it was quickly discovered, were more likely to succumb to the disease). Three of the outfits that dominate Ontario's private-sector nursing homes (Sienna, Extendicare, and Chartwell) had disproportionately high numbers of COVID-19 cases. They also, over the ten years leading up to the pandemic, had paid their shareholders over \$1.5 billion in dividends.[1]

A *Canadian Medical Association Journal* study, published before the second COVID wave hit, cited a dozen previous academic probes showing the higher prevalence of inferior care and mortality in profit-driven institutions. The study's own conclusions confirmed that this was the case during the 2020 pandemic in Ontario. For-profit status meant more outbreaks and deaths, though the McMaster University authors were careful to point out that private-sector institutions also tended to be older and more crowded.[2] They did not discuss the way the $1.5 billion payout reflected management priorities favouring shareholder satisfaction over much-needed facility upgrading for vulnerable seniors, often warehoused four to a room.

Aside from persistent poverty amidst overflowing wealth, the other durable feature of capitalism is its emphasis on *freedom*. Everyone favours freedom. Laudable though it surely is, freedom is nevertheless contested terrain, meaning different things to different people.

Free-market fundamentalist Milton Friedman[*] had since the 1960s been instrumental in persuading politicians and pundits of his interpretation of freedom. As early as 1962, the influential right-wing economist argued that true liberty means freedom from government regulation and freedom for capitalists to spend their money where, when, and how they desire. He insisted that "underlying most arguments against the free market is a lack of belief in freedom itself."[3]

Decades of rising inequality since then have exposed free-market fundamentalism, promoted so successfully by Milton Friedman and his acolytes, as a tragic failure. This book examines how a livable, obligation-free Basic Income, actually an old idea, offers a new way to promote a different interpretation of freedom—freedom writ large. From Thomas Paine in the eighteenth century to Karl Polanyi in the twentieth, some social analysts have insisted that the economy cannot be cut off from its social roots, that we owe our wealth and well-being to society and to one another. That we all have a right to a fair share.

"It is not charity but a right, not bounty but justice, that I am pleading for," wrote Paine, a leading figure in the American and French revolutions.[4] He supported a universal, no-strings-attached cash payment.

---

[*] A User's Guide to *The Case for Basic Income* starts on page 193. There you will find more information about some of the people (like Milton Friedman), concepts (like market fundamentalism), and organizations we refer to in this book.

The economic historian and social philosopher Karl Polanyi put forward a radical critique of free-market ideas and their socially corrosive consequences, laying out his complex understanding of the political origins of our times in his 1944 masterwork *The Great Transformation.* For Polanyi, allowing this thing called the market to take a primary role in organizing society was a historical aberration, unknown in the history of human endeavour before the late eighteenth century and the days of Dickens that followed. Polanyi would have seen Basic Income as part of an effort to re-embed markets in society and democratize prosperity.

It is our contention that the increasing chorus of voices supporting a livable Basic Income, amplified in the wake of the 2020 pandemic, is part of the double movement Polanyi talked about that re-embeds the economy in society: it would enhance freedom while also getting at the root of poverty: people not having sufficient money to live in dignity.

The Basic Income Earth Network (BIEN) was founded in the 1980s. Since then, many groups with a smaller geographical focus have formed, including the Basic Income Canada Network (BICN) and the Ontario Basic Income Network (OBIN). In 2013, the authors helped to launch the Kingston Action Group for a Basic Income Guarantee, based in Kingston, Ontario.

In 2015, a member of the Kingston Action Group, professor emerita Roberta Hamilton, met with James Janeiro, lead social policy advisor to then Ontario Premier Kathleen Wynne and an ardent Basic Income supporter. We would later tell ourselves that we had helped persuade Ontario's Liberal government to launch a Basic Income pilot project. We definitely succeeded in persuading Kingston City Council to unanimously support Basic Income, making our town the first in Canada to make this move. Given that the motion carried no financial costs, we had no illusions that the support, from across the local political spectrum, was more than symbolic; however, symbolism matters in politics. It also made us feel good, and in a long-haul political struggle, morale matters too.

After months of painstaking drafting by committee, we also concocted what we called, perhaps presumptuously, a "Charter" outlining our vision. The document calls for more than Basic Income, insisting that to be meaningful, unconditional Basic Income must be complemented by other measures to counter the broad effects of free-market fundamentalism. For example, the group identified the following additional needs, among others:

- Nonmarket housing (the private sector having shown itself incapable of building affordable shelter)
- Comprehensive, publicly funded child care and medication (both essential), and
- Higher taxes on capital gains, along with introduction of an inheritance tax (key elements in moving towards a fair taxation regime).

This book examines the politics of Basic Income, scrutinizing the way that a sclerosis of political imagination has paralyzed important parts of the left. Many potential allies worry that a Basic Income would somehow automatically forestall moves to extend public provision to crucial areas like those listed above. We also examine the stubborn sacralization of labour that prevents people more broadly from understanding how Basic Income would promote a decent society. For example, we seek to elucidate the following:

- Paid jobs are quite different from so much socially indispensable caring work—indeed, many that are highly paid are also quite useless (e.g., currency speculators, "strategic" communications types).
- The rise of precarious work calls for a thoroughgoing shakeup of labour regulation and strengthening of organized labour. Trade unions have for two centuries been indispensable—achieving shorter hours, better pay, and safer working conditions while promoting public policies for the common good. But labour has suffered catastrophic setbacks in recent decades.
- Finally, like many Basic Income supporters, we wonder about the coming impact of artificial intelligence and virtually worker-free factories.

We recount stories of people who briefly received a Basic Income as part of the 2017–19 Ontario Basic Income Pilot project, which was cut short by a newly elected government that had promised to carry the pilot through to its end. These stories speak their own truth about so much poverty in such an abundant country. We do *not* attempt to unravel Basic Income's tricky policy knots. If ever a proposal was subject to the old saw "the devil is in the details," Basic Income would be it, particularly in Canada with its overlapping—and often confounding—federal-provincial jurisdictional issues.

As we were starting to write this manuscript in early 2020, the pandemic arrived. Suddenly the overwhelming need for a Basic Income floor became obvious to most Canadians. Millions of jobs melted away, leaving workers with no income. Canada's Employment Insurance system, decimated by years of cuts, its surpluses diverted to pay down debt, was exposed as a sham.

The mass anxiety that accompanied the pandemic featured what we initially thought of as the "democratization" of insecurity. This gave us hope. Perhaps the sweeping wave of insecurity would lead to a widespread recognition that, for so many, insecurity had long been a way of life. Perhaps the democratization of insecurity would at last lead to the democratization of income security—in the form of a Basic Income.

Sure enough, Ottawa implemented the Canada Emergency Response Benefit. CERB paid jobless people $500 per week until it was replaced by similar measures. Talk of Basic Income, long confined to circles of apparently eccentric idealists like ourselves, popped up like so many rainforest mushrooms. Metaphors matter. The tired old "social safety net," so often described as frayed, now suggests people falling into an abyss. Maybe it is time for a firm Basic Income—a solid floor below which no one can fall.

Shortly after the pandemic hit, the *Financial Times* stated baldly that forty years of free-market fundamentalism needed to end. The world's business paper of record editorialized that "radical reforms" were required. These included "policies until recently considered eccentric, such as Basic Income and wealth taxes" that would have to be placed on the table. The paper acknowledged that such measures were "taboo-breaking,"[5] reflecting the way that more taxation and more robust public provision had for decades been regarded as laughable within the corridors of state and corporate power.

After neoliberal politics had so long hammered home the "you're-on-your-own" message, corporate titans and politicians were doing a sudden about-face. Cries of "we're all in this together" and "all hands on deck" were accompanied by the startling recognition that the women struggling to make ends meet as personal support workers (PSWs) were "heroes." Many were racialized newcomers who kept on working as nursing home residents for whom they had been providing intimate care started to die around them.

After decades of unquestioned pursuit of profit, a sub-microscopic infectious agent had suddenly cast a harsh light on the need for mutual survival. Public health. The common good. The collective ways we look after and care for one another. Long invisible low-wage workers who had been taken for granted—grocery store clerks, cleaners, PSWs, nurses, migrant farm workers, truckers, and so many others—enjoyed a brief flash of public recognition (though one newspaper's hero list also included bank managers).[6]

And yet, even as transparent plexiglass walls went up to help curtail the disease, a cashier at a Kingston Loblaws supermarket was still working while receiving chemotherapy treatment, her immune system dangerously compromised. For a few weeks, essential workers like her got a two-dollar-per-hour bonus. But Canada's largest food and drug retailer quickly took it away even though she was, presumably, still essential. The *Financial Times* put it succinctly: "Despite inspirational calls for national mobilization, we are not really all in this together."[7]

When free markets do not improve society's welfare, they can be said to fail. What is the purpose of markets unless they are rooted in society and are beneficial to all? Public policy is required to address these inherent shortcomings.

The 2020 pandemic exposed tragic market failure in Canada. The overwhelming majority of vulnerable elderly people left to die were living in so-called long-term care facilities. To call them "homes" would be a cruel hoax. The lethal places exemplify a market mentality that treats care, a basic human need, as a commodity:

- By June 2020, Sienna Living, one of the dominant businesses in the expanding sector, was ravaged by the disease. The provincial Ministry of Long-Term Care reported that 291 of its residents and three staff members had died of COVID-19. The federal government deployed the armed forces to two Sienna buildings to help deal with the catastrophe.[8] Two of its top managers resigned in disgrace.
- By Canada Day, seventy-eight residents of a Pickering, Ontario, long-term care facility (managed by the sprawling Extendicare firm, with net 2019 earnings of $28.6 million) had also died of COVID-19. One in three of the vulnerable customers had perished at the 233-bed place, where the military once again had to be summoned.[9]
- By October 2020, Ontario was reporting 1,909 deaths among residents in long-term care facilities. At the height of the pandemic's first wave, the overall case fatality rate was 28.4 percent.[10] Eight of the workers who had been trying to look after them had also died.[11] They were, it seemed, casualties of market failure.

In its formal legal defence against a class-action suit brought by the families of people in long-term care who were dead or had been sickened by this new plague, Ontario's government—which licenses, inspects, funds, and regulates these institutions—argued that no one backing the suit had "suffered any loss or damages."

The government then introduced Bill 218, indemnifying for-profit long-term care homes from liability for negligence during the COVID-19 pandemic. Premier Doug Ford had an abiding faith in the civilizing arts of commerce. While campaigning back in 2018, Ford had explained, "I believe in letting the market dictate."[12]

Basic Income offers one important path out of the let-the-market-decide mindset. We believe it is an idea whose time has come. It would strengthen freedom. Freedom to say no to a job that is poorly paid, boring, or simply nasty. Freedom to work caring for a relative or friend. Freedom to exit an abusive relationship. Freedom to try something new, like a small business. Freedom to do socially and culturally vital work that is unpaid or underpaid. Freedom from bureaucratic snooping by welfare officials. Freedom, to paraphrase Bertrand Russell, to be lazy.

As the pacifist philosopher wrote in 1932, "I want to say, in all seriousness, that a great deal of harm is being done in the modern world by belief in the virtuousness of work, and that the road to happiness and prosperity lies in an organized diminution of work."[13]

CHAPTER 1

A GOOD IDEA GOES VIRAL[1]

COVID-19 has revealed for all of us the cracks in our economic situation in Canada. Many people cannot pay their rent and can scarcely afford food. Now is the time to make a systemic change in the system that will remove the stigma of being poor and encourage a more equitable society.

—Rev. Lois Wilson, former United Church
Moderator and senator

When all this is over, it is to be hoped that more of us will have internalized the lies and the hidden contradictions that keep capitalism afloat, that more of us will remember that when the virus hit us, capitalism tested positive.

—Harry Glasbeek, Professor Emeritus and
Senior Scholar, Osgoode Hall Law School

THE CRACKS REVEALED

It took ten years for Leonard Cohen to write "Anthem," a hopeful song that featured on his otherwise foreboding 1992 album *The Future.* The song's chorus makes his hope clear. "There is a crack in everything, that's how the light gets in." For the profoundly spiritual artist, the light represents repentance, return, and resurrection. It also exposes "the brokenness of things."[2] In 2020 the COVID-19 pandemic, what earlier generations would have called a plague, showed how very broken things have been all over the world. Canada was no exception. The pandemic shone a light on some serious cracks indeed.

First, we saw that many of the people doing what we suddenly recognized as the most essential work—those in all aspects of health care (including cleaners and personal support workers), the food supply chain (from farm workers to grocery store employees) and the transportation sector (truck drivers, bus drivers)—work for low wages with few if any benefits. These people were suddenly considered "heroes." A light was now shining on the significant degree to which the smooth functioning of our society depends on people doing precarious, undervalued, and underpaid work.

Next, the plague cast racial inequalities into stark relief. It soon became clear that the pandemic was sickening and killing visible minorities in a wildly disproportionate manner. In Canada's largest city, 80 percent of COVID cases involved racialized people—who make up only 50 percent of Toronto's population.

Soon we learned that this was not only a racial plague; it was also a class plague. Fully half of COVID cases in Toronto involved people living in poverty, yet less than a third of Torontonians fall into that category. As part of this particular revelation, the disease cast a cold light on the scandalous housing situation in big cities, where so many low-income people cannot afford decent shelter. More than a quarter of COVID victims in Toronto lived in households with five or more people.[3]

And then, we see how all these strands are connected and interwoven. The families living in households with five or more people? They are generally not white. The people working as farm labourers, cleaners, personal support workers? They are also generally not white. These jobs are low-paying, involving hourly wages as opposed to salaries, along with the commensurate lack of benefits. So, we know that the people doing these jobs—the primarily racialized workers—are also low-income people.

Yet these same jobs had now been revealed as essential—essential to food production and distribution, to looking after the sick. The people performing these jobs had to keep working; everyone relies on them for their basic needs. Moreover, they could not perform these jobs from home; they would have to come in to work, thereby exposing themselves to additional risk. Additionally, as low-income people, they would tend to rely on public transportation and therefore have to expose themselves even further just to get to work.

Finally, we see how COVID-19 is not only a racial and class plague but also a gender plague. Another sector of jobs was revealed to be *non*-essential—jobs related to the hospitality industry; for example, jobs in hotels and restaurants. These jobs, also precarious and low-paying, were primarily held by women, who were laid off in staggering numbers—just one aspect of the gendered nature of this pandemic.

The Canadian Institute for Health Information reported that some ten thousand long-term care workers were infected. Nine died, along with thousands of elderly adults they looked after. Of the 8,454 Canadians dead from COVID-19 by late June, some 6,000 lived in long-term care institutions. While Canada's overall COVID-19 mortality rate was relatively low compared with the proportions in other OECD countries, we had the highest proportion of deaths occurring in long-term care. LTC residents accounted for four of five reported COVID-19 deaths in Canada, compared with an average of less than two in five LTC deaths in other OECD countries.[4]

Toronto's North St. Jamestown, home to personal support and retail workers as well as domestic servants and cleaners living in overcrowded apartments, was a raging COVID-19 hotspot, with 698 cases per 100,000 people in late May. For legions of these precarious service-sector workers, the notion of self-isolating by working from home was an absurd impossibility.

A short stroll north across Bloor Street one finds the lavishly wealthy Rosedale–Moore Park district. It had 72 cases per 100,000.[5] One Dale Avenue house that sold for $5.2 million at the height of the pandemic featured a nanny suite with a separate entrance, parking for four cars, and an in-ground pool on a 6,000-square-foot lot.[6] Rosedale hedge fund managers and others could, it seems, easily heed the advice of the authorities by working from their opulent homes.

There was nothing new in a plague having differential effects on rich and poor areas. A century earlier, during the Spanish flu pandemic of 1918–20, there was a broad popular and scientific consensus that "the flu hit the rich and the poor alike." Yet India's death rate was forty times higher than that of Denmark. In Norway, the flu killed most efficiently in Oslo's working-class districts. Chicago death rates were also highest among the unemployed and poor. People in crowded cities suffered more than those in the countryside.[7]

While doctors extolled the virtues of sunshine and pure air, working-class families living in slum areas not far from Queen's Park in Toronto inhabited overcrowded, vermin-infested row houses. Many had a single tap or an outside stand pipe. Toilets that did exist were often blocked in summer, frozen in winter. The air was choked by factory emissions and coal smoke. After the Spanish flu subsided, these were the conditions described in a report for the city conducted by Lieutenant-Governor Dr. Herbert Bruce.

The Bruce Report concluded by pointing to factors familiar to St. Jamestown residents when the COVID-19 crisis hit one hundred years later:

> Housing conditions are bad because there are many families which cannot earn enough to pay for decent and healthful dwellings. In the lowest income groups of society, the insecurity of employment and the inadequacy of wages do not permit the payment of rentals much in excess of $10 to $15 per month in good times.[8]

Similarly, during the COVID-19 crisis a century later, slogans such as "we're all in this together" quickly emerged. The virus "does not discriminate," maintained British cabinet minister Michael Gove.[9] However, Father Augusto Zampini, adjunct secretary for Pope Francis's COVID-19 response commission, had a different metaphor, one more

congruent with the social inequities that pandemics expose and reinforce. "We are all in the same storm, but we're in different boats. Those
who have big boats—with houses, income, and food—might get a little
seasick but don't worry about dying," he explained. "But other people
are in tiny little boats, some with oars and some just completely at the
whim of the giant waves."[10]

The plague of 2020 ravaged poor neighbourhoods. It was an ail-
ment of inequality, as are diseases like diabetes, hypertension, and
cardiovascular conditions familiar to so many disadvantaged Canadians
and their communities. The devastation was not inevitable. But it was
utterly predictable. In early March, just before the term COVID had
become common parlance, journalist André Picard wrote,

> Protecting seniors, particularly those in institutional care,
> from infection and death is an enormous challenge. So too is
> protecting staff, who work tirelessly and intimately with their
> charges. . . . Complicating the response is that many workers
> juggle shifts between various facilities, and their pay and ben-
> efits are so abysmal that they are reluctant to take time off if
> they are sick.[11]

Some people clean up other people's messes. Some don't. The pandemic tragedy had widened many a crack. The light got in.

NORMALIZED INSECURITY AND HELICOPTER MONEY

Late in the winter of 2020, it was dawning on Canadians that the
COVID-19 crisis was starting to shake things up in unimagined ways. A
Kingston man wheeled a supermarket cart groaning under the weight
of water, five cases of twenty-four plastic bottles. As he loaded it into
his late-model SUV, he was asked why he was buying so much—"Lots
of water in the tap?" His reply didn't catch the irony. It was sincere,
clearly anxious: "I *hope* so."

Gnawing insecurity abounded everywhere, daily certainties suddenly evaporating. Would there be enough food? How about public transit? Passing encounters with strangers in stores? What if they took the bus to get there? Jobs evaporated. Pop-up roadside signs blinked the insistent message "Stay Safe, Stay Home," municipal authorities carelessly assuming it was possible for everyone to do so. The stress pandemic quickly spread, the anxiety in part provoked by the sense that, suddenly, things seemed out of control.

For millions of Canadians who depend on precarious jobs or, even worse, social assistance, the stress of lives being out of control is hardly new. It's the commonplace stuff of daily life. Forget about hoarding food, or anything else for that matter. Providing food generates anxiety every single day. With the unexpected arrival of COVID generating mass anxiety, Canadians experienced what could be described as the normalization of insecurity. Unemployment skyrocketed as businesses from retailers to airlines laid off workers *en masse*.

Many could hope that the insecurity would, in the fullness of time, pass as things returned to normal. In the interim, the threat of Depression-level joblessness—coupled with a collapse of consumer spending—quickly gave rise to what Milton Friedman called, in a different context, "helicopter money," the image being that of a government helicopter hovering around tossing thousand-dollar bills onto people. The famous right-wing economist had a gift for metaphor.

In Canada, helicopter money took the form of public assistance to the unemployed as well as some underemployed gig and part-time precarious workers through the Canada Emergency Response Benefit (CERB), introduced in mid-March. By mid-April, 6.7 million Canadians had applied for either EI or CERB benefits; by early May, that figure had climbed to almost eight million.[12]

The launch of CERB demonstrated that previously inconceivable amounts of money could be mustered for social programs when the political will is strong. The obvious need for CERB exposed the utter inadequacy of the Employment Insurance (EI) system—and indeed the country's entire income security system. The speed of the emergency aid demonstrated that it is possible to do something that would have been unthinkable when market fundamentalism had reigned supreme, colonizing the imagination of the country's political class. The CERB lasted for months, supporting people in need, amounting to just the sort of no-strings-attached Basic Income that had already been gaining worldwide attention in the period before the pandemic.

The CERB amounted to a huge precedent, yet it did not reach everyone. It still left out those who had little or no "labour market attachment." Thus, 16 percent of jobless Canadians, about 1.4 million people, did not qualify either for the CERB or for EI. There are three main reasons why so many were excluded. They either: were out of work before March 15 but did not qualify for EI, did not meet the threshold of having made $5,000 in the past twelve months, or had quit their jobs recently.[13]

By focusing on people who had paid employment, the Canada Emergency Response Benefit maintained the stark division between the so-called deserving and undeserving, long a bedrock of income security programs. The "deserving" receive benefits from Employment Insurance, the Canada Pension Plan, Old Age Security, and the Guaranteed Income Supplement. The "undeserving" get miserly benefits in the form of social assistance, and as a consequence are stigmatized and subjected to suspicion and surveillance in the form of hundreds of rules. It's what many low-income people refer to as "the system."

No amount of established evidence about the costs of keeping social assistance recipients trapped in poverty—or the unfairness of a broken, punitive system—seems to change the dominant view. Twenty-first-century income security remains mired in nineteenth-century thinking—bourgeois moral values championing employment and, for those unable to work for pay, the workhouse. Or welfare.

There were other problems with CERB. It contained a strong disincentive for part-time employment: once a worker made more than $1,000 per month, CERB benefits were cut off. And laid-off workers could not refuse work and continue to collect CERB, even if they feared for their own or their loved ones' health and well-being. Nevertheless,

Basic Income proponents immediately noted that CERB was proof that Canada could bring in a no-strings-attached income floor. As they had been arguing for years, Canada already has a precedent for no-obligation, guaranteed benefits—except that people qualify for the universal Old Age Security and the means-tested Guaranteed Income Supplement only when they reach their later years.

THE 2010s: BASIC INCOME GAINS MOMENTUM

Most Basic Income advocates are aware that Basic Income can seem utopian and impractical in political cultures such as Canada's. Charity has stubborn traction, along with the shopworn nostrum "a hand up, not a handout." Such approaches appeal to widespread sympathy, reinforcing individualism. Plucky, striving folk just need a little bit of a boost.

Against this background, Basic Income campaigners often focus on poverty. Its elimination is an ambitious yet achievable goal in rich countries. With its insistence on seeing poverty as being about a lack of cash rather than a lack of character and making unconditional money available to all, Basic Income transcends conventional approaches to poverty. But a full-blown critique of treating labour as a commodity can seem a bit too radical. It suggests putting an end to that glorified thing known as "work." Even as wages stagnate, insecurity and inequality rise, and the labour market consistently fails to distribute prosperity, many cling to the idea that the ticket out of poverty is a job. As attention to Basic Income mounted in the 2010s, this was showing signs of changing.

It was a watershed period for thoroughgoing examinations of Basic Income by supporters. Guy Standing, whose pioneering book on precarious workers (*The Precariat: The New Dangerous Class*) had appeared in 2011, came out with *Basic Income: And How We Can Make It Happen* in 2017. Standing had established himself as a world leader in promoting Basic Income, spending nearly as much time in airports and hotels as he did at home. Along with the Flemish academic Philippe Van

Parijs, Standing had helped initiate the Basic Income Earth Network in 1986 (Van Parijs and Standing, both over seventy by 2021, were in it for the long haul). In 2017, Van Parijs co-authored *Basic Income: A Radical Proposal for a Free Society and a Sane Economy*, the most comprehensive analysis of the history and politics of Basic Income.

The Dutch writer Rutger Bregman's provocative and wildly successful *Utopia for Realists: The Case for a Universal Basic Income, Open Borders and a 15-Hour Workweek* included an important observation about just how stubbornly we can cling to fixed ideas such as the sanctity of paid labour. Citing the social psychologist Leon Festinger on cognitive dissonance, Bregman attacked the idea that free money makes people lazy. But he recognized the magnetic power of ideas, however outmoded: "When reality clashes with our deepest convictions, we'd rather recalibrate reality than amend our worldview. Not only that, we become even more rigid in our beliefs than before." Bregman, a clever writer and popularizer of complex ideas, went on to insist that old ideas are not immutable. They can be changed. "The question is *how*," he wrote four years before the 2020 plague. "Sudden shocks can work wonders."[14]

The prominent economic historian Adam Tooze observed that during the global financial meltdown of 2008, "We came as close as we have ever come in history to a total cardiac arrest, not just of the American economy, but the entire world economy."[15] The crisis was certainly strong enough to give market fundamentalism a shakeup, although governments that had long preached austerity for the citizenry were still quick to reward the bankers and speculators with an overdose of public money, even though their freebooting casino capitalism had set the economic earthquake in motion in the first place.

Rewarding greed and incompetence did not go unnoticed. The aftershocks included the Occupy movement of 2011 and the wild popularity of the slogan "We are the 99 percent!" It identified the overprivileged, overpaid 1 percent, bringing inequality into sharp focus. The idea came largely from Vancouver-based *Adbusters* founder Kalle Lasn, who worried about a "dark age coming for humanity."[16]

Bregman, the Dutch proponent of a radical Basic Income, joined the chorus targeting the 1 percent. He pointed to high-frequency traders, lobbyists, and corporate tax accountants—people who don't create wealth but whose jobs "mostly just shift it around." His picture of corrosive capitalism included law firms that buy up patents they have no intention of using, looking forward to the possibility of suing someone else for patent infringement. Bregman counterposed this sort of economic activity to the important yet undervalued work done by people such as garbage collectors, teachers, and nurses.[17]

The 2008 global meltdown cast a cold light on the brokenness of things, liquidating countless jobs and billions of dollars in personal savings. The intellectual fallout also included one of those books whose gravitas is irrefutable proof of any era's malaise. The French economist Thomas Piketty's bestselling 2013 doorstop of a book, *Capital in the Twenty-First Century*, clearly struck a chord. He showed that the gains that middle-income earners enjoyed in the three decades after 1950 were a historical anomaly. Capitalism has always tended to concentrate the gains of economic growth at the very top, perpetuating or increasing inequality. The so-called long boom of the postwar period was characterized by unprecedented taxes on capital and government control of wealth. This ended with the market fundamentalist onslaught after 1980. From there, the gains of wage earners ceased.

It was no accident that after 2010, Canadian political parties started to talk ceaselessly about "the middle class." Not the poor, mind. Their ox had never stopped being gored. The 2018 World Inequality Report by Piketty and four other economists showed that Canada's private wealth more than doubled between 1970 and 2016. Grouping Canada with the United States (where inequality "exploded"), the report indicated the top 10 percent of people received 34 percent of the national wealth in 1980. By 2016, this share had risen to 47 percent. Since the early 1980s, the income share of the top 1 percent had steadily increased in Anglo-Saxon countries, after its historically unique decline throughout the first part of the twentieth century. Oxfam's 2017 annual inequality numbers included a striking Canadian fact: Two Canadian billionaire businessmen (Galen Weston and David Thomson) had the same amount of wealth as the poorest 30 percent of the country.[18] It seems that Kalle Lasn had a point.

JOSEPHINE GREY AND THE LEAP DEBATE

During the 2015 federal election campaign, a group of prominent Canadian activists released a document they called the LEAP manifesto. It was an attempt to nudge the NDP, then led by centrist and former Liberal Tom Mulcair, to the left. Leonard Cohen was prominent among the celebrities who signed on. The call for radically egalitarian change included a keep-the-oil-in-the ground demand coupled with catchy turns of phrase, such as: "A Canada based on caring for the earth and one another."

The LEAP's principal organizers included the filmmaker and former television host Avi Lewis. The energetic activist, always intrigued by the shifting currents of radical thinking, moderated a 2017 Toronto debate, "Basic Income: A Way Forward for the Left?" The provincial government had just announced the Ontario Basic Income Pilot, so the issue was hot enough that the debate packed the six-hundred-seat auditorium. Lewis polled the crowd at the start of the debate session, concluding that over half the assembly favoured Basic Income. He also pointed to something fascinating about the LEAP manifesto—the way it deliberately fudged its call for a Basic Income.

Having helped author the document, Lewis was well placed to recognize the uniqueness of the Basic Income demand. Among the fifteen points, focusing on Indigenous rights, resource extraction, and an end to austerity, he explained that the otherwise forthright Manifesto's only "weasel words" appear with regard to Basic Income. This would ostensibly be because the policy of ensuring a no-strings-attached income divides the left. The Manifesto stated,

Since so much of the labour of caretaking—whether of people or the planet—is currently unpaid, we call for a vigorous debate about the introduction of *a universal basic annual income*. Pioneered in Manitoba in the 1970's, this sturdy safety net could help ensure that no one is forced to take work that threatens their children's tomorrow, just to feed those children today.[19]

The high-profile speaker against Basic Income was a well-known Toronto antipoverty activist, John Clarke. The affirmative side was represented by Josephine Grey, whose strong advocacy of Basic Income was informed by her life story.

Josephine Grey had been engaged in social justice work since the 1980s. Grey lives in St. Jamestown, the most diverse area in Canada's most diverse city, calling itself "the world within a block." Two of every five residents live below the (market basket measure) poverty line, with the median household income just over $40,000. Nine of ten residents are tenants living in tall 1960s towers. Two thirds of North St. Jamestown's residents are visible minorities. Grey and her kids had spent time in a shelter after Josephine, fleeing an abusive relationship, found herself with nowhere else to go. The Superior Court eventually ruled that women who had been subjected to domestic violence abuse could keep their homes; the abuser had to leave no matter whose name was on the lease. Grey recalled,

> My children's father was of African and Native descent from Canada's east coast. When I got into the relationship, I had no idea really what I was doing. I think the legacy of trauma and oppression really played out for him and his family. He was unfortunately quite abusive. I think it was a violence born out of pain and I understood. At the same time, I couldn't necessarily endure it.[20]

In high school Grey had become an early advocate for a curriculum shift that included the Black experience. She explains that her mother taught her not to allow herself to be unnerved by racism: "I am proud of my heritage and I clearly understand then and now that racism is usually the product of ignorance and miseducation."[21] Knowing the limits of simply denouncing racism and the cruelties of the welfare system, Grey sees her task as one of understanding, explaining and changing.

As she raised her family, first on what was then called "Mothers' Allowance," Grey had to endure the kind of government surveillance routinely visited upon women dependent on social assistance. The scrutiny was part of a system of moral regulation designed to draw sharp lines between deserving and undeserving women. Grey came to recognize that this system was not just a matter of snoopy welfare workers employed by the state to determine whether you were worthy of public support and living an upright life. It had deep roots in the broader culture, buttressed by public attitudes towards people—particularly women—unable to work.

Recognizing that people on social assistance do not have the same rights as everyone else would turn her into a human rights campaigner. "When you live on social assistance, you live in Stalinist Russia," she told a 1991 York University conference on democracy. "Your neighbour, your [social] worker, even your friend might report you. You live with all kinds of terrorist fears."[22]

Four years later, a devil-take-the-hindmost government turned a nasty system into one that was downright cruel. It restricted eligibility and cut social assistance rates by some 22 percent. The seventy-seven-year-old category of Mothers' Allowance was abolished altogether. Along with the usual tax cuts, market fundamentalism instituted "workfare," tying social assistance to work even as a good jobs/bad jobs labour market was steadily offering security to fewer workers.

In addition to appearing at the United Nations to explain that the human rights of Ontario's poor were being violated, Grey has long championed a livable Basic Income as the only way to abolish the welfare system while providing what people really need. She was an organizer of the 2018 North American Basic Income Guarantee (NABIG) conference in Hamilton and pushed Ontario to make its 2017 Ontario Basic Income Pilot (OBIP) a policy for everyone.

Together with many Basic Income advocates, Grey sees the idea as something that needs to go beyond social justice and a robotized future in which precarious labour becomes even more commonplace. For her, it's all about a bigger idea. Freedom. Not simply freedom *of* and *from*—freedom of speech and of worship, freedom from fear and from want—as Franklin Roosevelt famously promoted in 1941. Grey holds out hope for Basic Income as emancipatory in a different way.

"I think 'freedom to' as well as 'freedom from' is a very important thing," she said. "Freedom to grow your own food. Freedom to be there for your kids. The freedom to control your own time."[23]

Grey knows well that daily struggles to meet basic needs colonize the lives of her neighbours. If people were assured of a basic, no-strings-attached income, it would end the uncertainties. They would gain a measure of autonomy and, indeed, the opportunity to imagine a different future. Erich Fromm, the Jewish psychoanalyst who fled Nazi Germany, argued that once people unlearned their deep fear of scarcity and starvation, their newfound psychology of abundance would give them "initiative, faith in life, solidarity" and a renewed ability to find meaning and purpose in life.[24]

"Basic income is a wonderful space to allow us to dream," Grey insists, displaying the sort of optimism that makes for effective communication and organizing:

> When your community is hit with a bad storm, you can't wait for the people in authority and the first responders to come and fix things. You have to have community capacity to respond and help each other. That's just a new reality that we have to face. And Basic Income is the foundation for all of that.[25]

In the 2017 debate, Grey had a worthy opponent in John Clarke, a class-struggle activist with a decades-long organizing pedigree and a lengthy association with the Ontario Coalition Against Poverty. Clarke began his presentation by attributing the upsurge in interest in Basic Income in part to the "disorientation" felt by many on the left. Having been defeated by the austerity agenda, many had the sense that "we haven't been able to stop it, so maybe there's a social policy end-run around it."[26]

Clarke also emphasized the importance of understanding political context. The ascent of neoliberalism "has led to the explosion of low-paid and precarious work." He warned of Kathleen Wynne's "wily fox regime of austerity and privatization." His analysis had it that "some very evil people are cooking this up at the moment." According to Clarke, the key to social justice is mass mobilization and worker power, because the elites will never voluntarily relinquish power and privilege.

Clarke brought out a traditional shibboleth of many left arguments against Basic Income: the undeniable fact that Basic Income has had its supporters on the right. Hadn't some IMF economists backed it? Hadn't there been discussion of Basic Income at a recent World Economic Forum in Davos, think tank for the global elite? "Those evil bastards in the Swiss Alps know what they're doing." Clarke included in his axis-of-evil pantheon the economist Milton Friedman, at which point Grey responded that Basic Income is an idea that goes back to 1500, its proponents along the way including Tom Paine and Martin Luther King.

Grey found the unalloyed, fight-to-win anticapitalism approach provocative. "What I don't hear is, what's your alternative? What about women's unpaid work?" For her, a primary focus on the politics of opposition was insufficient and, indeed, frustrating. She described Basic Income not just as a solid foundation of individual and collective security that would get rid of the welfare system that creates "paper tigers to chase you through jungles of red tape." She made room for aspirational politics with the potential to mobilize across sectors.

How about a transition to a "liberating" income-security system, a move from "an economy that requires people to engage in destructive, insecure livelihoods and allows them to take the time to breathe and think about how they could enter green jobs?" Grey's Basic Income vision did not envision a panacea. Rather, it would "allow young people to take some unorthodox career paths towards more innovative livelihoods, like starting co-ops or creating food security." The current system, she said, frustrated people who did not have the space to imagine a different future. Instead, "They have to scramble from one shitty job to another."

At the end of the debate, Clarke and Grey were in agreement on one thing: the need for radical transformation. Clarke again warned of the foreboding forces on the right that back Basic Income, summing it up with the assertion that there is no social policy alternative to austerity and privatization. He did not answer Grey's question about what he was for.

Grey said she had not heard from her debating partner any demand that would bring people together, insisting that those backing the Basic Income vision included "an awful lot of good people." Moreover, she pointed out the context as she understood it. "We are at a political moment when there is enough popular support for the redistribution of wealth in a serious way." She reminded the audience of another moment that had arrived. "We've come to the point in human history where we are facing extinction or evolution."

Clearly, this point resonated with the climate justice message of the LEAP manifesto. Lewis took a new show of hands. The number of undecideds had declined; more people were holding up green cards, indicating support of Basic Income. Grey quickly jumped in to ask how many in the audience would support a Basic Income based on a human rights framework. Green card unanimity prevailed.

COVID PRESENTS AN OPPORTUNITY

Three years later, the context of the Basic Income debate had changed. Far from being made available to everyone as Josephine Grey had wanted, the Ontario Basic Income Pilot had been abruptly cancelled by the new Conservative government of Doug Ford. And then the 2020 pandemic raised the profile of Basic Income globally as even the most tight-fisted governments realized the depth of the crisis.

The CERB showed that unconditional state aid is both possible and necessary. It was an opening for the activists who had built Canada's Basic Income campaign. The timing was auspicious. Weeks before the pandemic, the Basic Income Canada Network (BICN) published the first-ever detailed set of policy options for a Canadian Basic Income, defined as an unconditional cash transfer from the state to individual people. The money would be unrelated to work status. It would enable everyone to meet their basic needs while participating more fully in social life—in essence, to live with a measure of dignity.[27]

"It is clear from child and seniors benefits that it works for many Canadians already," said BICN co-founder Sheila Regehr, who had also experienced poverty as a young parent. "The federal government's priority now must be to take leadership to make it work for everybody; we are all part of the future of this country."

Regehr and Ottawa policy analyst Chandra Pasma, together with a small team of Basic Income activists, used Statistics Canada's Social Policy Simulation Database and Model (SPSD/M) to develop three policy options. All depended on blending existing government spending with changes to the tax/transfer system, including tax fairness measures. The detailed recommendations spring from BICN's principles—more income security and less inequality.

There was a specific effort to appeal to middle-income earners, while ensuring that the wealthiest people and those legal persons called corporations contribute their fair share. All three options were based on an annual benefit of $22,000 for a single person, $31,113 for a couple. The level was below the up-to-$24,000 for which the 8.75 million Canadians eligible for the CERB could receive.[28] Canada has seven million people living in poverty, more than the combined population of the cities of Toronto and Montreal.[29] The BICN plan would virtually eliminate poverty in one of the world's richest countries, with the entire lower half of the income distribution seeing an increase in disposable incomes. For the lowest income families there would be an increase of more than 350 percent.[30]

The analysis, *Basic Income: Policy Options for Canada*, was detailed and indeed granular enough that journalists and pundits did not immediately grasp its significance. In the remarkable upsurge in interest in Basic Income generated by the pandemic, the number-crunching study still got lost in debates from across the spectrum about the plan's desirability and feasibility. It was left to the country's best-known Basic Income proponent to sum up the study's importance. Former Senator Hugh Segal explained,

> The BICN January 2020 report set aside for all time the grousing from the far right and far left, that Basic Income advocates are unprepared to deal with financing and tax implications. This, ironically, leaves the far left and the far right with the still unproven analysis of the real cost to productivity, literacy, the health and penal system, and society as a whole of the patchy, punitive, and work-discouraging welfare *status quo* . . . which they appear to favour.[31]

THE BASIC INCOME TAG TEAM

Like Sheila Regehr and Josephine Grey, Hugh Segal had first-hand experience of poverty. Segal had grown up in a "lower working-class family" and routinely referred to affluent purveyors of conventional wisdom as "swells" or "grandees." As of 2020, Segal had been supporting Basic Income for some fifty years. His long push for Basic Income stemmed from his understanding of the cruelties of rule-riddled social assistance systems and some stark images from the experience of growing up poor. "A bailiff arriving to seize your dad's car and empty the house of furniture is not something that fades into distant memory," he recalled in 2019. "It stays with you, like a dark spot at the edge of a slice of bread."

His tireless advocacy and political savvy combined with personal bonhomie made the happy warrior the dean of Canada's Basic Income movement. During his Senate years, the lifelong Tory gave over seventy-five speeches promoting Basic Income, talking to small church basement gatherings and delivering keynote addresses to international conferences. His timely 2019 memoir, *Bootstraps Need Boots: One Tory's Lonely Fight to End Poverty in Canada,* added to the political momentum. Politically hard to pin down—the Red Tory label doesn't capture his ideology—he denounced with characteristic flourish "the narrowness and selfish self-reference of neoliberal and neoconservative excess" in a book called *Beyond Greed.* Moreover, he knew that laissez-faire capitalism is abhorrent, describing "the excesses of the unmoderated marketplace" as "deeply harmful to the most serious driving force in any productive society: hope."[32]

Canada also has another high-profile Basic Income advocate: the health economist Evelyn Forget, professor of Community Health Sciences at the University of Manitoba and academic director of the Manitoba Research Data Centre. If there was anyone who has thought more about Basic Income than the voluble Segal, it is the understated Forget. When she was twelve, her mother was widowed and forced onto social assistance, subsequently taking a series of low-wage jobs. Forget recalled learning "very quickly how important money is, and how vulnerable anyone becomes when they have no money of their own. People with money have choices and opportunities that others don't have."

Her singular effort to unearth and interpret the findings of the 1975–78 Mincome Basic Income project in Manitoba was in good measure responsible for raising the profile of Basic Income more than thirty years after the project ended. Forget dug through the archives and sifted through and analyzed the raw data from the project, which was centred mainly on the town of Dauphin, Manitoba. She calculated the Dauphin experiment's positive findings—among other effects, hospital visits declined, as did high school dropout rates. In addition, Forget pointed to something that Segal always explained during his messianic pilgrimages in support of Basic Income: most poor people work. Many (like Lance Dingman, profiled in Chapter 5) struggle to do so in spite of often daunting physical and mental health obstacles.

Forget's point was essential in attacking the shopworn "if-you-just-give-them-money-they-won't-work" arguments against unconditional Basic Income schemes. Basic Income boosters call this the "zombie argument" as it never seems to die. The politics of Basic Income requires advocates to demonstrate clearly again and again that many people living in poverty are also employed, often part-time.

Forget further noted that because social assistance schemes are based on regulation and surveillance, they work "by taking away from recipients the ability to decide for themselves how to live their lives and how to spend their money." Her years of studying Basic Income in all its many variations made clear the importance of unconditionality: "The one bedrock agreement is that basic income should not depend on behaviour."[33]

OPPOSITION FROM BOTH ENDS

Hugh Segal was correct in looking both right and left to find opponents of basic income. Yet there are nuances that Segal, despite his sensitive political antennae, seemed to miss.

The right argues against Basic Income on the basis that it would cost too much and, more in tune with individualistic ideology, that it would lead to social decay because the inherently lazy elements of the undeserving lower orders would head for their couches, beer and video games ready to hand. When a business-page column looked at the way the just-announced CERB could possibly morph into a Basic Income, one typical comment had it that "the last thing we need is to expand a system that breeds dependency upon the government for a person's livelihood. It kills initiative and entrepreneurship in an individual," while another reader simply got mad. "Every lazy bum around will be on the dole and not looking for work at all. What a joke . . . the government never creates real jobs, it just creates itself!"[34]

Elements of the left oppose Basic Income because their ideological bête noire, Milton Friedman, had supported a minimalist version that would allow for the abolition of public provision—telling disadvantaged people that, given Basic Income, they were then free to simply buy what they needed in the marketplace. One of the authors recalls meeting— along with two other Basic Income supporters from Kingston—with a representative of the mildly market-critical Broadbent Institute, an NDP-affiliated think tank. The representative wanted to know how they possibly could support something favoured by conservative columnist Andrew Coyne.

Similarly, during the question period at a 2019 union meeting in Winnipeg, a young British Columbia delegate asked prominent Basic Income advocate Guy Standing, visiting from England, about the political pedigree of the idea he was promoting. The question was perhaps inevitable: Wasn't Milton Friedman an important supporter of what was then called a Guaranteed Annual Income? Standing readily agreed that this was so. But, he added, "Adolf Hitler supported a national public health care plan. Does that mean we should oppose it?"[35]

Others—particularly social democrats and trade unionists still grasping in vain for the chimera of full employment—believed that it could turn into a subsidy for low-wage bosses. Public sector unions in particular often oppose Basic Income because it could lead to job cuts for unionized welfare workers—including those tasked with policing the lives of the poor by enforcing the intrusive, often cruel conditions governing social assistance eligibility.

Believing that the labour movement is a natural ally in social justice struggles, many Basic Income supporters address the argument about welfare worker jobs being jeopardized by acknowledging that getting rid of traditional punitive welfare systems is one Basic Income goal. They often add that there are profound unmet needs among marginalized people struggling with disability, poverty, mental illness, and addiction. Public sector social service workers are trained to provide help. Because of its unconditionality, Basic Income would eliminate the soul-destroying task of policing the poor, freeing workers up for meaningful and important work.

Staying away from a Basic Income because of the inherent virtue of work is an idea that has traction on the left as well. In a 2020 story by the *Toronto Star's* Laurie Montsebraaten, explaining the way CERB could well usher in a Basic Income, Armine Yalnizyan—usually called upon by the media for her moderate left-of-centre viewpoints—was unequivocal. "Basic income helps people make the choice of not going to work," objected Yalnizyan, the Atkinson Charitable Foundation's fellow on the future of workers. "And when this is over, we are going to need all hands on deck."[36]

LOOKING PAST THE PANDEMIC

As the pandemic unfolded, the momentum behind a Basic Income grew steadily. Not surprisingly, people were given to wondering aloud: Just what kind of world would emerge post-pandemic? Would the megaphones of market fundamentalism holler about debt and deficit and the need to return to the decades of austerity, drowning out radical alternatives? Or would those who saw the plague as a canary-in-the-coal mine moment prevail?

For some, 2020 seemed to offer a once-in-a-generation opportunity to go beyond a gloomy, greed-fuelled vision of a Hobbesian war of each against all. Too early to tell, as it would take years for the dust generated by the pandemic's global earthquake to settle. But early on, two things could be discerned. Far-right demagogues in the United States, India, and Brazil, wedded to crazed patriotism and disease denial, were discredited. Also, centrists and social democrats started to show signs of creativity, realizing that the siren songs of unfettered globalization had fuelled raging inequality, stubborn poverty even in times of growth, and the inability of states hobbled by austerity to respond effectively to a massive public health crisis.

By the time Spain announced in early April that it intended to bring in a permanent Basic Income, it had come to light that rates of COVID-19 infection in Barcelona's working-class neighbourhoods were seven times those of affluent areas. Dr. Nani Vall-Ilosera, practising in one of Barcelona's poor quarters, explained something that would soon emerge as obvious everywhere. "Poverty and poor health are a vicious circle—the poorer you are, the more likely you are to have health problems. And so, the chances of becoming seriously ill with the virus are concentrated in poor neighbourhoods." Economy Minister Nadia Calviño of Spain's left-of-centre coalition said that her government was aiming for Basic Income "that stays forever, that becomes a structural instrument, a permanent instrument."[37] Hopes rose. Time, however, would tell.

Things unfolded slowly in Canada, with mainstream politicians still spooked by the idea of unconditional Basic Income despite the CERB precedent that amounted to a forced, if partial, experiment with the policy. Yet, in an adroit political démarche, two senators cobbled together a majority of their colleagues to sign an open letter to the government supporting Basic Income.[38]

Frances Lankin, before serving as an NDP provincial cabinet minister and head of Toronto's United Way, was one of the first female guards at Toronto's harsh Don Jail; Kim Pate was the former head of the Elizabeth Fry Society, which advocates for women in prison. Both were well familiar with poverty and social exclusion—and particularly the plight of some of the most despised and abused people in Canada, those who have been convicted of crimes.

The April 21, 2020, letter to Prime Minister Trudeau and Finance Minister Bill Morneau had but one careful mention of Basic Income, and that was in its salutation: "Subject: COVID-19 Pandemic—Minimum Basic Income." The rest of the appeal thanked the government effusively for the CERB, emphasizing how it reflected a "Team Canada" approach to social policy at "a unique moment in our history." This helped to generate a "climate of hope and optimism" at a time when such feelings were in short supply.

The letter's central ask urged the Liberals to "finish the work you have commenced by restructuring the CERB to ensure greater social and economic equity as well as greater efficiency." The efficiency emphasis was canny, highlighting the CERB's practicality. Civil servants could deposit money into recipient bank accounts "with little more than the push of a button." In this way it "liberated time and resources ... to help people not currently on the tax rolls to convert their applications to tax files." Many marginalized people, having scant income, do not file tax forms and fall outside tax-based income assistance. Getting that many senators on board was, Lankin enthused, "really quite extraordinary."[39]

A letter signed by senators across the political spectrum, from the controversial former conservative broadcaster Mike Duffy to the highly respected former judge Murray Sinclair, who had led the Truth and Reconciliation Commission into Canada's reprehensible residential school system, was bound to inject a dose of interest, if not legitimacy, into the case for Basic Income. Sinclair's commission was followed by the National Inquiry into Murdered and Missing Indigenous Women and Girls, whose report, published six months before the COVID crisis, included poverty as an important focus—and was clear about Basic Income: "We call upon all governments to establish a guaranteed annual livable income for all Canadians, including Indigenous Peoples, to meet all their social and economic needs."[40]

In the wake of the Senate letter, Toronto's YWCA weighed in as part of a what-is-to-be-done-post-pandemic thinkfest. Heather McGregor and Jasmine Ramzee Rezaee stated the case clearly in "A Feminist Approach to Ending Poverty after COVID-19," noting that the CERB recognized that a monthly income of $2,000 is needed to survive.

Moreover, they pointed to a longstanding if often neglected fact of life: "*Unpaid care work is a source of gender-based poverty and oppression*" (emphasis in original). In addition to the traditional feminist demand for universal child care, they added Basic Income. Ontario's pilot project had offered "wonderful findings," so they concluded that, "It is time for the provincial government to work with the federal government in developing a national guaranteed income program, or modify an existing income security program, that recompenses unpaid care work."[41]

Basic Income advocates who had long struggled, often in vain, to get people to pay heed, were amazed that the public square was suddenly echoing with discussions of the measure as part of what a "new normal" might look like. Well before the scale of the pandemic became clear, right-wing voices signalled a willingness to support a "crisis basic income" that would become CERB, although they added the caveat that it is "a bad idea in normal times."[42]

Hugh Segal and Evelyn Forget argued that the CERB amounted to "the largest experiment in basic income that anyone could imagine." The pandemic's "legacy" potential was, they maintained, generating a new awareness that anyone might need a Basic Income for reasons utterly beyond their control.[43]

During the height of the pandemic's first wave, one high-profile English Canadian pundit offered a pragmatic appraisal of Basic Income prospects. According to Andrew Coyne, backers claiming that all that was needed was political will (few if any ever made such a claim) were "talking through their hats." An actual Basic Income, "built to last," would be "not impossible, not undesirable, but difficult." This was something supporters knew well.

Coyne was aware of the market fundamentalist vision of Basic Income that would wipe out most if not all public provision, from nonmarket housing to free pharmaceuticals available to people on welfare, noting, "The more existing programs that were melted down into a basic income, the lower the overall cost." The political implications are obvious: "The minute you start talking about what programs you'd replace, you run into trouble. Welfare advocates worry that a basic income is a Trojan horse for gutting social programs. The people delivering those programs object to being made redundant." And then there are Canada's inevitable thorny jurisdictional issues: "Provinces—ah yes, the provinces."[44]

In spite of the unprecedented public conversation about Basic Income in light of the pandemic and the efforts of a small band of supporters, a program that would attack poverty, precarious work, and even inequality via giving people unconditional cash still seemed like a long shot in 2020. But maybe a little less of a long shot than it had been before.

As the pandemic's second wave gathered force in the autumn of 2020, Canada's chief public health officer, Theresa Tam, issued the Public Health Agency of Canada's annual report. It hadn't, evidently, been a very good year. She reiterated what was by that time common knowledge. The plague was worst for seniors, essential workers, racialized populations, people living with disabilities, and women. Her officials used arid, understated terminology that still described the way that the inequality baked into Canadian life hit some harder that others: "The structures of society influence exposure, susceptibility, and care related to COVID-19 for different groups of Canadians."[45]

Just as Ottawa's top public health agency pointed out the obvious, Evelyn Forget and Hugh Segal teamed up with veteran policy analyst Keith Banting to issue a report of their own, published by the prestigious Royal Society of Canada. It was another addition to the Basic Income chorus. In it they showed that from 1990 to 2018, Canada's spending on social protection as a percentage of GDP had flatlined, the lowest of a dozen OECD countries —even the United States had seen an increase.

Poverty rates were highest in the English-speaking countries like Canada that had most tightly embraced free-market fundamentalism. They pointed to the inescapable fact, long obvious to social analysts and victims, that the sharpest neoliberal cuts (they described them, delicately, as "retrenchment") had lacerated the poor and the unemployed, creating "disproportionate suffering . . . at the low end of the economic ladder." They concluded, "Never have the yawning gaps in our income security system been so glaringly obvious," describing decades of retrenchment as "not a mistake we can afford to make again."[46]

All of which brought to mind the title of another of Leonard Cohen's haunting musical insights: "Everybody Knows."[47]

CHAPTER 2

A BRIEF HISTORY OF BASIC INCOME IN CANADA

I am now convinced that the simplest approach will prove to be the most effective—the solution to poverty is to abolish it directly by a now widely discussed measure, the guaranteed income.

—Martin Luther King, Jr.

THORNY THICKETS

The idea of Basic Income is not new. It has been around for years—centuries even. In 1986, an assembly of academics and activists meeting in Belgium established what would come to be the Basic Income Earth Network (BIEN). As it happens, that meeting occurred nearly five hundred years after the publication of Thomas More's *Utopia*.

In Thomas More's famous tale, a traveller who had visited an unknown island called Utopia argued upon his return that petty larceny hardly justified the death penalty, commonplace in those days. "No penalty on earth will stop people from stealing, if it's their only way of getting food." Instead of killing people for theft, he reasoned that "it would be far more to the point to provide everyone with some means of livelihood, so that nobody is under the frightful necessity of becoming, first a thief, and then a corpse."[1] Not surprisingly, Basic Income promoters have become fond of the story.

Anxious to avoid being scorned as hopelessly woolly-headed uto-
pians, they also would recall the advice of the intellectual godfather
of neoliberalism. In his 1949 essay "The Intellectuals and Socialism,"
Friedrich Hayek told his fellow free-market fundamentalists to take
heart. Taxes on the rich were rising, along with government regulation
of business, but:

> The true lesson which the true liberal must learn from the suc-
> cess of the socialists is that it was their courage to be Utopian
> that gained them the support of the intellectuals and thereby
> an influence on public opinion, which is daily making possible
> what only recently seemed remote. . . . What we lack is a lib-
> eral Utopia.[2]

The first Canadian effort to create a policy vaguely resembling
a Basic Income scheme was spearheaded by William (Bible Bill)
Aberhart, Alberta's Depression-era Premier. Today's Basic Income promoters, however, tend not to hold up the charismatic fundamentalist
preacher (and onetime Ponzi scheme promoter) as a pioneering backer
of their plans.

When Aberhart's Social Credit party was elected in 1935, it surprised the political establishment, but not desperate farmers and workers reeling from the Depression. He devised schemes that included
twenty-five-dollar "prosperity certificates," available to anyone who
signed a "registration covenant" pledging allegiance to his government;
the certificates were dubbed "funny money." Many fearful Albertans
signed, but the plan collapsed—partly because the provincial treasury
was empty, but also because it fell afoul of Ottawa's responsibility for
banking and finance.[3] No doubt Basic Income in Canada will always confront the thorny thickets of federal-provincial jurisdictional conflicts.

The Depression didn't just grease the political skids of the Social
Credit movement—it also strengthened the left. Indeed, organizing
efforts by communists and social democrats proved crucial in laying
the groundwork for Canada's welfare state, as economic calamity was

followed by world war. Free-market fundamentalist capitalism had clearly failed. Ten years of Depression had eroded tired notions of individualism; victim-blaming had less traction in a world of mass victimization. What was the point of instructing people about a sturdy work ethic and the need to get a job when there was so little work to be had?

Crises tend to breed change. A few cases in point: In the wake of the Great War, Canada had seen the introduction of income taxes, the end of its two-party system, and voting rights for women. With the Great Depression, ideas long dear to the dominant class began to fade. Apparently working-class people were not basically lazy, sure to slack off if the public purse were to be opened a crack.

Unemployment insurance arrived in 1940. In 1945, Mackenzie King's Liberals reluctantly agreed to a family allowance or "baby bonus"—Canada's first universal social security program. Labour and social policy historian Alvin Finkel explored the complex political nuances of the program, writing in his exhaustive history of Canadian social policy, "Family allowances had the support of most business groups because of their ideological use in fending off arguments for the need for 'family wages' large enough to compensate fathers of big families. Unsurprisingly, then, the trade union movement was suspicious of family allowances."[4]

Despite its support for the family allowance, the business community generally remained distrustful towards the gradually arriving postwar social programs. The Canada Pension Plan (Quebec would develop its own system) and medicare, often taken for granted a half-century later, met stiff resistance from the right when they were introduced in the mid-1960s. Public health care was attacked by the Canadian Medical Association, the Canadian Dental Association, and the Canadian Chamber of Commerce. The insurance industry mobilized against medicare and found the idea of a national public pension plan particularly loathsome.

The enemies of public provision predictably cloaked unalloyed self-interest with virtuous-sounding claims: surely universal social programs would deprive Canadians of the freedom to choose their own insurance packages and deprive physicians of the freedom to practise without state interference. Yet new policies aimed at the public good had support from broad coalitions of labour, churches, and social democrats, with the CCF/NDP in the vanguard. Reform elements in the Liberal Party, long overshadowed by the chronic caution of King and his successor Louis Saint-Laurent, had gained influence. Moreover, the minority Liberals under Lester Pearson depended on the NDP for parliamentary survival for five crucial years (1963–68).

The era is often held up as a golden age of economic prosperity and progressive social policy in Canada. But in one arena—taxation—the corporate sector and the rich prevailed. The Royal Commission on Taxation, chaired by Bay Street accountant Kenneth Carter, studied the tax system for four years, submitting its report in 1966.

The Carter Commission's six-volume report included recommendations that would have reduced taxes on the bottom half of the population by over fifteen percent. Under its proposal, the wealthy would pay more through a simplified system, with corporations paying an additional twenty-five percent.

Oil and mining interests were so incensed that when one Sudbury legislator received the weighty response from Inco, he thought someone had sent him a case of beer. He concluded that "there must be some merit in the Carter Commission because it took them so many pages to criticize it."[5] Under Pearson's successor, Pierre Trudeau, the Liberals beat a fast retreat, and the decades that followed saw an increase in the unfairness and complexity of a preposterously skewed tax system that consistently favours corporate interests and those at the top.

Any transformational social policy like Basic Income will necessarily require thorough tax reform aimed at the privileges of the powerful. Basic Income advocates—along with others who support meaningful extensions of public provision—have consistently argued that the state's fiscal capacity must be concomitantly restored via tax reform. In short, we must amend the current system, through which the poor pay proportionately more while the rich take advantage of labyrinthine regulations containing favourable loopholes.

Right-wing think tanks and media trumpet "tax relief" as if taxes were akin to migraine headaches. At the same time, they denounce governments with the temerity to suggest raising taxes on the powerful while promoting the public good for having "tax-and-spend" tendencies. This ignores the inconvenient truth that it is the government's job to levy taxes and spend money—the issue being who gets taxed and at what rate, and how the resulting revenue is then allocated.

As the debate over tax fairness consumed lobbyists for the affluent in the late 1960s and afterward, Canadians concerned about widespread poverty turned their attention to the Special Senate Committee on Poverty headed by Senator David Croll. The committee issued its landmark report in 1971, pointing out that poverty was not confined to people on social assistance and unemployment insurance. Rather, there were millions of "active labour market participants" such as single mothers, who remained in poverty, working—often sporadically—at low-end jobs. "Unless we act now, nationally," the Croll Report warned pointedly, five million Canadians "will continue to find life a bleak, bitter and never-ending struggle for survival."

The committee's main policy recommendation involved introducing a national Basic Income plan. It would be income-tested and funded by the federal government, with net expenditures declining as it replaced the Family Allowance and Old Age Security. The senators envisioned that this version of Basic Income would eventually be extended to all citizens. Being politically pragmatic, however, they also added some water to the wine—the plan would exclude single people under forty.[6]

Aside from generating a flurry of inconclusive bureaucratic and political infighting that produced little meaningful action on poverty reduction,[7] the Croll Report and its Basic Income recommendation went nowhere in Liberal Ottawa. Yet thanks to the political dynamics of the day between the Liberals and the New Democrats, along with the personal relationship between then Prime Minister Trudeau and the New Democratic Premier of Manitoba, Ed Schreyer, a project emerged a few years later that would become Canada's—and arguably the world's—most important Basic Income experiment.

A LANDMARK EXPERIMENT

In February 1974, Ottawa and Winnipeg announced the joint Mincome project, with seventy-five percent of the funding coming from the federal government. The 1975–78 project was similar to Ontario's 2017–19 Basic Income pilot to the extent that it was a carefully designed social science research experiment that included a small-town "saturation" site in Dauphin, where almost everyone could collect the unconditional payments. Sadly, both projects were terminated soon after right-wing governments took office. The Manitoba government of Sterling Lyon never bothered to analyze the masses of data that were collected about the results of the Mincome experiment. Premier Doug Ford cancelled the Ontario Basic Income Pilot before intervention data could even be gathered.

Mincome would become a global reference point for Basic Income supporters in the decades that followed, particularly after the University of Manitoba's Evelyn Forget undertook the mammoth task of unearthing and analyzing the Mincome results, digging through eighteen hundred dusty bankers' boxes containing the raw data.

Forget had been twelve when her mother was widowed and forced onto social assistance, subsequently taking a series of low-wage jobs such as those highlighted in the Croll Report. Her mother had been savvy enough to encourage Evelyn to live at home, even when she was old enough to work, so that she could continue pursuing her education. Evelyn recalled learning "very quickly how important money is, and how vulnerable anyone becomes when they have no money of their own. People with money have choices and opportunities that others don't have."

Forget was a first-year college student in 1974 when a professor described the new Mincome project and then proceeded to explain things that the undergraduate knew well—for example, that welfare was a form of social apartheid that separated the poor from those with money, eroding independence; that getting a job did not mean getting out of poverty; and that people are always worse off when they get help in the form of charity instead of more money because they know better how to spend that money than government officials or charitable outfits. Poverty seemed to be about *money*. Forget switched her major to economics.

Some twenty-five years later Forget, now a health economist, was working at the University of Manitoba medical school, studying the intimate links between poverty and ill health. Poor people die sicker and quicker, costing the system unnecessarily large amounts of *money* along the way. Deprivation leads to higher rates of stress, diabetes, hypertension, cardiovascular disease, and other chronic illnesses. "I wondered whether reducing the poverty in which people lived would actually improve their health," she wrote. "Then I remembered Mincome."[8]

Forget's training emphasized evidence, and she wanted to find out if Mincome added to the growing mountain of evidence—cited tirelessly but fruitlessly by social justice activists—that poverty is costly. Her archival excavations paid off, providing clear evidence that the Basic Income project worked to improve both health and educational outcomes.

The Mincome project had used the small city of Dauphin as its saturation point, and the data included everyone living there. Mincome also had a control group to buttress its findings. The data showed that over the course of the project, high school dropout rates had declined, reminding Forget of her own decision to stay in school rather than quit to take a job as a telephone operator or a bank teller. Hospitalization rates fell 8.5 percent compared to the control group. Physician visits also declined.

Poverty produces uncertainty and insecurity, generating anxiety that, in a perverse cascade effect, produces stress-related disease.[9] The reliability of Basic Income offered people the ability not to worry so much about money, providing what Forget termed "insurance." Describing the feeling of security as more important than the actual money, Forget knew the prairie town's agricultural economy played a key role: a poor grain crop might slash incomes for truck drivers, labourers, shopkeepers, and hairdressers.

Forget helps us connect the dots: "If this was the nature of small-town employment forty years ago, it is increasingly coming to characterize a much larger segment of the labour market today."[10] Back when the Manitoba Conservatives consigned the Mincome evidence to archival obscurity, notions of "precarious work" and a "gig economy" were unknown, although working-class people had long been familiar with insecure jobs that pay poverty wages. Sterling Lyon's new government at the time had no apparent interest in reducing poverty—or even reviewing evidence of how this could be done.

THE ASCENDANCY OF MARKET FUNDAMENTALISM

The early 1980s marked the start of what came to be called neoliberalism, a sustained ideological and political offensive that can also be described as "market fundamentalism." The left-wing Canadian economist Mel Watkins had a much pithier name for this campaign to turn back the clock on social progress: "madness and ruin," also the title of a collection of his post-1980 writings.[11]

The 1985 report of Ottawa's Royal Commission on the Economic Union and Development Prospects for Canada, chaired by Bay Street Liberal and former finance minister Donald Macdonald, proved a notable milestone for market fundamentalism in Canada. The commission recommended free trade with the United States and a Basic Income that it called a Universal Income Security (UISC) Program. Brian Mulroney's Progressive Conservative government didn't bother with the Basic Income portion. Instead the Tories spent their political capital on the free trade recommendation, ultimately fighting and winning the bitter 1988 election on the issue.

The proposed UISC was a classic right-wing version of Basic Income—the kind that Milton Friedman and his acolytes had years previously imagined as one way of eviscerating public provision and the gains of the Keynesian welfare state. The Macdonald Commission's UISC would have:

- Eliminated the vitally important Pearson-era Canada Assistance Plan, a cost-sharing arrangement under which Ottawa underwrote provincial social programs. *Jean Chrétien's subsequent Liberal government, also in thrall to let-the-market-decide thinking, ended it anyway in the 1990s.*
- Killed nonmarket housing programs. *These were also terminated under Chrétien.*
- Eliminated the venerable family allowance program. *This was replaced by tax-based measures in the last days of the Mulroney government.*
- Replaced the Guaranteed Income Supplement, a notable success in cutting poverty among seniors. *Cutting benefits for seniors was a non-starter, and this survived.*

Throughout the 1980s and 1990s, both Conservative and Liberal governments deployed individualist rhetoric that urged those sinking to the bottom to stop depending on the state. One Liberal discussion paper on the unemployment insurance program—which the Chrétien government gutted, diverting the UI fund surplus to deficit reduction—urged "individual responsibility and self-sufficiency." The same document admitted that many were "losing ground," but explained that it was because they lacked the skills being demanded by the market. Conservative talk focused on "breaking the spiral of dependency," a line picked up by Lloyd Axworthy after he became the minister responsible for "Human Resources Development" under Chrétien. Axworthy, although not a business Liberal in the mould of Donald Macdonald, still resorted to that "cycle-of-dependency" shibboleth.

All of this ignored the reality of the split-level labour market emerging during those decades. As early as 1993, a Statistics Canada report showed that it was "quite clear" that unequal access to hours of work was a major cause of rising inequality; increasingly, a core of full-time workers was surrounded by "increasing numbers of part-time, part-year, or contract workers."[12]

Both the trade union movement and the antipoverty advocates with whom it might have been allied with respect to Basic Income and poverty were scrambling. While the union movement stuck with the good-jobs-for-all approach, some social reformers recognized that full employment was no longer in the cards. In the 1980s, one venerable Ottawa social policy shop, the Canadian Council on Social Development (CCSD), backed a guaranteed annual income initiative it called a "CORE income." It would have been means-tested and aimed at people for whom the labour market meant market failure.

CCSD figured that its CORE idea would improve welfare benefits while providing "a financial incentive to seek additional earnings." The logic was that the labour market excluded valuable activity that commodifying capitalism does not value or even recognize as work because it is unpaid. It is also mostly done by women. According to the CCSD, such activity included "starting one's own business" as well as an amorphous category of "community development," along with "voluntary work, education and training, and child rearing."[13]

Such proposals attempted to navigate a middle way. On one side, traditional social democracy celebrated the glory days of something approaching full employment via limitless growth—even though the postwar boom had, as the Croll Report showed, still left millions mired in poverty. On the other, right-wing proposals like the UISC would have done nothing for marginal workers, cementing increasing inequality. CCSD pointed out that neither pole recognized that "conventional notions of work and employment and their ties to income need rethinking."[14]

UNION RESISTANCE

Perhaps contrary to what one might expect, the official labour movement response to any Basic Income proposal was automatically and consistently negative. Trade union officials equated Basic Income with its Friedmanite, market-fundamentalist variant. From the 1970s onward, this ideology dominated the public square, and some labour intellectuals seemed unable to imagine an alternative.

One academic analysis of the way organized labour treated Basic Income after the 1970s referred to union analysis of social policy as "reactive and indistinct."[15] Unions were on the defensive. Their core membership was starting to shrink in the face of transformed labour markets, job flight in the wake of free trade, corporate campaigns for "flexibility," and, increasingly, technological change. Union intellectuals came to regard Basic Income, then still being called a guaranteed annual income or GAI, as simply part of the onslaught. The Canadian Labour Congress had it that "a right-wing version of GAI" would be an "excuse for dismantling programmes such as UI and Family Allowances"—something that market fundamentalist governments, uninterested in Basic Income, were doing anyway.

Instead of seeing an egalitarian Basic Income as a way of *countering* market fundamentalism, the labour line lumped the two things together. In labour's view, the solution to poverty and inequality was, as it had been since the days of the now long-gone boom of 1945–1980, a job. "For most adult Canadians" argued the CLC, "the primary source of income security and the first line of defence against poverty is a secure, well-paying job. . . . Restoring and maintaining full employment is the most fundamental consideration in attacking the root cause of poverty."[16] The job-equals-ticket-out-of-poverty sentiment would be repeated by Ontario's Conservatives when they killed the Basic Income pilot.[17]

DEVELOPING A BASIC INCOME MOVEMENT: THE PEOPLE AND GROUPS THAT POWERED ITS GROWTH

Basic Income activist, busy academic, and longtime co-chair of the Basic Income Earth Network Karl Widerquist believes the movement in favour of a Basic Income has undergone three distinct "waves," which he describes as follows:

- The first wave began in the early twentieth century, with thinkers from Bertrand Russell to Virginia Woolf in *A Room of One's Own.*

The idea was later picked up by populist politicians like Louisiana's Huey Long in his 1934 make-the-rich-pay "Share Our Wealth" plan.

- The second wave began in the 1960s. Proponents included Martin Luther King, more than a dozen economists who would be awarded Nobel Prizes, futurists like Buckminster Fuller, and right-wing libertarians, most famously Milton Friedman.

- Interest in the idea of a BI subsided during the 1980s, with Widerquist marking the beginning of the third wave—the largest—in 2006, when Namibia implemented its basic income project, followed by Brazil and India.

It took decades, experiments, and a grave pandemic for an unconditional, livable Basic Income to make its way onto the mainstream political agenda, becoming a serious option. During this time, a global movement to promote Basic Income took shape, with engaged intellectuals launching what would become the Basic Income Earth Network (BIEN), the primary vehicle and coordinating arm of this burgeoning movement.

The movement became more interconnected over time. This was due in part to the new tool that was the internet and in part to the ever-clearer contradictions manifested by globalizing capitalism. The years before the 2020 plague were generally characterized by neoliberal dominance, but rising inequality and the growth of green consciousness slowly began to erode its hegemony. Perseverance by several key organizations and individuals also played a key role in expanding the movement over the years.

The National Council of Welfare (NCW) was an Ottawa fixture for nearly fifty years. Established through legislation in 1962, it published reports on poverty, organized workshops, and made formal presentations to parliamentary committees on topics ranging from the need for a national antipoverty strategy to the ineffectiveness of social services for Indigenous children. The NCW was committed to working within the system to advocate for powerless people in the midst of an Ottawa lobby scene dominated by interests that represented the polar opposite. Stephen Harper's government killed the Council in its first budget after gaining its 2011 majority.

The National Anti-Poverty Organization (NAPO), a related group, began at a 1971 national gathering of poor people with an emphasis on giving voice to those with direct, personal experience of poverty. NAPO reflected the spirit of participation, which the National Council of Welfare complemented with detailed research. It was from such organizations, along with a small band of activist intellectuals, that Canada's Basic Income movement would slowly emerge.

Sheila Regehr had her feet in both camps. In 2006, the savvy policy analyst who had become Executive Director of the NCW saw the shift in the political winds with the election of the first Harper government. The Council had just completed a survey showing that welfare was Canada's most broken social program, followed closely by the shrinking Employment Insurance program. The research demonstrated further that a Basic Income program offered the best fix.

Regehr, figuring that the Conservatives would soon clamp down on government travel, noticed that an upcoming Eastern Economics Association conference in New York would include sessions on Basic Income. The Canadian contingent in attendance included Regehr, NDP MP Tony Martin, Rob Rainer of NAPO, and Hugh Segal, the witty raconteur and longtime Conservative appointed to the Senate by the Liberal government in 2005.

Two years later, a handful of people from Canada's fledgling Basic Income movement attended the annual Basic Income Earth Network (BIEN) gathering in Dublin; Hugh Segal was a keynote speaker. Segal knew that Basic Income had supporters on the right and left but that there was also sturdy opposition from both sides—not to mention ever-cautious finance ministers who generally tend to lean starboard. He was also aware that the Harper government was "deeply inhospitable" to any kind of social assistance reform.

With his penchant for ironic understatement, Segal recalled the crowd's reaction at the University of Dublin's business school when he told them of his long-time commitment to Basic Income. They looked "bemused, sympathetic, or curious—the way you might look when you saw someone walk absent-mindedly into a telephone pole." The Canadians later met over a bagged lunch and resolved to form what would become the Basic Income Canada Network (BICN), affiliating with the BIEN.

One local participant at the conference was Sean Healy, a Catholic priest who regularly excoriated the Irish government, then riding the wave of the Celtic Tiger's buoyant economy. Father Healy argued that public policies were widening the gap between rich and poor. Within months of the BIEN congress, the Tiger would be brought down by the near-collapse of casino capitalism in 2008. At one point, Father Healy looked at Segal and asked in a bemused Irish lilt, "So, you're a conservative senator, are yeh? And you care about the poor? How very interesting. Well, good luck to yeh."[18]

Basic Income advocacy had never been a broad-based social movement, and its primary support was scattered. It resided in parts of the academy, particularly among those studying and teaching social policy and social services; in assorted pockets of the left; and among people simply offended by persistent poverty—in countries both rich and poor.

Some of the most stubbornly committed Basic Income supporters, like Evelyn Forget and Hugh Segal, had themselves grown up in low-income homes. For her part, Sheila Regehr, who went on to lead the BICN, had struggled as a single mother during the depression of the early 1980s. At the time, unemployment hit 13 percent, and inflation was not far behind. Interest rates hovered around 20 percent. Market fundamentalist dogma had started to take hold. A commission of Canada's Catholic bishops denounced the Liberal government's "survival of the fittest" mentality that "has often been used to rationalize the increasing concentration of wealth and power in the hands of a few."[19]

Regehr found herself with two children and too many marginal jobs. She sometimes relied on social assistance, then known in Ontario as Family Benefits. She also got a student loan to support her graduate studies. Later, recalling what would happen when Ontario's hard-right government made this illegal, she said,

Many still recall the 2001 suicide of Kimberly Rogers who was charged with fraud for doing what I did legally. I had a *de facto* basic income. It was not generous by any means, and it tortured me to not be able to provide my children with some of the most basic pleasures that other kids had, like ice cream cones from a park concession stand on a hot day.

Regehr did, however, have sufficient autonomy to buy time to work at home, be with her children, and avoid child care costs. When she did get a federal government job, it remained temporary for much of the period she was repaying her student loans: "Most of my career from then on was related to gender equality issues and income security."[20]

After Hugh Segal became a senator, he used his position to up the ante with respect to Basic Income advocacy. This in spite of his understanding that the Canadian Senate often serves as a place where important ideas go to die—a case in point being the Croll Report of 1971 and its guaranteed annual income proposal, which had been consigned to the political boneyard. But Segal was stubborn. He began to make common cause with another prominent senator, the Liberal Art Eggleton. While Segal had never won an election of any sort, Eggleton had moved from being Toronto's longest-serving mayor to a senior cabinet post under Jean Chrétien. Their 2009 Senate report *In from the Margins: A Call to Action on Poverty, Housing and Homelessness* included a call for a guaranteed annual income pilot project and a revamping of social policy. Still, Segal described the report as being "weak-kneed" on the GAI.[21]

Segal's aide Rose Brisson discovered a Manitoba newspaper story about Evelyn Forget's research on the 1970s Mincome project and brought it to his attention. The pilot project the senators were recommending had apparently already been done! From then on, Segal and Forget became a high-profile tag team instrumental in keeping Basic Income in the public eye until interest finally blossomed in the wake of the 2020 pandemic—including in the Senate, from which Segal had resigned in 2014. In July 2020, the Senate's Finance Committee looked forward to the looming need for permanent measures on which people could rely. Mass insecurity was clearly not going to go away anytime soon, and the senators urged the Trudeau Liberals to "give full, fair and priority consideration to a basic income guarantee."[22]

The sudden upsurge in mainstream legitimacy for Basic Income was stoked by the pandemic, but the period after the global meltdown of 2008 witnessed gradual recognition that some sort of Basic Income would eventually come to Canada. Forget's discoveries about Mincome were instrumental. She brought an understated passion to the issue, her work becoming widely recognized after 2011—when the interdisciplinary journal *Canadian Public Policy* published her findings about how a Basic Income had had such glaringly positive results in Dauphin, Manitoba.

The main part of her title, "The Town with No Poverty," neatly encapsulated her findings—it is, apparently, not that difficult to reduce if not eliminate poverty in one of the world's richest countries. Forget and other advocates pointed to one of the world's great social justice martyrs, citing Martin Luther King's full-on support of Basic Income not long before his assassination. King attacked inequality and the accompanying need to "compress our abundance into the overfed mouths of the middle and upper classes until they gag with superfluity." Forget outlined the advantages of Basic Income in plainspoken terms, explaining that it "addresses deprivation at its source, while the current system waits to address the consequences of poverty by spending more on our health services, special education, and the judicial system."[23]

A SPARK IN CHARLOTTETOWN

As Forget's revelations about the Mincome experiment added legitimacy to the Canadian case for Basic Income, Rob Rainer, Executive Director of Canada Without Poverty (formerly NAPO), decided to step down from his job of "putting out fires" dealing with poverty's manifestations. He would instead focus upstream—on poverty elimination. After hearing a 2007 speech by Hugh Segal about Basic Income, Rainer was "sold, then and there." He embarked on five years of intense advocacy to raise awareness and promote the idea of Basic Income.

In the spring of 2013, Rainer was invited to Charlottetown, P.E.I., by Marie Burge, a former Sister of Saint Martha, and Cooper Institute, an education and social justice centre that Burge had cofounded in 1984. She had organized two public talks for Rainer, meetings with local community members, and a discussion with the provincial Liberal cabinet, headed by Premier Robert Ghiz.

Cooper Institute's Catholic founders named it after William Cooper, who, after moving to Prince Edward Island in 1820, became an energetic advocate for tenant farmers to have the right to purchase their land. His campaign, fiercely opposed by the dominant class, won the day in 1853. Institute founders wanted to honour someone who "challenged power and proposed alternatives from the bottom up"— and to follow in his footsteps.[24] "We haven't had an idle day since we started," said the irrepressible Burge.

Burge had spent five transformative years in the Dominican Republic in the early 1970s, learning from the people in El Doce de Haina, a poor barrio just outside the capital of Santo Domingo. The mission program in which she worked was informed by the principles of liberation theology—the revolutionary Catholic movement that analyzed the structural causes of poverty, oppression, and colonization. Its key principle, the "preferential option for the poor," emphasized an assault on suffering by working directly in solidarity with people at the bottom of the social pyramid.

Burge integrated liberation theology into her thinking and way of living. The bright-eyed octogenarian was "amazed" by what people in the Dominican Republic taught her about "international capitalism and how Canada is guilty of draining the resources of the South." Every day, she watched as trucks rumbled along the main highway, heading for the port with loads of nickel destined for smelting at Falconbridge in Canada. She was "surprised and horrified" to learn from the people in the Dominican Republic about corporate Canada's corrosive role in the Global South.[25] Burge came home to P.E.I. knowing she had to continue social justice work by taking her direction from marginalized people: "I'll have that mission until I die."[26]

Rob Rainer's visit to Charlottetown was a turning point both for him and for Cooper Institute. "My experience there, with such enthusiasm for BI among those I met," Rainer recalled, "marked the beginning of a new, national, sustained 'push' for BI."[27] Rainer's campaign unquestionably helped to increase public support for Basic Income. He also sparked the 2013 founding of the Kingston Action Group for a Basic Income Guarantee.

The Kingston group was led by retired law professor Toni Pickard, whom Segal described as bringing "the diligence of a good lawyer, the vision of a worldly observer, and the determination of a disciplined humanitarian to her role—a true shepherd for the plains, valleys, and hills the effort for Basic Income must confront."[28] The group's principles for a Basic Income also informed the development of BICN's foundational document, *The Basic Income We Want*.

Other local groups and a provincial organization, the Ontario Basic Income Network (OBIN), followed. Also in 2013, the same year the Kingston group got started, Luc Gosselin co-founded Revenu de Base Québec, along with Alexandre Chabot-Bertrand, Jonathan Brun, and Alex Bigot. By 2020, two new national networks had formed to push basic income: Coalition Canada Basic Income–Revenu de Base and Basic Income Canada Youth Network.

As for Cooper Institute, Rainer's visit marked a shift in its work on livable income, which had begun in 2002 with a focus on the minimum wage. After his visit, Cooper Institute set up the Campaign for a Basic Income Guarantee PEI (C-BIG-PEI), following its usual way of working. Institute activists began consultations with people living in poverty to inform development of its position on basic income. Then they lobbied politicians, communicated with the media, and developed national connections. Burge said that when she and other members of C-BIG-PEI go to politicians, they can say, "This is what the community tells us."[29]

Before long, all four provincial parties in P.E.I.—the Liberals,

Progressive Conservatives, Greens, and New Democrats—had endorsed Basic Income. In 2016, the provincial legislature unanimously agreed to seek federal government support to launch a Basic Income pilot. The federal government offered no funding, only logistical support.[30] In the fall of 2019, the P.E.I. Legislative Assembly set up a special committee to explore the issue of poverty, with unanimous support from all parties. The committee developed a fully costed plan for a Basic Income pilot on the island. The interim report, issued in the summer of 2020, adopted, almost word for word, the principles for a Basic Income program that C-BIG-PEI had put forward—the same principles that they adopted originally from the Kingston Action Group for a Basic Income Guarantee.[31]

LAYING OUT PRINCIPLES

The Basic Income We Want, issued by the BICN in 2016, addresses inequality and the inadequacy of existing income security policies. The statement is straightforward, describing a Basic Income guarantee as a policy that would ensure that everyone gets sufficient income to live a dignified life, regardless of work status. This "autonomous income" would mean that people could decide for themselves how to meet their basic needs. The BICN went out of its way to insist that Basic Income had to be solidly welded to existing and proposed public services. It was not meant to replace universal social programs like public pensions, Employment Insurance, and aid to families with children. It could, however, replace "income provided through social assistance systems that impose paternalistic and stigmatizing conditions not applicable to other Canadians."

The statement is emphatic, affirming that a good Basic Income is one that "leaves no one receiving income support worse off than before a basic income program was implemented" and "substantially improves the wellbeing of those in deepest poverty." A Basic Income would likewise not replace minimum wage regulations and similar measures aimed at making sure that labour markets operate fairly. "Nor does good basic income program design remove the need for an affordable housing strategy, and the need to combat racism, other forms of discrimination and other factors linked to inequality."

The BICN was aware that the state's capacity to bring in creative policies aimed at making Canada a fairer country had been decimated by decades of tax changes that had lightened the load on the wealthy and the corporate sector. The BICN therefore made it clear that its design for expanding public provision for the common good would be "based on fair and progressive taxation."[32]

A half century after the Carter Report, Canada still had no inheritance tax, allowing rich people to pass on their fortunes to their children tax free—the U.K. and U.S.A. each tax inheritance at 40 percent, Japan at 55 percent. In 2020, with government balance sheets shredded by the pandemic, former bank chief economist turned iconoclast Jeff Rubin calculated that if Shopify founder Tobias Lutke, Canada's richest person, were to pay an estate tax at the American rate, the government would take in $4.5 billion—the equivalent of what 125,000 average Canadian households pay annually in income tax. Rubin also calculated that the system is so unfair that rich people whose taxes have been steadily falling since 1990 earn most of their money not from wages but from capital gains. Only half of such income is taxed, compared to 100 percent of the wages of ordinary workers. With a $343 billion deficit, Rubin was certain taxes would be heading up: "The question is, who is going to pay them?"[33]

The Basic Income We Want also lists jurisdictions that had implemented different forms of Basic Income. The twenty low- and high-income countries included Canada because of its public pension benefits and the by-now inevitable nod to the Mincome experiment and its encouraging Dauphin results.

INITIATIVES IN THE GLOBAL SOUTH

Prominent on the BICN list of worthy Basic Income initiatives was Brazil's targeted, countrywide *Bolsa Familia* program. This program, instituted by the Workers' Party in 2003, had reached some 80 million people, producing dramatic reductions in poverty and inequality and a forty percent decrease in infant mortality over ten years. Grade school enrolment hit nearly 100 percent. And, for those still worried that giving people money would encourage them to quit their jobs, a 2020 International Monetary Fund report on the impact of the program on formal labour market participation found "positive and significant" effects, particularly among younger workers, both female and male. The research determined that Bolsa recipients were more likely to get work than non-beneficiaries.[34]

As the globetrotting Guy Standing, the world's most zealous Basic Income promoter, noted, the *Bolsa Família* increased women's autonomy by helping with child care and public transit expenses. Standing argued that the effects were similar to those for Basic Income pilots elsewhere in the Global South, in that they increased "women's ability to claim equal priority for health care, countering the tendency to give priority to 'the breadwinner.'" An academic study added that the *Bolsa Família* "significantly increases women's decision-making power regarding contraception."[35] In 2019, the far-right government of Jair Bolsonaro dramatically downgraded the program, slashing the number of new families accepted for the benefits from 275,000 per month to fewer than 2,500.[36]

The BICN's list of countries with successful Basic Income schemes also included Namibia, the arid country northwest of—and once ruled by—South Africa. Its two-year 2008–09 Basic Income test in the village of Otjivero-Omitara generated the usual results. School attendance rose, as did use of the village clinic. Petty crime declined. With fewer stolen vegetables, people planted more food and bought more fertilizer. Women's status improved, as did nutrition. Basic Income encouraged collective action, and villagers initiated a Basic Income Advisory Committee, which further enhanced the program's effectiveness.

Zephania Kameeta, a bishop of the Evangelical Lutheran Church, had been jailed by apartheid South Africa for organizing against South African rule over his country. The former school principal was part of the central committee of the South West Africa People's Organisation, which eventually liberated Namibia. In 2015, at the age of seventy, he became Namibia's Minister of Poverty Reduction and Social Welfare, having been instrumental in promoting Basic Income in the desert land.

An eloquent speaker, Bishop Kameeta had a ready biblical insight into poverty reduction and Basic Income. He noted that before the pilot project started, opponents said that if you give people—especially poor people—money, they will sit down and become lazy. The bishop pointed to Exodus 16, which recounts the people of Israel's long journey out of slavery, including how they received manna from heaven. He noted that the manna did not make them lazy. Instead, it enabled them to be on the move to travel through the desert: "In Namibia, we know how harsh the circumstances of the desert can be. In this context nobody would say the manna made the Israelites dependent."[37]

Despite the Bishop's efforts and the success of the pilot, Basic Income in Namibia had not gained traction. By 2016, it had been consigned to the back burner as the government moved to prioritize food banks. However, the COVID-19 pandemic gave Namibian Basic Income advocates new impetus. A 2020 posting to the Basic Income Guarantee (BIG) Coalition website exclaimed, "Due to the social and economic situation exacerbated by the Covid-19 crisis, civil society is re-launching the BIG coalition. The introduction of a universal basic income grant for all in Namibia is a matter of urgency!"[38]

The same push was being felt in other parts of the world as well, including by governments. In South Korea, the Gyeonggi Provincial Government hosted the 2020 Korea Basic Income Fair online. Half a million people from all over the world attended virtually, five times the expected turnout. The governor gave the opening address, advocating the importance of Basic Income not only as a solution to the "pandemic-induced economic crisis" but also in response to the "development of AI and robot technologies."[39]

CANADA HOSTS THE WORLD SOCIAL FORUM

In 2016, the twelfth World Social Forum (WSF) took place in Montreal. Started in 2001, the global gathering is often regarded as the left's version of the global corporate elite's annual extravaganza in Davos, Switzerland. Previous WSFs had been held in the Global South; Montreal was chosen in part because of the successful 2012 "Maple Spring" student uprising against a Quebec tuition hike. Sessions addressed causes ranging from indigenous issues to climate change, neoliberal capitalism to women's rights. Basic Income had a significant presence, garnering attention from many among the thirty-five thousand delegates.

The WSF differs from Basic Income Earth Network congresses in that it casts its political net well beyond committed Basic Income activists. The Montreal gathering thus provided an early opportunity for Rutger Bregman to test-drive the ideas in his just-released *Utopia for Realists,* a book that would soon help to expose Basic Income to a broad reading audience. The Dutch journalist used his knack for popularizing complex issues to argue that moralists repelled by "money-for-nothing" proposals are sacralizing labour, holding it up as virtuous in and of itself.[40]

Veteran Canadian social justice activist and Basic Income organizer Tara Kainer, who also attended the 2016 gathering, recalled that many participants agreed with the idea of dissolving the connection between labour and money. Furthermore, she noted, "For the majority of those in the discussion groups I attended, Basic Income is a grassroots movement that should be independent of formal politics." Kainer's observation shed light on the thinking of many attending the WSF, though not necessarily those in the Basic Income movement. How Basic Income—by necessity a state program—could be distinct from big-P Politics remained unclear.

Kainer also noticed something important: Basic Income is a big tent. The wide range of opinions among WSF participants, themselves scattered about on the political left, suggested that Basic Income, rather than being a single idea, encompasses a panoply of ideas. Some at the WSF insisted that a Basic Income would give people the power to say "No!" to bad jobs. Others argued that it would offer people the power to say "Yes!" to new careers or hobbies or even following new life paths that they could not otherwise undertake. If there was a common denominator at the WSF—and indeed among many Basic Income proponents—it was the appeal of a venerable political ideal: Freedom.

TURNING POSSIBILITY INTO REALITY?

By 2020, Basic Income was an idea that been tested and studied, analyzed, and discussed. And often trashed, though it had never been implemented in any comprehensive and decisive way. It had also become a minor academic industry. Scholars regularly submitted articles for peer review to *Basic Income Studies*, published in Berlin. As far back as 2012, Palgrave Macmillan had offered up a collection with the lofty title *Basic Income Guarantee and Politics: International Experiences and Perspectives on the Viability of Income Guarantee*. The academic examinations contrasted with the sometimes breathless titles on the parade of volumes soon to appear. Journalist Annie Lowery travelled the world to produce *Give People Money: How a Universal Basic Income Would End Poverty, Revolutionize Work and Remake the World*. A blizzard of YouTube offerings, TED Talks, and internet memes began to make landfall in the 2010s.

Two of Basic Income's leading promoters in the early twenty-first century—Belgian scholars Philippe Van Parijs and Yannick Vanderborght—saw a surge of interest in their foundational idea as uncertainty grew during the 2020 pandemic. Inequality, which had been growing steadily since the early 1980s, exploded.[41] Traditional walls of social protection were crumbling as trade unions and the welfare state came under assault. Precarious jobs paying miserable wages had become the norm for many, particularly younger working-class and racialized people. Yet in their 2017 book *Basic Income: A Radical Proposal for a Free Society and a Sane Economy*, Van Parijs and Vanderborght still managed to convey a sense of optimism, a key ingredient in energizing a patient politics of proposition. "Utopian visions," they write, "do not turn real in a day, but they guide us and strengthen us through the effort."[42]

Van Parijs and Vanderborght imagine Basic Income as a "floor"—something more solid and permanent than the "safety net" metaphor commonly used to describe the welfare state. A safety net conjures up the image of a circus tightrope walker, with all the risk that implies. Importantly, the floor envisioned by Van Parijs and Vanderborght is not composed of a single board, or a few sub-floor joists, for that matter. Agreeing with the argument that Basic Income must be implemented in conjunction with other measures, the two also advocate for universal basic health care and education, lifelong learning, universal access to the internet, a healthy environment, and savvy city planning.[43] To which can be added universal child care, publicly subsidized housing, pharmacare, and other measures. Notably, many of these elements of a free society have something in common: the need for them stems from market failure.

One contribution to the Palgrave Macmillan volume, "On the Political Feasibility of Basic Income: An Analytical Framework," was co-authored by prominent Basic Income supporter Jurgen De Wispelaere. De Wispelaere was working at McGill while helping in the early stages of BICN by joining its board and organizing the 2014 Basic Income Earth Network congress in Montreal. He and sociologist José Antonio Noguera outlined the formidable challenges that stand in the way of turning hope into reality with respect to a Basic Income scheme. The two theorists outlined three key political obstacles facing Basic Income proponents:

- The first obstacle is *political feasibility*. To overcome this, supporters need to build robust, enduring coalitions based on an ideological agenda. Such coalitions need the capacity to undertake sustained campaigns, taking into account differences between the partners. Such partnerships could include egalitarians struggling against inequality while promoting an expansion of social services and right-leaning libertarians inclined to individualism. To develop a minimal basis of unity, each set of political entrepreneurs would need to compromise, while emphasizing aspects of Basic Income that would appeal to their partners. For example, in 2019, a business-oriented group called UBI Works took shape in Canada, following in the footsteps of CEOs for Basic Income, which had been initiated by Floyd Marinescu, CEO of C4Media. He had been appalled by the cancellation of the Ontario Basic Income Pilot by Doug Ford's government. UBI Works was separate from the loose BICN umbrella organization that is more inclined to a social democratic approach.
- The next obstacle is *institutional feasibility*. This means overcoming concerns, even anxieties, about implementation of a Basic Income program. Any major recasting of public policy will predictably ruffle bureaucratic feathers and, as any experienced lobbyist or advocate knows, the civil service can be a formidable ally or an equally staunch opponent. Even with substantial bureaucratic and political support, there is truth to the old cliché: the devil is in the details. Many proponents argue, correctly, that a Basic Income could simplify needlessly complex welfare systems. That does not mean an unconditional program would be simple to implement. "The sheer size of the program in practice means that few instruments currently in place have the comprehensive reach that a universal BI requires...," wrote De Wispelaere and Noguera. "Hard choices between setting up new institutions from scratch or recombining several administrative instruments in novel ways [are] fraught with complexity and risk." Devils, details, indeed.
- A third challenge is the all-important *psychological feasibility* of

Basic Income. Convincing influential politicians and civil servants that an unconditional Basic Income is the key to real poverty reduction is only one step. A significant bloc of public support is also required, and that would call for an effective campaign to explain the principles and values underpinning what remains, for many, a novel idea: "Psychological feasibility entails the capacity to mobilize positive perceptions, emotions and reasons such that the proposal does not generate strong social opposition." That means dealing with the fact that the mass of working- and middle-class people would be paying taxes so that others would be able to do a bit better. Basic Income campaigners are intimately familiar with arguments about the work ethic and the principle of deserving-ness, and ignore them at their peril.

"So where is the income coming from to sustain this basic income for people who have no desire to work productively?" asked one keyboard warrior in response to a conservative columnist writing positively about Basic Income during the 2020 pandemic.[44] De Wispelaere and Noguera pointed out a hard fact of cultural (and hence political) life. Many, if not most, hold fast to the idea that work is a central obligation to society and that social assistance should be confined to the needy or "deserving"—that is, those who are unable to work.

As Basic Income supporters, De Wispelaere and Noguera did not just offer a pessimistic shrug. For them, "framing" is crucial: "Carefully framing BI proposals to avoid triggering negative perceptions, values, and beliefs, and instead trigger positive dispositions may significantly improve the psychological feasibility of BI." The positives might include promoting the policy as an antipoverty measure or as a natural social dividend—a share-the-wealth argument that can be linked to tax fairness. Another method of boosting public acceptance would be to introduce it gradually, linking it conceptually to universal child benefits and universal pensions.[45]

The BICN picked up on this when it insisted that Canadians already have a Basic Income after age sixty-five. Framed in this manner,

Basic Income becomes simply another step that follows previous social achievements that are now widely accepted. Canadian Basic Income promoters have often likened it to public health care, a sort of public insurance that everyone supports through the tax system and only uses when needed.

Even so, the framing issue and the very feasibility of Basic Income are bound up with two factors that so often prove decisive in resolving political issues: values and self-interest. Appealing to values like fairness and a sense of justice is important. But poverty and food insecurity are *not* issues of direct concern to most Canadians. Unlike issues such as health care, housing, the economy, jobs, and the environment, they rarely if ever make it onto those top-of-mind lists typically offered up by pollsters. As insecurity, inequality, and precarious work increased, becoming more acute with the 2020 pandemic, Basic Income enthusiasts finally got a golden opportunity to link their issue with those affecting a broader public.

GUY STANDING PULLS THE STRANDS TOGETHER

The world's most prominent Basic Income promotor is an animated English economist who grew up playing in Greenwich bomb sites downriver from London. The scars of war festered beyond urban streetscapes. When Guy Standing was born in 1948, rationing of staples as basic as bread was just ending. He was an involuntary vegetarian until he was eight: "We didn't get much milk, never had butter. It was margarine for us."[46]

His mother had been thirteen when she left school, a product of England's rigid class system. Education was not for people of her social rank, so she bitterly opposed Guy's decision to go to university: "A working-class boy did not go to university. She was absolutely furious and wouldn't speak to me for ages." His parents had separated, with Standing's father cobbling together a meagre living working in offices and hotels, playing piano when he could get a gig. He reached retirement age just when Margaret Thatcher took office and proceeded to gut public pension benefits. His son supported him for the last twenty-five years of his life, working at the International Labour Organization. "You never forget those things," Standing recalled. "He left a legacy of me being a dissident."

A child of the 1960s and politically on the left, Standing upholds Basic Income as an instrument of liberation from the shackles of capitalism. For Standing, Basic Income in its ideal form really *is* revolutionary, utopian in the sense of something that may seem unrealistic at first glance but remains an ideal worth pursuing. He traces it back to the essence of ancient Greek democracy, yet is particularly intrigued by its medieval roots in England and the 1217 Charter of the Forest, which was issued alongside the Magna Carta and asserted the rights of commoners to subsistence in the commons.

By 2019, when he came to Winnipeg at the centenary of the General Strike, Standing had come out with yet another book boosting Basic Income, *Plunder of the Commons: A Manifesto for Sharing Public Wealth.* Within a year he had another one. *Battling Eight Giants: Basic Income Now* listed eight evils that subsistence income for everyone would banish: inequality, insecurity, debt, stress, precarity, automation, populism, extinction. No one could accuse Standing of not casting his net widely. With a Cambridge PhD and thirty years at the ILO, he was offering new meaning to the notion of the public intellectual.

Standing had been in good measure responsible for bringing the notion of precarity into debates about the brave new world of work. *Precariat* is a clever portmanteau blending proletariat, that venerable term for the working class, with people forced into precarious work. Not long after Standing published *The Precariat: The New Dangerous Class* in 2011, discussions of a "gig economy" began bubbling up. Uber and Taskrabbit had yet to achieve prominence, Brexit was not yet a word, and Donald Trump was still a bombastic reality television performer when Standing began to warn that the precariat is "prone to listen to ugly voices." Many whose lives had become more insecure, watching resentfully as inequality deepened, listened to voices that fuelled their resentment.

Guy Standing has featured in a seemingly endless number of YouTube videos, in which he passionately urges viewers worldwide to support the Basic Income concept. A cofounder of the Basic Income Earth Network, Standing emphasizes the corrosive effects of precarious work. As more people lose hope for secure employment, work-based identities fade away, as does a socially rooted sense of self. Standing outlined four "*A*s" experienced by the precariat:

- Anger—rooted in frustration at the inability to achieve a meaningful life.
- Anomie—the passivity born of despair.
- Anxiety—generated by chronic insecurity.
- Alienation—the awareness that one is a mere subject whose life is directed by others.

Standing issued a strong warning in 2011: "The very success of the 'neoliberal' agenda, embraced to a greater or lesser extent by governments of all complexions, has created an incipient political monster. Action is needed before that monster comes to life."[47] By the time he touched down in Winnipeg in 2019 to address a national union convention, populist monsters were striding across the globe and Standing's *Precariat* book had been translated into twenty-four languages.

The National Union of Public and General Employees had invited Standing to Canada because of his analysis of precarious labour, not his Basic Income advocacy. Like many unions, NUPGE was ambivalent about Basic Income. Standing began his speech by pointing to the centenary of the Winnipeg strike and the lasting image of a streetcar being overturned by strikers, two of whom were killed by law enforcement. The NUPGE delegate kits included a graphic history of Canada's most famous strike.

Standing went on to tell the story of another labour demonstration that took place one hundred years before the Winnipeg strike, likely unfamiliar to the Canadians in the room. In 1819, some hundred thousand protesters gathered in St. Peter's Field in Manchester in their Sunday best to demand electoral reform and improved working conditions. At what became known as "Peterloo," the forces of order responded with a cavalry charge that killed nineteen, injuring hundreds more. For Standing, Peterloo 1819 was a "statement of rebellion," while Winnipeg 1919 marked the beginning of "a period dominated by laissez-faire, right-wing market fundamentalism" and a gilded age of inequality and insecurity—which led to Depression, which led to fascism and world war.

Standing's wide-ranging remarks covered gains made during the welfare state's promising era and the flash of hope during the Occupy movement's attacks on the new gilded age: "The left progressive movements have only made progress when they have class-based politics driving them on, and when they have a vision of a better tomorrow, not [using] words that suggest they want to create a lost yesterday." For Standing, that did not mean the traditional union focus of jobs-for-all but redistributing wealth so everyone could gain "basic security—a human need and a superior public good."

It was here, as he approached the end of his talk, that Standing departed from his analysis of precarious work to discuss the need to develop a strategy to provide everyone with that security. "Can we honestly say that is what the unions have been doing? Or labour parties or social democratic parties?" he asked, his voice rising, arms windmilling. A job focus is a dead end, he argued: "If you do jobs, you get security. If you don't, well, you'll take the consequences." This constituted one of those lost yesterdays, he insisted, calling for a far more systemic approach: "This is one of the reasons, one of the many reasons, why I support Basic Income."

There was a short, sharp burst of spontaneous applause, prompting the speaker to offer a sort of embarrassed half-smile, a shrug, and a quiet "Thank you" before recounting the story of one of his periodic dustups with trade union officials over Basic Income. At one interna-

tional gathering, an Italian labour official had told him that after thinking it over, he figured one reason unions tend to resist Basic Income is
that, if people had one, they would not join unions. Standing's rejoin-
der was that this was "immoral" and "fundamentally wrong." Standing
exclaimed, "People who have basic security are *more* likely to join and
support collective bodies fighting for rights." This generated another,
longer round of applause.[48]

Standing added a snippet of inspirational verse. It is not every
union convention that features romantic poetry from the podium.
Perhaps it helped stretch the lengthy queue of union members who
later waited for him to sign a copy of his book on the precariat. The
radical romantic Percy Bysshe Shelley wrote *The Mask of Anarchy* in
the immediate aftermath of Peterloo:

Rise, like lions after slumber
In unvanquishable number!
Shake your chains to earth like dew
Which in sleep had fallen on you—   .
Ye are many—they are few!

CHAPTER 3

BASIC INCOME COMES TO ONTARIO—BUT BRIEFLY

Let's vote for a poverty free Ontario.
—Roadside campaign sign

THE ANNOUNCEMENT

It was perhaps an odd place to announce a new pilot project designed to provide more money to people colonized by stress and uncertainty because of poverty—a project for people who must think every day about paying for food, shelter, and other basics, and a great leap forward for Basic Income in Canada.

Ontario Premier Kathleen Wynne made her excited presentation at LIUNA Station, an event venue that promised the "extraordinary luxury and opulence of a golden era," including Italian marble floors and flowing Versace™ draperies, a place that boasted "180,074 lobster tails served."[1] Back in the 1930s, the station's original owners, Canadian National Railways, directly or indirectly employed some ten thousand people in Hamilton.

The sprawling extravagance of the LIUNA Station in Hamilton's gentrifying North End testified to the success of an entrepreneurially minded construction union. By the time Premier Wynne's entourage arrived to make the Basic Income announcement, LIUNA (the Laborers International Union of North America) Local 183 had refurbished the derelict station into "Ontario's Premier Venue." Local 183 also owned and operated hundreds of nonmarket housing units in Hamilton.

LIUNA, a heavyweight outfit in the Toronto-Hamilton construction sector, was also a stalwart supporter of the Ontario Liberals, having given $182,350 to the party by 2016. That was four times the amount it had donated to the New Democrats, labour's traditional allies.[2] Much had changed since 1995 when 96 percent of all Ontario union contributions had gone to the NDP. It was all about strategic voting and labour's general political defensiveness in the face of neoliberal attacks, as some unions adopted ABC (anything-but-Conservative) multi-partisan tactics. It was not necessarily a case of "vote Liberal," but pragmatic support for the party most likely to defeat Conservative candidates in particular ridings. For this reason, by 2003, Ontario's Liberals had eclipsed the NDP as the main recipient of union campaign money.[3]

At the April 2017 event, Wynne announced that four thousand people across three Ontario cities (Hamilton-Brantford, Lindsay, and Thunder Bay) would be eligible for the $50 million pilot, designed to test how unconditional money would improve their lives. Under the plan, a single person on Ontario Works would receive about $17,000 per year, an amount the Premier described as "not an extravagant sum by any means."[4] An understatement, to be sure. Those with a disability were eligible for up to an additional $6,000 per year.[5]

"It wasn't just an announcement, but a full-on keynote speech," recalled Liberal political staffer James Janeiro, a millennial who had been keen on Basic Income since his university days. Janeiro had organized Toronto's west end for Wynne's 2013 leadership bid. During the 2014 general election, he had been at Liberal central, briefing candidates and writing social policy material. After Wynne's 2014 election victory, Janeiro made it up to the Premier's Office. The Basic Income Pilot became, albeit rather belatedly, a centrepiece of her government. Janeiro was over the moon by the time of the Hamilton announcement, saying, "We filled the room with people from all over."[6]

RELUCTANT CONVERTS

A smiling Deirdre Pike was among the demographically mixed group carefully selected for the TV-friendly background, positioned behind the Premier. The veteran Hamilton social justice campaigner had long been sceptical of the Ontario Liberals. They had been in office since 2003, first under Dalton McGuinty and then under Wynne, and their antipoverty record had been spotty at best.

When Mike Harris's right-wing Progressive Conservatives ran successfully on an austerity platform in 1995, the Liberals denounced the heartlessness of the Tory "welfare diet," which claimed that a single person on welfare could eat well for $90 per month. Pasta perhaps, but certainly no sauce.[7]

Wynne herself would later admit that when she was first elected in 2003 as a star candidate for the McGuinty Liberals, "poverty reduction was not part of our platform." She also conceded that when, seven years after being elected, the McGuinty government launched a comprehensive probe of Ontario's welfare system—famous for the eight hundred rules that trap people in a web of state surveillance, harassment, and intimidation—the commissioners "were not given the permission to talk about adequacy of rates."[8] And by the time Wynne made her BI announcement in 2017, social assistance rates were *still* abysmally inadequate, far behind even what they had been when the Harris government launched its deliberate attack on the poor more than twenty years earlier.

Against that background, Deirdre Pike had helped to organize a "mock trial" of Kathleen Wynne as part of Ontario's Put-Food-in-the-Budget campaign. "Where is this social justice Premier?" the activists asked, recalling that during her leadership campaign Wynne declared that social justice "is what drives me" and would be her political legacy.[9]

Pike, a longtime staffer at the local Social Planning and Research Council (SPRC), was also a columnist for the *Hamilton Spectator*. Like Tom Cooper of the Hamilton Roundtable for Poverty Reduction, she had long been sceptical about whether a Basic Income was the way to attack poverty.

Still, Basic Income campaigners had been pointing to Evelyn Forget's findings about the positive results of the 1975–78 Mincome experiment in Dauphin, Manitoba. Forget's observation that Mincome "made a profound financial difference [for] working people" who suddenly had "the freedom to spend their time and money as they saw fit" appealed to Pike's sense of fairness. Perhaps a Basic Income could, after all, help to liberate people for whom the SPRC had long been advocating. "I'd heard about the Dauphin, Manitoba thing," she said.[10]

Yet Basic Income still remained a tough sell for Pike. She saw its potential but worried about what another right-wing government committed to decimating other social programs might do with it. She had what she described as a "fear spot." The "wrong hands" might use Basic Income to "cancel all the other government programs, saying 'Well, we gave you this money, now you just have to go buy [things] for yourself.' That's the great danger."[11]

Prominent Hamilton social justice activist Tom Cooper also showed up for the Premier's Basic Income announcement. He was campaigning for a Living Wage for Ontario workers. Distinct from a minimum wage—fixed by political factors—Living Wage activists calculated hourly rates on a city-by-city basis according to what it actually costs to get by. His vision, however, went beyond such important advocacy efforts. It was underpinned by an egalitarian value; people living in poverty's grip have the right to a say in the decisions affecting their lives. Solidarity, not charity. Empowerment aimed at asserting people's agency. It works best when people are not regarded as passive victims but become actively engaged participants.

By the time Wynne came to town to announce the Basic Income pilot, Cooper had gradually become intrigued by the idea of giving people more money, no strings attached. Though a former Liberal himself, Cooper was suspicious of Liberal intentions. His attitude reflected that of Tommy Douglas, the first NDP leader and "father of medicare," who had a favourite quip about Liberal promises: "There's a lot of noise on the stairs, but no one's coming into the room." Cooper's scepticism had extended to Basic Income: "I thought that maybe this is just an excuse to get rid of public health care, let people buy it from the private sector, that sort of thing."[12]

But this scepticism had gradually given way to cautious openness when the Hamilton Roundtable for Poverty Reduction sent two activists to Winnipeg and the Congress of the North American Basic Income Guarantee (NABIG) in 2016. By this time Cooper was the Roundtable Director, and the Wynne government had surprised everyone—not least the growing Basic Income lobby—by including a BI pilot in its most recent budget.

A few months after the Premier's LIUNA Station announcement, Deirdre Pike was working with a group called HOPE (Hamilton Organizing for Poverty Elimination) on an "empty fridges/empty promises" effort to bring attention to huge numbers of low-income people *not* participating in the OBIP. Aiming to demonstrate that the $721 provided monthly by Ontario Works was laughably inadequate to pay for a healthy diet, they urged supporters to take photographs of the contents of their refrigerators and send them to the government. Most of the pictures showed few if any fresh fruits and vegetables.

The media-savvy effort also urged better-off Hamiltonians to send photos of fully stocked fridges, pointing once again to the savage inequality that the *Spectator* had for years been exposing. Holding a sign reading "Will vote to end poverty," Pike insisted that *everyone* should get the amount that people signing up for Basic Income were soon to get.[13]

Cooper and Pike ultimately decided to back the Wynne government's Basic Income pilot after concluding that it was a necessary—although far from sufficient—way of addressing longstanding problems like food insecurity and the sorry neglect of nonmarket housing for low-income people. They recognized that Basic Income held some promise for getting rid of the "terrible" social assistance system that delivered only "income insecurity."

By June 2018, Ontario was preparing to go to the polls. The opposition Progressive Conservatives and New Democrats both said they were firmly committed to supporting the Basic Income Pilot for the full three years. Fully convinced by now, Pike threw her hat in the ring and actually ran for the Liberals in Hamilton against NDP leader Andrea Horwath. Horwath's NDP had come down resolutely on the fence with respect to poverty reduction in general and Basic Income in particular. Longtime friends who supported the NDP considered Pike a traitor, turning their backs on her. She lost to Horwath; the Liberals were defeated; and the Progressive Conservatives ended the Basic Income Pilot within a few short weeks of coming into power—a move that Hugh Segal, who had played an important role in getting it started, called "beyond tragic."

THE LONG ROAD TO THE ONTARIO PILOT

While it took Hamilton activists a while to come around to supporting Basic Income, the Wynne Liberals had taken three years after being reelected with a solid majority to make their move. This despite the conventional wisdom that a newly elected government should make its big moves early in its mandate.

Wynne's Liberals needed to convince people, themselves included, that the time had come to launch a Basic Income experiment. Would a comprehensive Basic Income research study provide crucial evidence about whether Basic Income actually works? Though supporters continued to argue that their favourite policy prescription had been tested *ad nauseam*, only the Green Party was offering explicit support. And it had never elected anyone to the Ontario Legislature.[14]

Kathleen Wynne herself was certainly open to Basic Income, suggesting that the government's women's caucus had long been pushing poverty reduction and recalling that she had wanted to examine the policy ever since becoming Premier. Indeed, for a government leader she had a granular understanding of just how distorted the social welfare system was. "The people who are working in social assistance delivery are actually not doing the things they need to be doing. We need people to be supporting, guiding, and facilitating" people struggling on welfare "as opposed to punishing, shaming, and demeaning."[15]

With support from the top, it might have seemed that starting a Basic Income pilot would have been a done deal. But James Janeiro knew that things are never straightforward in government, in part because of bureaucratic and political inertia. So, the government called in long-time Basic Income supporter Hugh Segal, the former senator and high-profile Progressive Conservative who had been promoting Basic Income since the dawn of time. Or at least that is how it seemed to a millennial like Janeiro—understandably, since Segal had been an adviser to Progressive Conservative Premier Bill Davis back in the 1970s.

Segal prepared a report for the Liberals, titled *Finding a Better Way*, which provided the basis for the pilot project. He told the Liberals in 2016 that they should be inspired by Ontario's introduction of the Guaranteed Annual Income Supplement for seniors in the 1970s, which, he wrote, "radically reduced poverty for this group" and led the way to the federal Guaranteed Income Supplement. What's more, Segal was explicit about the need to do away with the state's "welfare cop" surveillance approach. He made it clear that the OBIP's main purpose had to be to test "replacing the broad policing, control, and monitoring now present in Ontario Works and the Ontario Disability Support Program."[16]

Segal arrived at the Ontario Legislature from nearby Massey College where he held the arcane title of "Master." He brought along Evelyn Forget, who had just come from Winnipeg for a stint as a visiting scholar at Massey. After meeting Segal and Forget, the Premier pulled Janeiro aside and said, "Okay, I think we gotta do this."

"I'm like in heaven because this is the kind of policy thing I've been thinking about since I was in undergrad," said Janeiro.[17]

The government asked Segal to look into what it would take to conduct a Mincome-style study in Ontario. He did so, with assistance from Forget and the young health economist Maripier Isabelle, who was working on her PhD at the University of Toronto. There were many details to work out: what data sets would be needed; how to recruit participants to generate a solid sample; how to recruit researchers and analysts who could gather quantitative and qualitative data via administrative records, questionnaires, and interviews; how to evaluate the costs and benefits of replacing social assistance with a Basic Income. But in spite of the complexity inherent in this sort of social research, the underlying question was straightforward: "Will a Basic Income reduce poverty more effectively, encourage work, reduce stigmatization, and produce better health outcomes and better life chances for recipients?"[18]

Segal was aware of the project's pitfalls. There would be:

- the usual queries about the cost—the "classic bugaboo of the right"
- concern that a money-for-nothing scheme would breed sloth, and
- objections from unions about job losses among public service workers who oversee traditional welfare.

In the short term, however, the canny political operative predicted a question from cynical reporters and Basic Income opponents: "How much is this former senator being paid to help the poor?" To which he could reply, "Nothing." His requirement for the assignment was that his work would be *pro bono.*[19]

The initial application for the pilot ran to seventy-five pages, creating a steep barrier for potential applicants. The hefty package included detailed questionnaires and endless fine print—hardly a reliable way of reaching out to low-income people, who often harbour deep-seated and well-founded anxieties about the state's intrusive welfare regime and the aggressive surveillance of some welfare officials. Desperate to get the pilot going, the government had to get creative. Officials in Hamilton headed out to food banks, meal programs, and church basement gatherings with simplified descriptions and big signs reading, "Ask me about Basic Income." Enrolment jumped.

THE YEAR OF THE PILOT

By 2017, an international spate of interest in testing Basic Income had given its boosters reason for hope. Basic Income Earth Network cofounder Guy Standing dubbed 2017 "the Year of the Pilot."

The previous year, a Basic Income referendum in conservative Switzerland had been defeated by a three-to-one margin. Yet supporters had ignited a lively national conversation with their happy campaign that included dumping eight million gold-coloured five-centime coins—one coin for every Swiss—into Geneva's largest square (the famous Swiss banks refused to cooperate). Meanwhile, several Dutch cities were developing experiments, despite opposition by the senior partner in the coalition government of the day.

Finland's no-strings-attached experiment lasted two years. It was basically geared to ascertaining whether a Basic Income would encourage people to take low-wage or precarious jobs without fear of losing unemployment insurance benefits. Its outcomes were limited because participants came from a small and narrow group, and benefits were fixed at subpoverty levels.

During the scheme's first year, about 18 percent of unemployed Finns got jobs—around the same rate as the control group. The next year saw 27 percent of people working, slightly higher than the control group.[20] Yet the Finnish scheme came to an ignominious end in late 2018, the victim of internal politics, bureaucratic problems, and—most importantly for BI advocates—the way that the unconditionality crucial to Basic Income schemes clashed with social norms.

Support for income security programs tends to be grounded in the notion of reciprocity. The American socialist publication *Jacobin* ("Reason in Revolt") argued that people will back such programs "as long as they reasonably believe that recipients of these benefits are trying to get a job and will eventually pay into the system. Since a Basic Income does not impose that requirement on recipients, it can be quite difficult to build support because it violates the reciprocity norm." Clearly, this *quid pro quo* comes into play even in a country with a political culture like Finland's, where issues of fairness and worthiness are central to policy debates.[21]

Guy Standing flagged the Ontario Pilot as "the most promising of those planned to start in 2017," his Year of the Pilot.[22] Frustrated that their proposal had been studied to death, Basic Income advocates knew that they still needed a solid body of evidence to prove that their unconditional proposal would shatter the widespread caricature that a money-for-nothing plan would turn recipients into slackers lazing on the couch scarfing bonbons or, worse, drinking beer.

Against this background, Ontario's Basic Income pilot had a specific political goal: it was designed to provide evidence. Would an unconditional income, well above traditional miserly welfare rates but by no means generous, be a disincentive to work? Would the results of the experiment fly in the face of the view that if the state gives people money for nothing then they would do, well, nothing? Does this commonly held view reflect a profound insight into human nature? Or was it just a popular misconception based on prejudice against low-income people?

Of course, simply providing irrefutable evidence that Basic Income is a fine idea would certainly not guarantee success; after all, even though an avalanche of evidence has proven that human activity is causing global heating that threatens life on earth, governments have continued to allow CO_2 emissions to rise.

James Janeiro, as responsible as anyone for bringing the Basic Income Pilot to Ontario, had a grasp of both the policy issues and the politics of Basic Income. He knew that deep poverty is endemic and that social assistance kept people trapped there. For years, the government had had a comprehensive report in hand, co-authored by newly minted senator and former NDP minister and labour activist Frances Lankin, that provided clear evidence that welfare was a toxic mess.[23]

Janeiro was also aware that the labour market was keeping many trapped in poverty—no matter how many jobs they had. And he knew that the federal Liberals and Conservatives had over the years gutted the Employment Insurance system, cynically using the fund's surplus as a tool to cut the deficit. "People are being left with a very frayed social safety net and nothing underneath if they fall," he said. "The Feds have never really taken a serious stab at adapting [Employment Insurance] to gig work or precarious work." He offered a blunt summary: "People just don't have enough goddamned money."[24]

SHIFTING CURRENTS

Hugh Segal's decades of BI promotion were based on the idea of providing an amount approaching a livable income to people who had long been struggling with dysfunctional social assistance systems. But things had changed for working-class people in the half-century since Segal started to ponder what was, back in the late 1960s, called a guaranteed annual income. The cliché was that, once upon a time, one could quit a job in the morning and get another that same afternoon. In the brave new world of work, the boss now had the upper hand. The labour market had become very much a buyer's market.

As the main policy staffer driving the Basic Income bus for the Wynne Liberals, Janeiro also knew that in this world, precarious and displaced workers are being left behind. And as a partisan politico, he was also familiar with his party's failure on this front. The federal Liberals in particular had been in good measure responsible for turning the Employment Insurance system into a cruel hoax: while everyone is legally required to pay insurance premiums, by 2017 EI was excluding over half of contributors from benefits. The Chrétien Liberals had also been in charge of the program's Orwellian name change from Unemployment to Employment Insurance.

Janeiro had considered the potential political advantages of putting forward a Basic Income program. He anticipated that Ontario's opposition Progressive Conservatives under their new centre-right leader Patrick Brown might complain that Basic Income would bankrupt the province, while the NDP might do some handwringing about possible social service job loss. He noted, "I wanted this political fight that never actually came. It would give us a chance to be full-throated in defence of people who would benefit from Basic Income."

The Basic Income effort had another, albeit minor, political advantage: it would garner support from social justice groups. For the past several provincial elections, lawn and roadside messages that read, "Let's vote for a poverty free Ontario" had started to appear alongside partisan campaign signs. Clearly, ideas related to Basic Income were gaining steam. It also couldn't hurt to have faith communities that had been lobbying the legislature since the late 1980s onside.

Ted McMeekin, a Hamilton MPP and former Liberal Community and Social Services Minister, was a keen Basic Income supporter with strong connections to church circles. McMeekin was something of an outlier: he could quote scripture and had voluntarily left the Cabinet so Wynne could promote a woman.

The former Hamilton city councillor had been an MPP since 2000. Faith community antipoverty activists lobbied him regularly, and he was instrumental in making sure that the government picked Hamilton as a site for the Basic Income pilot. McMeekin saw the OBIP as a singular political achievement, particularly since his party had been in office for fourteen years when the Premier made her announcement. His years in public life had given him a slightly jaded perspective on government: "You become more concerned about holding onto power than doing the right thing."[25]

The Pilot was poised to secure approval during the third year of the Liberal mandate. McMeekin and other reform elements in the caucus, including Deputy Premier Deb Matthews, were convinced the government was on the right path. Liberal polling showed that public support for Basic Income had legs, although it was hardly top-of-mind for most voters. Nonetheless, there was no apparent downside. The government had political and policy opportunities.

BASIC INCOME 101

A three-hour lineup stretched out onto the street outside the columned entrance to Lindsay's public library. It was early November 2017.[26] Like many old Carnegie-financed libraries, its well-proportioned classical façade conveyed a sense of solidity. The *public* in public library conveyed a principle close to the hearts of Basic Income boosters: everyone can use it; everyone contributes to its support.

The people queuing up were not waiting to borrow the latest Stephen King novel. They were hoping to sign up for Ontario's Basic Income pilot program. At the other end of Kent Street West that afternoon, a hundred people gathered to learn more about OBIP at the Celebrations event venue, a former church tucked along the side of the Scugog River. The space wasn't nearly as opulent as Hamilton's LIUNA Station, but the sense of anticipation was just as palpable.

Few were as keen as Roderick Benns. The entrepreneur and journalist had just launched the *Lindsay Advocate,* a vehicle for local news and no small measure of Basic Income advocacy. Benns, a Lindsay native, assured the gathering that low-income parents know how to spend extra money, citing the recently introduced Canada Child Benefit that was arriving without judgment or behavioural control. "Despite the mythology of what 'poor people' might do with money, I understand what that mythology means. Growing up right here in what was then called the East Ward, with a hard-working mother and a hard-spending alcoholic father, I lived it."[27]

The event, sponsored by the fledgling Ontario Basic Income Network and the Basic Income Canada Network, was introduced by the chair of the regional community development corporation. It was a kind of Basic Income 101 seminar. The audience, some of whom had just signed up for the Pilot, heard about its advantages from the perspective of law enforcement and social justice, health policy, and political philosophy.

Dr. Bert Lauwers, CEO of Ross Memorial Hospital, had been practising family medicine in Lindsay for twenty-five years. He started his remarks with a nod to a prominent nineteenth-century German physician. Dr. Rudolf Virchow was a cellular pathology pioneer—and also a political radical. After engaging in street demonstrations during the 1848 revolution, Virchow cofounded the weekly *Medical Reform* under the banner "the physician is the natural attorney of the poor."[28]

Dr. Lauwers agreed with Dr. Virchow's understanding of medicine as a social science. He then laid out the grim situation in Lindsay and the surrounding cottage country area. The population was about ninety thousand. Among them were 11,615 low-income people—a poverty rate of 13.16 percent. Allowing this level of poverty, he stated, constitutes "a policy choice." The physician continued, nodding once more to Virchow, noting that "politics is nothing else but medicine on a large scale."

Dr. Lauwers, clearly a stickler for accurate data, introduced "something called the social determinants of health": Food insecurity. Unaffordable housing. Social exclusion. Unemployment. Inequality. All, he said, were linked to unequal distribution of wealth and income. People at the very bottom have far poorer health than people at the top. To put it in graphic terms, their lives are shorter.

"We believe we're a first-world country and that the type of poor child health that exists in third-world nations is not happening here in Canada. But we're wrong." He explained that children living in poverty get admitted to hospitals like Ross Memorial at higher rates than other children. They have lower birth weights and more mental health disorders that give rise to more addiction. They have disproportionate rates of asthma, injury, and learning disabilities. Later in life there is more heart disease, diabetes, and even cataracts. The proof, he noted, is in an extensive Canadian trial that started long before anyone began to ponder testing Basic Income. "The greatest example of this [is] a centuries-old social experiment in what's happened to our First Nations people."

Dr. Lauwers brought up another experiment, the 1970s Mincome project in Manitoba, through which people received a Basic Income, no questions asked. Hospitalization rates of recipients declined markedly. He looked forward to similar savings at Ross Memorial in the next three years. Pointing out that that health expenditures took up 38 percent of the provincial budget, he said, "You know, I think there are going to be some strong economic reasons why this is going to be a successful project.... Plus, you get the added bonus of these people actually living in dignity. What could possibly be better?"

Another panelist at Celebrations that day was John Hagarty, the Police Chief for the community that includes Lindsay, soon to retire after thirty-five years in law enforcement. The homespun philosopher understood the role of chance in life. That November afternoon, he had a twinkle in his eye and a poppy pinned to his black uniform. He also had a self-deprecating food story.

It seems that one day Hagarty glanced at an incident report that had come across his desk. A couple had been caught shoplifting, having stolen a half-pound block of butter. Active on Twitter, he couldn't get over it: "I thought it was hilarious. So, I tweeted about it. 'Who would steal butter?' It didn't make any sense to me at all." It didn't take long for another tweet to arrive: "Maybe they were hungry."

"Here I was, having a great, elitist time. Hee-haw! I apologized."

The Chief took a closer look at the incident report. The couple were recovering addicts with a couple of children at home. They had been returning from the food bank where they had been allowed to procure some bread. "They had the bread, but that's all they had. No fault of their own, they were trying to do the best they could. They thought they couldn't just take some bread home, so they stole some butter."

Hagarty decided not to charge the couple, provoking a sharp response from the grocery store owner. He shrugged and sent out another apologetic tweet, reiterating what he described as his mistake in not taking the episode seriously. Not with respect to the three-dollar chunk of butter, but the food insecurity reflected in the act of stealing it.

The Chief then described the opioid crisis. During his first ten years as a road cop, he had never responded to an overdose incident. In 2016, his force had two overdose calls in ninety days. In 2017, during the same period, they responded to fifteen overdoses. This led Hagarty, a born raconteur, to bring up a parable that he figured would shed some light on how to deal with the growing problem of addiction and its chronic cousin, impoverishment.

"Let's speak about cathedral thinking," he said, invoking a thirteenth-century building project—one of those towering gothic structures that attract so many twenty-first-century tourists. The aristocratic financiers knew they would never see the finished churches, complete with gargoyles, rose windows, and countless minute details. Nor would the masons, carpenters, and all the others who did the actual work. It took some two hundred and fifty years to build the magnificent York Minster in northeast England, from 1220 to 1472. Cathedral thinking was all about vision, planning for the long term.

"To me, cathedral thinking fits into this Basic Income idea. I probably won't see the benefit of Basic Income as a police chief. Many of you will not see the benefit for five years, ten years, twenty years." Hagarty was thinking of the children of the couple who had been caught stealing butter. His analysis summed up the arguments in all the studies, academic papers, and books about Basic Income:

> I think the main beneficiary of this will be the children of those that are receiving social assistance—that they'll have proper housing, that they'll have proper nutrition. They'll have proper care. That they'll have proper education. . . . It's hard to focus if you're hungry or stigmatized. So that's why I think a Basic Income will help in our community. I'm talking about hope and doing the right thing. So that's why I'm here. I just wish it wasn't a pilot.

The meeting organizers had reached out beyond small-town Ontario, inviting Josephine Grey from downtown Toronto. The social justice activist had recently visited the area to speak about Basic Income and the right to healthy food in nearby Peterborough. She knew that the Kawartha Lakes Food Coalition (farmers, local food promotors, restaurateurs, gardeners, food security activists) had been partly responsible for persuading the Wynne government to make Lindsay the Pilot's "saturation site." As a result, two thousand people would soon be receiving no-questions-asked payments.

Grey told the Lindsay gathering she was "really thrilled" that the politics of food had been instrumental in getting the Basic Income experiment to Lindsay. "Access to healthy food without a decent income is impossible," she said. "Basic Income is not just a good idea, it's a human right."

For Grey, human rights had become the lens through which social justice is reflected. She was a cofounder of the Hemispheric Social Alliance, a network of over three hundred national organizations working on alternatives to neoliberal free-trade regimes. She was part of the planning group for the North American Basic Income Guarantee (NABIG) congress, scheduled for Hamilton the following summer.

Despite the fresh hope that the Basic Income pilot seemed to represent, Grey agreed with Chief Hagarty. Why keep studying something with such obvious benefits? "I don't really think we need to test the theory. We all know it's a wonderful thing that should be done," she said, adding that she knew that social science experiments, like drug studies, need control groups: "We're not lab rats, thank you very much. I don't know who wants to be under that microscope: 'Watch me suffer for three years.' Really?"

Coming to Lindsay just as people were eagerly signing up for the Basic Income pilot was, Grey said, "probably one of my happiest days." She had been an active supporter of Basic Income for over thirty years: "I got really tired of being in the antipoverty movement and the whole issue of fighting against things. I always wanted to fight *for* things. Economic security should be a human right. Access to healthy food and shelter should be a human right."

She insisted that the problems confronting the planet require an effort that, during the 2020 pandemic, would come to be routinely described as an "all-hands-on-deck" approach. "We don't have a lot of time," she said.

> If we're going to get through climate chaos, if we're going to become greener, a lot of people are going to have to change what they do for work. And in order to be able to make those changes, we're going to need the freedom and the time to decide how we're going to be part of a greener economy.

This was an angle that few Basic Income supporters had considered as integral to their advocacy efforts. The Lindsay organizers, however, had invited another social justice organizer from Toronto, whose thinking about Basic Income was remarkably similar. Tim Ellis was an expatriate American who had worked on the 2016 Bernie Sanders campaign and would do so again in 2019. Ellis had married a Canadian and considered his work as a staff campaigner for Vancouver-based Leadnow as his dream job. It was all about "mobilizing the democratic power of an engaged public." He had previously worked as a rave DJ, a gym technician, and a bond market analyst.

Ellis described Basic Income as one way to contend with the "automation revolution" and the changing nature of work. Two generations younger than Grey, he added that he was seeing a shifting understanding of the value of different kinds of work: "There's a lot of work that gets done every day that isn't paid. Parenting—really valuable work." Ellis argued that the way we understand work reflects dominant values.

"Basic income," Tim Ellis said, "offers people the freedom to pursue those kinds of work that people do value but profit-seeking enterprises do not." Capitalists routinely replace labour with capital in the form of robots and myriad other information-driven technologies. Ellis regarded this as, potentially at least, a good thing. Less work? Great. Yet people suffer when their labour is no longer required, even as productivity increases: "So Basic Income, done right and as part of a progressive framework, is the way to address that. It's kind of 'How do we get from where we are to Star Trek?'"

Not long after the Basic Income 101 gathering, people in Lindsay began receiving their first regular payments. Roderick Benns recalled that the start of registration for the Ontario pilot project in his home town was "a day full of hope and promise."[29]

THE CANCELLATION

The hope and promise were short-lived. On July 31, 2018, eight months after participants had started receiving Basic Income and just two months into its term, the newly elected government of Doug Ford announced that it was cancelling the OBIP. Few foresaw the abrupt move. Ford (an alleged high-school hash dealer[30] and university drop-out who had inherited part of a multimillion-dollar business from his father) had promised during the campaign to continue the Pilot.

The government offered up weak reasons for the cancellation, all of which have since been shown to be unsubstantiated. Lisa MacLeod, the Minister of Children, Community and Social Services famously offered that the best way out of poverty is a job. Never mind that over a million Canadians living in poverty already have jobs.

Clearly the government was ideologically opposed to the idea of "money for nothing." After a press conference about the OBIP cancellation, media outlets circulated a photo of MacLeod positioned in front of a government sign that appeared to say "Live in Poverty." While the full sign had a different message, government critics suggested that the way the shot was framed revealed the government's actual message to the four thousand OBIP participants.

CHAPTER 4

LINDSAY
The Saturation Site

Money in people's pockets is money they'll spend.
> —Bill Scott (seven-term former federal
> MP—Progressive Conservative Party)

SMALL-TOWN VALUES

The Lindsay Exhibition, or LEX as it's known, advertises itself as the largest single event in the City of Kawartha Lakes, the amalgamated municipality that includes the town of Lindsay, some ninety minutes northeast of Toronto. The fourth biggest fall fair in Ontario, the LEX draws some forty-five thousand to the big fairground each September. The fair includes tractor pulls, a midway, 4-H events, and a demolition derby. Some three hundred volunteers help to organize the fair, which has taken place every year since 1854.

Situated on the traditional territory of the Anishinaabe Mississauga First Nation, Lindsay was settled by Europeans in the early nineteenth century, initially as a lumbering centre. William Purdy and his sons built the first sawmill on the Scugog River in 1827. Other mills, along with farming and manufacturing, soon followed. Lindsay's main drag, Kent Street, is reputedly the widest downtown street in Ontario, designed in the 1860s to allow a wagon team with six horses and a carriage to make a 180-degree turn (the LEX is a proud member of the North American Six-Horse Hitch Classic Series).

Though agriculture continues to be an important aspect of Lindsay's economy, it is now also an important hub for cottagers and outdoor recreation in the Kawartha Lakes area. Mike Perry, Executive Director of the City of Kawartha Lakes Family Health Team and former Lindsay + District Chamber of Commerce president, likes to call it the "Norman Rockwell town of the north."[1] Local lore has it that once you've lived in Lindsay, you always come back. In no small measure, the local Lindsay identity is defined *against* the nearby big city. People from Lindsay tend to abhor pretension and big city ways. Even those inclined to frown at the town's conservative politics are proud of Lindsay's small-town qualities—the friendliness and hospitality, ease of getting to know one's neighbours, ready access to outdoor recreation, a relaxed way of life.

Local lawyer Leslie Frost, who was Premier of Ontario from 1949 to 1961, is said to have driven his well-worn car from town out to the countryside to meet his driver and plush government limousine for the trip to Toronto and his office at Queen's Park. A genial pragmatist who presided over the height of Ontario's postwar boom, Frost was the second of four successive Progressive Conservative premiers who kept the party in power for forty-two years. Sometimes held up as the personification of small-town values, he came to be known as Old Man Ontario.

Frost's biographer, Ron Graham, described Lindsay as a place whose people "shared a civic loyalty and community pride, a belief in honest toil and fair dealing, and a feeling of satisfaction with things as they were."[2] The town's civic pride extends to sweet treats: Local restaurants, even chains, wouldn't dream of serving anything but Kawartha Dairy ice cream.

Lindsay residents were proud that their modest town, with a population of about twenty-one thousand, was selected as the saturation site for the Ontario Basic Income Pilot. It brought provincial, national, and even international attention to a quiet spot that rarely makes the news.

THE SALES PITCH

Mike Perry, a former Ottawa civil servant, was a key player in the initiative that brought the Ontario Basic Income Pilot to Lindsay. A lawyer and social worker by training, Perry is one of those born in the area who went away and then returned to become a proud Kawartha Lakes booster.

When the Basic Income Pilot project was announced in the 2016 Ontario budget, Perry was the volunteer chair of the Kawartha Lakes Food Coalition (KLFC). He was pondering issues related to food insecurity and had noticed the OBIP announcement in the provincial budget. Realizing the potentially positive food security impacts for Kawartha Lakes and its residents, Perry brought the idea to the KLFC. The group set a goal of educating local residents about Basic Income and gauging local support.[3]

Their first public education event in September 2016 was a presentation (by this book's co-author, Elaine Power) about Basic Income and food insecurity. It filled the Fenelon Falls Community Centre and generated an impromptu petition asking the provincial government to make Kawartha Lakes a Pilot site.

Shortly afterward, when Karen Glass, the Wynne government's top civil servant responsible for poverty reduction, arrived in town for another event, the group buttonholed her with a five-minute sales pitch. In October, Perry and a group that included people living in poverty made an appointment with Glass at her Toronto office, offering a slick PowerPoint presentation about why Kawartha Lakes should be selected as one of the test sites. They left her with a spiral-bound pitch document outlining the presentation's highlights.

The lead slide in the deck ticked some important boxes: "Select the City of Kawartha Lakes for the Basic Annual Income Pilot Program: *Close. Rural. Measurable.*" It was heavy on results-based evidence and evaluation and offered a blizzard of source references, from the local police to social services. The overall argument was designed to appeal to anyone concerned about testing the evidence in a social experiment that emphasized the possible health effects of Basic Income.

The group had also given their presentation documents to their MPP, Laurie Scott, who committed to sharing copies with her Liberal colleagues across the floor. The Progressive Conservative, whose father had served as the local Tory Member of Parliament for twenty-eight years, soon declared her public support of Kawartha Lakes as a test site. She had held the riding for seventeen years by the time Perry and fellow basic income advocates came knocking in search of her support for the Basic Income Pilot—the Kawartha area was known to be a formidable bastion of Conservative support.

In January 2017, the Ontario government announced province-wide consultations on the design, implementation, and evaluation of the Basic Income Pilot, but there was no mention of Kawartha Lakes. Unwilling to be left behind, Perry and his group organized their own community consultation at Lindsay City Hall. An official from the province's Poverty Reduction Strategy Office accepted an invitation to attend both day and evening sessions and appeared suitably impressed by the overflow crowd and participants' enthusiasm.

Perry still felt he needed to do more. He worried that the province might just pick the pilot communities, without an application process. One of Ontario's most experienced lobbyists donated a half-hour of his time after Perry put the touch on him. He got the name of James Janeiro in the Premier's Office. Perry was delighted to learn that Janeiro spent part of his annual summer vacation at a Kawartha Lakes area cottage. He hounded Janeiro, leaving so many messages that Perry said he was sure the cops were going to come knocking.

Eventually, he got a call from Janeiro, requesting an in-person meeting the next day. Perry and two others arrived at Janeiro's office with a litre of famous Kawartha Dairy ice cream and their pitch document. Janeiro explained that although he had spoken with representatives from other communities, Kawartha Lakes was the only one with that kind of document—and presumably the only delegation that brought ice cream!

The efforts paid off. Perry, an organizer savvy enough to spread the credit, said it was a "community effort for a community win." But the payoff would not likely have happened without Perry's dedicated and energetic leadership.

As Janeiro described it, the initial version of the Pilot included two thousand people—one thousand each in Hamilton and Thunder Bay. He and his staff had all the details nailed down, including the locations, budget, benefit amounts, and delivery mechanism, all packaged up "with a nice bow." This two-thousand-person, $25 million Basic Income Pilot was about to go to Cabinet when the Premier took Janeiro aside and told him that she thought the plan was missing something.

"Wasn't Dauphin used as a saturation site in the Mincome experiment?"

"Yes."

"We don't have that here."

"No, we don't, Premier. We've got North and South." (The plan had called for Hamilton and Thunder Bay to be the Basic Income test locations. Both are medium-sized cities, one with a significant Indigenous population.)

Janeiro mentioned the problems with getting approval from the deficit-shy finance ministry, a predictable roadblock to new spending programs. To make the task even more difficult, this one would have limited political payoff with the voting public. Even though Basic Income seemed popular, it was hardly top-of-mind with the general public. Low-income people tend not to vote, in good measure because of cynicism about government.

Wynne told Janeiro to find a small city like Dauphin where four thousand people had incomes low enough to qualify for Basic Income. Two thousand people could still be signed up as planned, along with another two thousand to serve as a control group. "Okay, it's $25 million a year now," she said to Janeiro. "Let's take it up to $50 million."

Janeiro jumped at the idea. Wynne seemed to understand that a saturation site like Dauphin could measure broad community spinoffs, not just individual and household effects. When she doubled the budget and the enrolment numbers Janeiro realized that Lindsay matched up perfectly and also fit other criteria related to loss of manufacturing jobs and rural location. And it had clear community buy-in. Janeiro said that Wynne didn't care that the community was a Conservative stronghold; she did not want the Pilot to be about politics.

At Wynne's direction, Janeiro sold the new plan for the Basic Income Pilot, with Lindsay included, to cabinet members. Polls were showing that Ontarians approved of Basic Income, and the Pilot received enthusiastic cabinet support.[4]

THE SUPPORT NETWORK

Laurie Scott's enthusiastic endorsement of the Pilot was important. The Progressive Conservative MPP was a former nurse, who apparently understood that bringing people out of poverty would lead to better health for recipients and thus would provide savings in the health care system. Her position was aligned with that of local hospital CEO Bert Lauwers, who had spoken out about the need to put more money into the social determinants of health, including adequate income, rather than spending on acute health care in hospitals.[5]

This was hardly a novel idea; the 1971 Croll Report on poverty in Canada included the same recommendation, made by the then Director General of Medical Services Branch of the federal Department of National Health and Welfare. Scott also knew that the infusion of provincial money into the local economy would provide an economic boost. In an interview with the *Lindsay Advocate*, she quoted her late father, former federal MP Bill Scott, who was fond of saying, "Money in people's pockets is money they'll spend."[6]

Police Chief John Hagarty was also a key supporter of the Pilot. He expected it would create a healthier community, providing people with concrete means to help break the corrosive cycles of hopelessness and despair that lead to substance abuse and dysfunction: "We need to think further out and take a leap of faith when we believe in what the expected results will be, even if we may not see the benefit."[7]

Larry Hope, the aptly named Director of the Trillium Lakelands

District School Board, also expected that the Pilot would provide tremendous opportunities for individual and community good. As an educator, he understood that people tend to meet expectations of those around them, whether positive or negative. Hope's philosophy is that "most people will do well if they possibly can." The confidence generated by Basic Income support, he suggested, would lead them to become "contributing and participating members of society."[8]

Despite all of the potential for personal and community benefit, Mike Perry noted that Mayor Andy Letham and several municipal councillors offered only tepid support. One councillor called Basic Income "ridiculous" and "all fluff," worrying that municipal taxpayers would end up footing the bill. Unlike most other Ontario municipal councils that supported Basic Income in principle, the City of Kawartha Lakes simply voted to "receive" the request, declining to take any further action.[9] That feeling of satisfaction with things as they are was, it seemed, still well entrenched. The lack of Council support for Basic Income made the success of Perry's advocacy efforts all the more remarkable.

However, the final win was bittersweet for those who had campaigned for the entire Kawartha Lakes municipality—not just the town of Lindsay—to be designated as the Pilot site. Perry regretted that people in places like Fenelon Falls, Bobcaygeon, and Omemee would not be eligible to participate. He lamented that this created a backlash, a sense of "deserving" and "undeserving" among low-income residents of Kawartha Lakes. Those left out wondered "what about the rest of us?" Maybe the government could be persuaded to expand the number, or, at least, create a waitlist for people in neighbouring communities in case there wasn't enough uptake in Lindsay. Officials seemed initially amenable to consider expansion outside Lindsay but the Pilot filled rapidly. Perry noted that the long line of applicants outside the Lindsay library was "a good thing" for the Pilot, at least to the extent that the clear demand for the program disproved the sceptics who had predicted that no one would sign on. It also suggested desperate need.

ANOTHER VOICE FOR BASIC INCOME

Another local Basic Income booster was self-described former "Red Tory" Roderick Benns, who had been reading about Basic Income but started to think much more about it after leaving a job as a senior writer with the Ontario Ministry of Education. Having trouble finding more than "a gig here and a gig there," Benns came home to Lindsay, with his wife Joli Scheidler-Benns and their elementary-school-aged daughter, after Lindsay was chosen as an OBIP site.[10]

Benns and Scheidler-Benns were already Basic Income activists. Scheidler-Benns had started her doctoral studies at York University's Health Policy and Equity program, where the social determinants of health are a central analytical pillar. She also began teaching courses on equity, diversity, and social justice at Ontario Tech University in Oshawa. For the energetic Scheidler-Benns, Basic Income is a necessity because "no one is going to be able to care [about all of society's broader challenges] unless they have their basic needs met."

In 2015, Benns had started to interview Basic Income advocates and politicians, asking about their reasons for supporting the idea and publishing the results on his "Leaders and Legacies" website. Scheidler-Benns developed a Basic Income survey, inviting some three hundred mayors from across the country to participate. Benns followed up by doing interviews with engaged respondents and published comments by mayors, including those in Edmonton, Calgary, Halifax, Charlottetown, and Victoria. In 2016, he collected the columns into a book, *Basic Income: How a Canadian Movement Could Change the World*, reflecting Benns's pride in his country and his determination to make it better by providing income security for all.

After moving to Lindsay, the couple launched the *Lindsay Advocate*, a free online monthly magazine chockablock with advertising and coverage of local issues. The startup flew in the face of the ongoing decline in local media, gutted in small-to-medium-sized Canadian cities by corporate chains and online advertising. The *Advocate* began with a strong emphasis on stories about Basic Income, poverty reduction, and social issues, but carefully included other news, features, and opinion pieces.

After several months online, with growing ad revenue, Benns began to publish a glossy print monthly that won the local Chamber of Commerce "New Business of the Year Award" in 2019. By 2020, the magazine had added podcasts featuring local stories. With its emphasis on progressive causes, "putting human values ahead of economic values,"[11] the *Advocate* was attempting to shift the political discourse of the conservative town, promoting civic pride and public engagement along the way.

THE RECRUITER

Every now and then, agencies and communities celebrate their volunteers—the social glue that does so much to keep communities together and functioning. They are sometimes called "heroes," but the crucial work they do is often invisible, unpaid, and unrecognized. Tracey Mechefske qualifies. She has done packaging and delivery for the Good Food Box, served on the boards of both the Lindsay Community Gardeners and the Community Care Garden Group, chaired the Program Committee of the Kawartha Soroptimist Club ("Best for Women"), and worked on cooking and personal care sessions for the mental health promotion group Reach for Recovery. She had been a member of the United Church Women at Trinity United in nearby Bobcaygeon and president of the Kawartha Lakes Haliburton Housing Corporation Tenants' Association. But Mechefske did not even consider the work she did to get other low-income people in Lindsay to sign up for the Ontario Basic Income Pilot "volunteer work."[12]

Mechefske is no stranger to adversity and anxiety. She began psychological counselling when she started university, not long after a sexual assault at seventeen. The sessions soon moved on to her abusive childhood. She is reluctant to say much about her "shitty childhood," but it is clear that her father was violent. Though she remained close to her mother, it was only in the last three days of his life that she felt seen and understood by her father. She was able to forgive him just before he died.

By the time Mechefske started counselling as a student, stress had taken its toll on her body. She suffered from migraines and debilitating bouts of physical pain from inflammatory bowel disease (IBD), which eventually forced her to quit her university studies. Later, she had to quit college but eventually earned a diploma in children's literature. She was fired from a job as a retail clerk because the disease would flare up unexpectedly and she would have to take three, four, or five days off work at a time. Being told she was "unreliable" was humiliating, gnawing away at her self-esteem.

Physicians have been able to help Mechefske control the disease's symptoms, but there is no cure. To make matters worse, her anxiety flares on the days she has to stay home because of painful gastrointestinal problems stemming from the IBD. She has also developed anaphylactic reactions to sulfa and sulfites, which are added to almost all processed foods, including baked goods, canned and frozen fruits and vegetables, cereals and crackers, and tomato sauces. Combine this factor with needing a special diet to treat her bowel disease, and Mechefske's dietary options are extremely limited.

In the language of trauma researchers, Mechefske's ACE score was high. "ACE" has come to be known as more than a top card. It is an acronym for "Adverse Childhood Experience," such as experiencing or witnessing abuse or violence as a child or teen. In the mid-1990s, a massive study of 17,000 people in California showed that ACEs are a powerful predictor of serious social and economic problems, as well as physical and mental health issues in adulthood.[13] The original research identified ten family and household ACEs within three main categories:

- Abuse (physical, emotional, and sexual)
- Neglect (physical and emotional), and
- Household dysfunction (including mental illness, an incarcerated

relative, domestic violence, substance misuse, and instability resulting from divorce).

Other researchers have subsequently added ACEs that originate from toxic social stressors such as poverty, violence, unemployment, structural racism, historical trauma, poor housing, and poor schooling, all of which in turn contribute to household traumas. Environmental factors that include events related to climate chaos have also been identified as ACEs—in 2020, temperatures near Los Angeles came close to 50 degrees Celsius. International researchers have also added war, human rights violations, and forced migration as important ACEs.[14]

While most people experience some adversity in childhood, this research shows that the likelihood of health problems in adulthood increases in direct correlation to the number of Adverse Childhood Experiences encountered. Those with an ACE score of four have a 700 percent increased risk of alcoholism and are 1,200 percent more likely to attempt suicide. Risk of heart disease and lung cancer doubles, independent of other risk factors. Those with an ACE score of five or more are seven to ten times more likely to use and inject illicit drugs than those who have zero ACEs.[15] Pioneering addiction medicine specialist Dr. Daniel Sumrok explains that addiction is the wrong term: It is, rather, "ritualized compulsive comfort-seeking."[16]

Not all people with high ACE scores are addicts, but practically all addicts have high ACE scores. Canadian addiction treatment specialist Dr. Gabor Maté, who works in the Downtown Eastside of Vancouver, understands addiction as "neither a choice nor an inherited disease, but a psychological and physiological response to painful childhood life experiences." According to Dr. Maté, treating addiction, a symptom of childhood injury, without treating the underlying pain dooms addicts to repeated cycles of suffering and premature death.[17] He also argues that traumas that provoke addiction are not just the result of horrific events:

Trauma can occur not only when bad things happen, but also when the parents are too stressed, too distracted, too depressed, too beset by economic worry, too isolated to respond to a sensitive child's emotional need to be seen, emotionally held, heard, validated, made to feel secure.[18]

This relatively new science reveals the multiple adverse effects of toxic stress in our homes, institutions, and environment. It is a way to understand how the social becomes biological, how our environment and traumas "get under our skin" and become "biologically embedded" in our bodies.[19] Even beyond individual ACEs, another relatively new science called epigenetics indicates that we may literally carry the traumas of our ancestors—from wars, genocides, slavery, witch hunts, pogroms, forced migrations, starvation, deprivation, abandonment, and other forms of violence—in our genes and in our bodies.[20]

Everyday stress can be normal and healthy. But toxic stress—stress that is repeated, intense, or chronic—damages health in many ways. In children, toxic stress erodes the healthy development of the neurological system, disrupting learning, behaviour, and growth as well as the immune and endocrine systems. Children who are exposed to multiple ACEs are more likely to have learning challenges, behavioural issues, sleep disturbance, and problems such as asthma and mental illness— any and all of which make succeeding at school much more challenging. Education is another important determinant of health: those with some postsecondary education are likely to live longer and healthier lives than high-school dropouts.

There is an adage in the world of trauma research: "Hurt people hurt people." Adults with high ACE scores who are self-soothing with substance addictions, acting violently, or suffering mental illness repeat the cycle with their own children—who may also have inherited the epigenetic susceptibility to physiological reactivity. It is even more troubling to consider that adults with high ACE scores who gain positions of power, such as former US president Donald Trump, can inflict widespread trauma through public policy, especially on those who are already marginalized, from policing and immigration to access to public services and health care.

Some forms of trauma are disproportionately experienced by whole groups because of structural inequities—for example, women, Indigenous peoples, Black people and people of colour, and people with disabilities. Some have their own legacies of historical trauma that can intersect, adding complexity. Such groups are almost invariably at higher risk of poverty.

These new understandings of trauma and ACEs again show the limitations of "individual responsibility" for health, well-being, and material prosperity. They point instead to the need for action "upstream"[21] to address the underlying structural factors that contribute to and perpetuate the conditions that give rise to Adverse Childhood Experiences and traumas. Access to affordable housing and child care can help promote healing and even allow some people to flourish. But solving the puzzle requires income security, as briefly experienced in Lindsay by two thousand Ontario Basic Income Pilot participants.

Tracey Mechefske learned about the Pilot through a friend, who had picked up a postcard about it at the LEX. She immediately recognized the flaws in recruiting registrants at the fair—the people who needed Basic Income the most couldn't afford to go: "It's ten dollars to get in, but that doesn't cover ride tickets, parking, or food. It's fourteen dollars for a hot dog with a drink, twenty dollars for a small book of tickets—all told, about forty dollars for the day." For one person.

Instead, she and a friend went to social housing complexes, gave people information about the Pilot, and recruited them to sign up. As Mechefske explained, her activism and volunteerism had long been about "finding a better way for people to live." She was convinced that Basic Income was a better way, one that ideally would support all Canadians who needed it. "I was all in," she said. "I was so driven about this program, I just told everyone."

Mechefske found it much easier to recruit the working poor—"the people who used to be middle-class who now can't make ends meet"—

than the lowest-income people, who were on social assistance and disability. Those who already had plenty of contact with the social assistance bureaucracy were much more cynical; they usually responded with some variation of, "Yeah right. Free money. There's got to be a catch." People receiving money through the Ontario Disability Support Program (ODSP) were especially wary because they usually had had to fight so hard to qualify for a disability cheque in the first place. The idea that they would have to reapply for ODSP after the three-year Pilot was over cast a nightmarish shadow over discussions about Basic Income.

Mechefske herself was sceptical about moving off ODSP onto the Pilot until she realized that the reapplication to ODSP only included a financial review, and not a review of the medical information, which would require appearing in front of a formal tribunal. She reassured herself that "there was no real downside" to enrolling in the Pilot. It paid more than ODSP.

THE EFFECTS

With two thousand people in the Pilot, about ten percent of Lindsay's total population and about twenty percent of its working-age population started receiving Basic Income payments. Mike Perry said that after the Pilot started, "the renewed sense of hope was palpable." People who got the Basic Income were looking healthier, eating better food, getting more rest, thinking about the future more. "They were less stressed because—time and time *again* I heard it—'I paid off my bills.' They got out from underneath that cycle."[22]

Most stores along Lindsay's main street likely didn't notice the effects of the Basic Income Pilot. The home décor and stylish clothing stores that cater to cottagers and tourists didn't see much change in business when some 15 million extra dollars began flowing into town during the first year of the program. Traffic at the food bank, however, dropped. Local grocery store owners saw an uptick in business. The Buy and Sell shop, featuring used furniture, small appliances, and kids' bicycles, saw more people buying and fewer anxiously selling off their possessions to make ends meet.

After a few months on the Ontario Basic Income Pilot, Tracey Mechefske and her husband Kurt hadn't felt so well "for as long as we could remember." They paid off their credit card and hydro bills, purchased supplements and prescription medications, and headed to the grocery store instead of the food bank. Kurt was able to have a long-delayed hernia operation and take the required six-week recovery off work as a delivery driver. Their relationship improved because they no longer argued about money. They went on date nights at the drive-in and were able to have a niece come live with them when her home life became "intolerable." Confident in the government contract that guaranteed three years of OBIP money, Tracey took out a line of credit to start up a home business in all-natural skin care products, prompted by her severe allergy to sulfites, which can be found in almost all skin care products including soaps and shampoos.

Sixty-two-year-old Bob Frew had been working in the kitchen at Kelsey's for three years and was volunteering at the local shelter, A Place Called Home, where nineteen beds are available for single people, couples, and families. Frew said that after Basic Income hit town, fewer people were going to "the Home" for meals. Although surprised when his own OBIP application was accepted, he said, "I bought new boots. I bought new shoes. I bought clothes. I eat better."[23]

William Whiston struggled with physical and mental illness and had been able to move from disability assistance to Basic Income. "My depression and anxiety have gone way down because I'm not using the food bank anymore," explained the fifty-one-year-old Whiston. "I'm eating properly. I'm getting my meds that I need, because I've got osteoporosis as well. I have to buy vitamins, and I couldn't buy them before this. So, it's helping my bones as well. This program is working." Basic Income had enabled Whiston to move up a bit, to get "up there by the middle class, instead of being in the bottom class."[24]

The owners of one Kent Street restaurant benefited from the OBIP personally and their business benefited indirectly. Fresh Fuell was started by husband and wife co-owners Luis and Leanna (the two "Ls" in "Fuell") Segura in 2015, born out of their frustration with trying to find healthy, affordable, on-the-go food for themselves and their children. Fresh Fuell began simply—with wraps, smoothies, and salads. The Seguras opted for plant-based ingredients and biodegradable packaging.

Luis and Leanna met while working at a Toronto gym, Luis explaining that they have "always been about health and being active." Family is central. Leanna is originally from the Lindsay area; her parents owned a nearby Foodland supermarket. Luis's family came to Canada from war-ravaged El Salvador when he was nine. The couple moved back to Lindsay when they decided to have their first child. "Toronto was just not the place for that," he said. "So, we moved up here, bought our first home, had our first child, and worked at Foodland."[25]

When Leanna Segura's parents retired from the grocery business, the young couple could have taken over the store, but they wanted to start their own business. They were already two years into running Fresh Fuell, with three kids under the age of six, when the Pilot came to town. The extra $800 a month that the Pilot provided took a huge burden of stress off the young parents, allowing them to cover childcare and activities for their children. They even had a fourth child. They described the Basic Income as a "blessing" because it allowed them to stop worrying about household expenses and focus on "catapulting" the business to success. After the Pilot began, they saw that people were spending more money. They also noticed new customers.

The couple began hiring more staff. They renovated a second-hand food truck and started bringing their fresh offerings to events like the LEX. They sold lunches for school kids. They made smoothies for local sporting events. They provided catering services. Fresh Fuell won a "best new business" award and a "customer service excellence award," planting the family firmly in the community. Luis Segura figures that by the time the Pilot was cancelled, their income had grown to the point that they probably wouldn't have been eligible for continued benefits.

Basic Income also affected Lindsay in ways that no one had considered. These are the kinds of effects that Kathleen Wynne was curious about when she directed James Janeiro to find a saturation site. Rod Sutherland is the welfare boss ("Director of Human Services") for the City of Kawartha Lakes. According to his calculations, 366 local cases (families and singles) left Ontario Works (social assistance) to enrol in the OBIP. The city was able to change its service delivery model, allowing Sutherland to offer more concentrated staff support for the remaining Ontario Works recipients. Staff morale improved as case-loads dropped. Stronger, more positive connections between workers and clients developed. Clients began experiencing more success. Sutherland was pleased that at least a few clients were able to secure employment for the first time in years.[26]

The Kawartha Lakes Haliburton Housing Corporation, which runs rent-geared-to-income housing, also saw unexpected positive benefits. Tenants enrolled in the Pilot saw a big increase in their incomes, which meant that they paid more rent. Sutherland estimated that the Pilot created a $300,000 unbudgeted surplus for the Housing Corporation, which it was able to invest in its capital project reserves.

THE DOWNWARD SPIRAL

When the newly elected Ford government announced on July 31, 2018, that the Pilot was being cancelled, Tracey Mechefske was devastated, her hopes shredded. Feeling she had to do something, she immediately wrote a letter to Premier Ford, describing the positive benefits of the OBIP and asking him to reconsider his decision. She perhaps naively expected a reply; she received none. OBIP participants learned about the cancellation of the Pilot through the media. It took two months for Mechefske's official notice to arrive.

In documents gathered by Toronto law firm Cavalluzzo LLP to support an ultimately unsuccessful class-action lawsuit against the government for breach of contract, Mechefske and three other former OBIP participants—Dana Bowman, Susan Lindsay, and Grace Hillion, all from Lindsay—told of the effects of the Pilot and its cancellation.[27] Mechefske described how she now had to juggle bill payments—cell phone and hydro one month, line of credit and internet the next. She cancelled her cable and membership in the Rec Centre to pay for vehicle repairs.

In her statement of claim,[28] Dana Bowman described the benefits of being on the OBIP after twenty years of being on ODSP. There was no more anxiety generated by the rushed need to respond to regular inquiries from officials about her disability benefits. She was suddenly able to afford proper food and basic clothing, including undergarments. Her long-time goal of enrolling in college to become a social services worker was no longer a vague dream. She could even pay for transportation to visit her daughter and help care for the grandchildren.

Following the cancellation, Bowman suffered a persistent deterioration in her mental health, as did Hillion and Lindsay. The court filings stated that "the cancellation resulted in Lindsay losing her sense of self-worth and increased her fear and anxiety."

After the pilot ended in April 2019, Tracey Mechefske found herself back on social assistance through the Ontario Disability Support Program. She had taken out a line of credit to start her new skin-care business, Raventree Naturals, but she could not afford to run it on social assistance. Her new sense of identity as a business owner vanished, along with the self-confidence it brought. "I know that I am the same person on ODSP as on Basic Income," she said, her voice breaking. "That hasn't changed. But the way others look at me has changed. I feel as if I'm taking money out of other people's pockets and begging for money to live."

For the first eight months back on ODSP, Mechefske did almost no grocery shopping—milk and eggs and not much else. There was simply no money. When Christmas approached, she and her husband used the money they had set aside for gifts to buy fruit and vegetables. Everything else came from the food bank. "Try to stay healthy on that," said Mechefske, her voice dripping with sarcasm.

Once a month, Tracey and Kurt got four bags of groceries from the food bank. The bags included "a couple of cans of fruit, a couple of cans of vegetables, a couple of cans of tuna. The rest is just filler to make you feel like you are eating." Hardly enough to last the month that clients are required to wait until the next visit. Lindsay food bank users can return weekly for bread. Limited by her sulfite and sulfate allergy, Mechefske could usually find one or two "bread-like" items. The monotonous, unhealthy diet, the strangulating restriction of choice, and the indignity of returning to the food bank were particularly crushing after the sense of freedom and well-being that Mechefske had experienced on OBIP.

Mechefske's mental health also spiralled downward. She had long ago realized that swimming helped with stress, but the arrival of cooler weather meant she could no longer swim outdoors. Insomnia hit, followed by panic attacks and alarmingly high blood pressure. She was admitted to Ross Memorial and prescribed medication.

Speaking to the gains that the OBIP had made possible for his family, Luis Segura is convinced that Basic Income supports entrepreneurial initiative, shaking his head at the OBIP cancellation. "It would have been amazing to see how many more ideas, how many other businesses would have come out of it," he said, adding that a fast-changing economy offers a seedbed for fresh ideas for new businesses. "How do you encourage people to do that without the fear of falling?"[29]

Segura is also a musician with the Toronto-based Latin hip-hop collective Los Poetas (The Poets). The group represents a celebration of Latinx heritage, capturing "life's beauty, intensity, anguish and hope, from the far-flung streets and corners of their birth countries to the land where they found their voices."[30] Segura understands the value of Basic Income for artists. "When you don't have that financial stress, creativity thrives," he said.

While some remain convinced that Canada can't afford Basic Income, Segura figures that they just don't get it: "They are seeing numbers, and they're forgetting the people and the human experience" that translates into happiness and confidence. "Confident communities, healthy, mentally, emotionally—that's huge." The father who had watched as war and revolution swept through his homeland asked whimsically, "Why wouldn't you want to be known as a country that could do that?"

LIFE AFTER BASIC INCOME

A few months after the Pilot was cancelled, Mechefske started swimming regularly at the Lindsay Recreation Centre—after an anonymous benefactor offered to pay the monthly twenty-five-dollar fee that she could no longer afford. Several months in, friends were noticing a marked improvement—her eyes shone brightly, and she smiled readily. Mechefske said she could hardly believe the muscles she had developed, exclaiming, "I've never been healthier!" She decided to compete in an indoor triathlon at the Rec Centre. It featured a swim, cycle, and run based on a limited time, with points for mileage rather than a specified distance.

Mechefske made the triathlon a forty-eighth-birthday present to herself. There were, however, two possible stumbling blocks: She was not sure she could do the run portion, given the plates and screws in one leg following surgery because of a congenital bone disease. A friend gave her a guest pass to the gym so she could try the treadmill; she decided she would do a brisk walk for the triathlon rather than run.

The second stumbling block was the sixty-dollar entrance fee. A utility disconnection letter had threatened to cut off her electricity, so Mechefske made the wrenching decision that the triathlon fee was not on. When a friend offered to kick in twenty dollars towards the fee, however, she decided to ask other friends for help and soon came up with the balance.

On a wintry Sunday afternoon, as she deposited her wet winter boots in the bottom of her locker at the Lindsay Recreation Complex, Mechefske commented that someone recently had their boots stolen from the open cubbyholes outside the change rooms. Someone else lost designer jeans that weren't put in a locker. Her observations were matter-of-fact, suggesting familiarity with the everyday desperation that has risen since the OBIP cancellation.[31]

The pool is often busy with parents and kids. Mechefske had only been in the pool for a few minutes when ten-year-old Grace popped up like a seal, interrupting her usual training schedule. She engaged Mechefske in a range of mini-competitions: who could sit, then lie, on the bottom of the pool at the deep end the longest; who could travel the farthest underwater after diving in; who could do the most head-over-heel underwater tumbles.

Mechefske explained that kids seem attracted to her. It's not surprising. She accepts kids as they are, asking caring questions. She is also a fierce truth teller, as evidenced by her determination to bring the Ford government to account for its betrayal of OBIP participants. With their highly attuned sensitivity to adult bullshit, kids appreciate this, aware that they can trust this surrogate aunt. She pays attention, engaging them on their own terms, treating them with respect. Mechefske worried about Grace and her younger sister, who are often left unattended at the pool on weekend afternoons.

Most Sunday afternoons, Mechefske brings another "niece" to the pool. Amber, the twelve-year-old daughter of a neighbour, had spent several months living with her recently because of problems at home. But lately, Amber tells her that her social schedule is "full" and she doesn't have time to go to the pool with her "aunt," leaving Mechefske feeling deeply concerned. She never had kids of her own, and she hasn't been able to find paid work that can accommodate her often precarious health condition. But along with her informal mentoring of the girls at the pool and her care for her niece, Mechefske's volunteer work is as important to her as her exercise regime. She is the sort of person who, when asked, jumps into any campaign.

Mechefske was nervous on the morning of the much-anticipated triathlon. She had had a stressful week, preparing for being cross-examined in the class-action lawsuit. When the whistle blew to start the swim segment, Mechefske started out with a strong front crawl, but it quickly became clear that she was in trouble. After the first lap, she stopped. The pool staff talked her through her first panic attack in over a year. In the end, she finished the fifteen-minute swim but was upset because that should have been her strongest leg of the race. The race volunteer consoled her that it was very unusual for anyone to finish after having a panic attack.

Mechefske regained her usual exuberance on the bicycle, plugging into ear buds with upbeat music and the encouragement of a trainer. She completed 7.5 kilometres on the spin bicycle, which she had never used before, and went on to a strong finish on the treadmill, despite not being able to run. She was exultant: "I woke up an ordinary person, and now I'm a triathlete!" It was a huge accomplishment, not least because she had pushed through the panic attack. By the end of the day, Mechefske was already planning her participation in next year's triathlon.[32]

THE RESISTANCE

On August 7, 2018, a week after the OBIP cancellation was announced, Tracey Mechefske joined several hundred other people who had gathered across the street from the Lindsay Public Library at Victoria Park. The boisterous crowd was there to protest the Ford government's decision to kill Basic Income in Ontario immediately after an election campaign during which the Tories had pledged to keep the Pilot going.

One little boy, about five years old, sported a Batman ball cap. His sign read, "I am LEARNING to keep PROMISES." A middle-aged woman with a shopping buggy held up a sign that said, "Make true on your promises, Laurie Scott, Doug Ford." Another woman stood beside a fellow in a red mobility scooter. Her sign had more of an edge: "#Doug Fraud." Other signs played on Ford's promise of one-dollar beer: "We are worth more than a can of Coors Light." Aside from the obvious broken-promises anger, a striking theme at the rally was the link between poverty and the job market. "Basic Income: When a Job Isn't Enough" read a sign held up by a grinning thirtysomething fellow.

Bob Frew waved a sign that said, "I have a job, but I still need Basic Income."

William Whiston did something he'd never done before when he heard that the OBIP was cancelled. He called Laurie Scott's office, describing his mental illness and the way Basic Income had helped. He gave Scott's secretary his contact information and was told that if anything changed he would hear from them.

Laurie Scott never did get back to people who contacted her about the OBIP cancellation. Children, Community and Social Services Minister Lisa MacLeod said she would be pleased to meet with OBIP recipients, but she never did, despite numerous invitations from angry people in Lindsay. Although the strong public outcry likely pushed the government to wind the Pilot down more slowly, with a nine-month runway to the end (April Fool's Day 2019), that was its sole concession. The Ford government did not change its mind. When Windsor-area New Democratic MPP Lisa Gretzky demanded in the Legislature that Minister MacLeod apologize for the premature OBIP cancellation, MacLeod responded that she would "never apologize."[33]

On the day of the last Basic Income payment, Mike Perry organized a group of recipients to gather in front of Laurie Scott's constituency office. They entered her office and stayed all day, waiting for an apology from Minister MacLeod for the government's shabby treatment of the OBIP participants. With no apology forthcoming, the protestors refused to leave until a Kawartha Lakes police officer showed up at the end of the day to escort them out, helping them with their belongings. The *Lindsay Advocate* ran a photo of the constable handing the protestors coffee.[34]

After that, Scott's staff locked the doors, leaving the demonstrators—and everyone else—on the sidewalk. By day three, one protestor carried a hand-lettered sign reading "Where? Are?? You?? LAURIE SCOTT???" The *Advocate* documented dozens of inquiries from constituents through letters to the editor and on social media. But Scott remained hidden away; there was nothing but silence from her and her staff.[35]

It remained unclear whether the dustup over the cancellation of the OBIP would hurt Scott in the next election, scheduled for 2022. The old Tory town is, after all, a hotbed of social rest and political complacency. But it was very clear that Basic Income had improved the lives of "the bottom class." Luis Segura summed it up at the Lindsay rally. The refugee, restaurateur, hip-hop artist, volunteer firefighter, local club supporter, and father of four concluded,

We're all family. We're all a community. What affects you affects me. So, I stand here in solidarity with those that have a worse situation than mine. And how much cutting this program affects you. I will not let a political party or an ideology create a divide and make me build hate in my heart. There's a lot of that already going on.[36]

HAMILTON I
The Freedom to Live with Some Dignity

> Overcoming poverty is not a gesture of charity. It is the protection of a fundamental human right, the right to dignity and a decent life.
>
> —Nelson Mandela

LANCE DINGMAN'S BUMPY ROAD

Lance Dingman is a numbers guy. He keeps score, readily listing the times he went down over the course of a two-year period: seventy falls. "It's best to land on your side. And the prosthetic side is the best side, because it's not going to hurt the prosthetic."

Dingman was twenty-seven when he took his life-changing fifty-foot fall while sleepwalking. The disastrous tumble resulted in a compound fracture of his right femur. Eighteen surgical procedures later, he asked the doctors to remove most of his leg; he could no longer handle the pain. He's been falling ever since.

At sixty, Lance has carefully slicked-back black hair and an enthusiastic mien. He uses a wheelchair and a walker but gets around with a cane when he can. Even though he's eligible for discount taxi chits because of his disabilities, he takes public transit as often as possible. It's about sociability as much as transportation: "If you live alone, you want to get out and walk. You go to the bus stop or you go to a public area. You know the people who want to talk and those who don't. If you don't talk, you meditate. And enjoy yourself."[1]

American bluesman Albert King's classic 1967 recording of Booker T. Jones's "Born Under a Bad Sign" includes a line that resonates with Dingman's bumpy road: "If it wasn't for bad luck, I wouldn't have no luck at all." Dingman's physical challenges alone would be daunting enough, but he has also been dealing with schizophrenia since he was diagnosed at eighteen. He attributes his big fall to sleepwalking during a particularly vivid dream sequence. A regular at the Crossfire Church ("Engaging our world with the extravagant love of Jesus"), located in a converted cinema not far from his rent-geared-to-income apartment on gentrifying Locke Street, Dingman jokes that "The only thing I fear is, someday, I'm going to go up and Jesus is going to go, 'Lance! No more colour dreams.'"

It would be hard to find anyone in Hamilton more familiar with the health care system than Lance Dingman. He has undergone countless surgeries. His 2019 prescription list ran to some two dozen entries, and he has had to learn how to walk with his prosthesis. Dingman has a remarkable ability to remain positive and actively contributes to Hamilton self-help and advocacy efforts, but physician and hospital visits, along with Schizophrenia Outreach, remain a regular feature of his life.

Dingman takes two primary psychiatric medications; in 2019, he was also taking four kinds of pain-management medication. "None of them are opiates," he exclaims, pumping a fist. "Yeah!" Dingman is proud of his accomplishments, including his ability to face up to the ways that life has dealt him a bad hand. In a town that has more than its share of people struggling with disability and poverty, he is a poster boy for what social workers and psychologists herald as "resilience."

Dingman combines his self-awareness with hard-earned self-es-teem. He works at an array of jobs—some paid, some volunteer. On two occasions he managed to reduce his social assistance payments to zero, briefly free of the need for public assistance because his earnings as a peer support coach and a security tenant in his building surpassed his usual Ontario Disability Support Program (ODSP) payments. That definitely generated a sense of accomplishment.

There have also been years of work to overcome what he acknowledges as dyslexia. Dingman has taken a full slate of literacy courses, but it took a while. "I finally finished it two years ago," he says. "I can read, write, and do grammar and, yeah, I'm not doing too bad now. My spelling ain't the best, but I'm doing better. Because of my dyslexia, nouns are hard for me."

The walls of Dingman's modest one-bedroom apartment are amply adorned. They include a photo of his late mother with a sign that says simply, "Believe." He has numerous hockey-related posters, with a nostalgic focus on old NHL arenas like the Montreal Forum and Maple Leaf Gardens. There are also numerous records of his accomplishments on display, the credentials he has earned by taking various workshops and short courses, such as Suicide Prevention and Safe Talk training: "I feel very strongly about my certificates, and I go over them all the time. I feel like I need to. It pumps me up, you know. There's seventy-two of them. I've done this. I've done that." His voice trails off as he nods.

A partial list of his credentials, dating back over the years, includes the Mental Health Rights Coalition; the Peer Support Caring Program, Certificate of Completion Peer Support Worker; the Certificate of Appreciation in recognition of continued Generosity of Spirit & Faithful Ministry to the patients of St. Joseph's Health Care; Certificate of Completion of the McMaster Discovery Program; Certificate of Participation, Mental Health First Aid; and fourteen Certificates of Completion, CORE Collaborative Learning.

Despite a life fraught with daunting obstacles, Dingman remains remarkably upbeat. His spirit refuses to fade in the face of so many falls, so much pain. If there is a word that describes his worldview, it is hope. "If I work hard at my volunteer work, if I work hard getting back to more school, I could get a decent, decent job with some decent, decent hours," he says, adding that he would ultimately like to get off social assistance. "That's my hope. I'm not going to give that up."

FROM STEELTOWN TO RUST BELT

Downtown Hamilton is remarkable for its ramshackle streetscape. High above the sidewalks are façades that recall parts of Lower Manhattan. Ornate stone cornices are a reminder of the city's glory days and long-forgotten financial outfits like the Landed Bank & Loan. Down at street level, however, today's businesses have names like Looney Land and Ca$h-4-you. Tattoo parlours sit beside variety stores that trade mainly in smokes and lottery tickets. At the heart of the city centre, the sidewalks around King and James adjacent to Gore Park—actually a paved plaza featuring patriotic statues—are crowded with legions of ragged people. Lots of smokers with sandpaper coughs. Wheelchairs, walkers, and motorized scooters are commonplace. People shout at each other. And at themselves.

Hamilton's health care system has become seriously stretched as poverty and inequality take their grim toll. Emergency room visits for psychiatric issues jumped by some 60 percent in the decade between 2006–07 and 2016–17. In the lower central city, life expectancy actually *declined* by 1.5 years in the decade ending in 2018.[2]

The city where Lance Dingman lives was once Canada's most important manufacturing hub. The biggest employers were the massive steel mills on the deep-water harbour. Their toxic emissions seemed to be a fact of life. Other manufacturers—elevators, rail cars, agricultural implements, fences, tires—generated thousands of decently paid, stable, and secure union jobs. The epic eighty-one-day 1946 strike at Stelco had given the United Steelworkers a firm foothold in manufacturing. Hamilton's identity was wrapped up in a masculine, muscular image of a blue-collar town.

But this identity has faded into oblivion as Hamilton's reputation shifted from lunch bucket to rust belt. The city became a petri dish for the deregulated capitalism of the late twentieth and early twenty-first centuries. Globalization, automation, and the internet all contributed to wage stagnation and the rise of precarious work.[3]

GETTING ONTO THE PROGRAM

In late 2017, Lance Dingman joined some four thousand other Ontarians previously dependent on paltry social assistance payments in the new provincial government experiment—the Ontario Basic Income Pilot. Announced in Hamilton that spring by Premier Kathleen Wynne, OBIP meant in concrete terms that Dingman, who had been getting some $1,200 monthly on disability support, would for three years be receiving $1,700 per month. People on general welfare had been receiving $640 monthly under a program dubbed, with classic Orwellian doublespeak, "Ontario Works." OBIP—which enrolled one thousand people in each of Hamilton and Thunder Bay and two thousand in the "saturation site" of Lindsay—doubled that rate to $1,300.

When the Basic Income pilot came to town in 2017, despite the promise of a 40 percent increase over his monthly payments from the Ontario Disability Support Program, Dingman was initially reluctant. He learned that not every medical support that had been covered by ODSP would be paid for by Basic Income. He would have to save. He was, however, used to managing on a tight budget, saving when he could, getting some extra money from occasional work. He also figured that it wasn't all about the money.

"Lance was unsure," said his friend Tom Cooper, Director of the Hamilton Roundtable for Poverty Reduction. "He wanted to be talked through the process." Cooper had met Dingman some twenty years earlier while working as an organizer at a community legal clinic on Main Street in the working-class east end; Dingman, then in his late thirties, was chairing a residential care home tenant group.

The people in the home suffered from both mental illness and physical disabilities, both of which Dingman was familiar with. Like so many such unlucky people, the residents had been consigned to run-down care homes—out-of-sight-out-of-mind and largely forgotten by society. The owner-operators of the homes offered little support. Dingman stepped up because peer support is one of the volunteer jobs that have helped him keep going.

After Wynne's announcement that Hamilton would be a Pilot site (and once Cooper himself was convinced), Cooper set out to convince Lance Dingman to take the plunge by signing up. The two realized that, while the $650 silicone liners for his prosthetic would no longer be covered, Basic Income would have offsetting advantages. "New things were happening," recalled Dingman. Well accustomed to the reams of paperwork confronted so often by people on social assistance, Dingman filled out the application. "It was a very, very smart application. I had to go back to the office the next day with my T-4, and then everything was fine. In three weeks, I got a reply saying I was accepted."

Cooper was glad to see hope rekindled, not only for Dingman but also for the dozens of others he had come to know in the course of various social justice campaigns. Many signed up for the pilot. Among other projects, the Hamilton Roundtable had helped to organize low-income people into a Speakers' Bureau and later the Living Proof group, the idea being that the voices of those with lived experience must be central to any public discussions of poverty. This meant that when the Basic Income cheques started rolling in and various media outlets came calling, no one had any trouble finding articulate voices to describe the way lives were improving.

For Dingman, the benefits were immediate and tangible. He was able to buy a new stereo. New pictures appeared on his living room wall—glossy colour photos of the stars who played at those long-shuttered NHL arenas. He was also able to make important improvements in his diet—receiving a Basic Income allowed Dingman to stock his fridge with fresh produce. Having always recognized that his multiple medications played havoc with his metabolism, Dingman knows he needs fresh produce to try to maintain an equilibrium. The extra money provided by Basic Income clearly made a difference.

The way Dingman saw it, the Basic Income pilot offered a measure of hope to people in Hamilton, Lindsay, and Thunder Bay lucky enough to be accepted into the three-year program. "Let's provide an example to show that these four thousand people, we're a good, working-class part of society. A lot of us can't work full time, but a lot of us can work. A lot of us can go to school."

The prospect of an obligation-free Basic Income—especially in an era of insecurity, inequality, and precarious work—was giving new life to the old idea. It did not take long for Ontario's Basic Income Pilot to start attracting international attention. When word started to spread, Tom Cooper and the local Roundtable began fielding media queries from all over the place. The *Wall Street Journal* called. Television crews arrived in Hamilton from South Korea's KBS and Japan's NHK. Dingman talked to Al Jazeera. A ten-minute segment aired on the American Public Broadcasting System's *Newshour*. Pilot participant Jodi Dean (featured in Chapter 6) told BBC Scotland's chief correspondent about how the program had assured her family a reliable grocery supply and help for her daughter, who has a severe disability, noting "Basic Income basically changed our lives."[4]

After six months on the pilot, Dingman got a call from the *Guardian*. He described how he was now able to plan ahead, especially for food. His overall health was improving because his diet was better. But, he added, the new program went well beyond what he could now purchase. As Dingman explained to the English reporter, during an election campaign that would bring a new government to power, he'd previously been trapped by Ontario's traditional social assistance system:

> Basic income has given me freedom to live with some dignity with a little extra money to buy the essentials in life. I want to make the most of this opportunity and work up to a full-time job eventually. . . . I feel much more in control of my own life.[5]

Lance Dingman's feelings about public support hadn't changed that much. As with the old social assistance system, he still felt a pressing need. "I want to work off of BI," he explained after he had been on Basic Income for some nine months. "I think that's the main purpose of BI, to get as many people off it as possible. It's a system that works if you can make it work."[6]

THE LIMITATIONS OF CHARITY

Corporate-sponsored food bank appeals regularly refer to "tackling hunger"—an appeal that may have traction in a football-mad town like Hamilton. With respect to the food banks scattered across Hamilton's charity landscape, however, Dingman was clear about his feelings. Adamant about maintaining his autonomy, he declared, "I never, *ever* go there. I didn't feel I needed to. I wouldn't do it. Because *I* took people to food banks. I'm a peer support coach."

Dingman is far from alone among people whose incomes limit their grocery store purchases but are food bank refuseniks.[7] It's partly about the limited food bank selections on offer in a consumer society that screams "choice" at every turn. It's partly about pride, with people like Dingman not wanting to be the objects of anyone's charity. And it is also about the understanding that food banks do nothing to address the deeply embedded cycles of poverty.

According to a 2020 report from the PROOF research group, headed by prominent food insecurity researcher Valerie Tarasuk of the University of Toronto, there is "a four-fold difference between the number of people living in food-insecure households and the number receiving assistance from food banks. Further, there is no evidence that food charity is able to move households out of food insecurity."[8] *Food insecurity* is the jargon term that academics and Statistics Canada use when people don't have enough money for food, or they are worried about where the next meal is going to come from.

Someone once defined insanity as trying the same thing over and over again and expecting different results. The observation is often erroneously attributed to Albert Einstein, but it does not take a genius to understand the importance of poverty in determining the poor health of so many. Most poor people cannot afford healthy diets. If they had enough money, they could. Evelyn Forget has pointed out a basic truth of health economics: "Poverty relentlessly drives up the cost of delivering health care." As food insecurity, a sensitive marker of deprivation, worsens, health care costs increase. Adults who are the most food-insecure have health care costs that are almost 2.4 times those who are food-secure, especially with respect to medications.[9]

Insanity comes in with the dominant tin-in-a-bin approach. It may make individual donors who toss the canned tuna into the food bank bin feel good, offering the illusion that they've done something important. But the food bank experiment has been stubbornly repeated for some four decades with no apparent improvement in the food security of low-income Canadians. Insanity?

"It's a systems problem," said Dingman. "If we can't make that revolving door stop, that's a hell of a problem." Long active in antipoverty work, Dingman has twice headed out in his wheelchair to assist with a "point-in-time" homeless count. The idea was to take stock of the city's most visible manifestation of destitution, with a view to helping desperate people get off the street.

In 2018, he and his fellow volunteers, together with social service staff, surveyed 386 families and individuals. Of this group, 78 percent had insufficient money for shelter. Forty-five percent suffered from chronic illness, double the national average. Five years earlier, Hamilton's activist Social Planning Council revealed that 5,400 households were on the waitlist for social housing. In one year, 5,653 individual men, women, and children were sleeping in emergency shelters. Some 21 percent of tenant households were paying more than half their income on rent. Meanwhile, the benchmark for determining housing affordability is spending less than 30 percent of one's income on shelter.[10]

"Doing the survey made me feel great, but Jesus, Jesus. When I came home, I cried. You meet people and their clothes are rotting. They stink. They're picking up pop cans and drinking the last bit. They're finding pizza in the garbage."

FOOD BANKS PROLIFERATE, FOOD INSECURITY REMAINS

Lindsay saw a 30 percent increase in food bank requests in April 2019. Heather Kirby, General Manager of the Kawartha Lakes Food Source, had never seen such a jump in demand.[11] Although Lindsay could identify a unique reason for the change, the cancellation of the OBIP, it came as part of a broader general trend.[12] Across Toronto in 2017, one in five food banks had to turn people away because they had no food.[13] Food Banks Canada reported that 47 percent of food banks across the country reported an increase in visits in 2019.

There is no better symbol for government abandonment of the welfare of its poorest citizens than the food bank. The first food bank in Canada was established in Edmonton in 1981, during the deepest recession since the 1930s. Bob McCarty, director of a Phoenix, Arizona, food bank—the first in the United States—arrived in Edmonton to advise the Edmonton Gleaners Association. Within a decade, there were hundreds of food banks.[14]

Food banks present themselves as a means to address poverty-induced hunger when the market has nothing to offer hungry Canadians with no money to shop for groceries—a community solution to market failure. These charities are built with the labour of kindly volunteers and individual donors. They also offer self-interested corporate supporters a handy, tax-deductible alternative to adequate government spending on income security programs.

Early food bank volunteers expected they would close their doors as soon as the economy recovered. Instead, food banks became part of the social wallpaper. These growing institutions bought properties and vehicles, expanded freezer and storage capacity, and hired permanent employees; they planted themselves firmly in the imaginations of Canadians as the only way to address hunger. By the turn of the century, young Canadians were routinely advised that good citizenship meant participating in school food drives. Contests became common, with prizes for kids raising "the most" (i.e., the heaviest) food. Sometimes bottled water counts.

Food banks are convenient for corporate Canada. Manufacturers with products that are edible but not saleable can donate them to Food Banks Canada, get a tax benefit, avoid landfill tipping fees, and present themselves as fine corporate citizens. Grocery chains can package up non-perishable items and encourage customers to buy them for the local food bank, benefiting the stores' bottom line. Other companies can use food drives as team-building exercises, burnishing their brand credentials by "giving back." Corporate Canada gets to maintain the illusion that food banks are taking care of hunger. It's better than paying more taxes to support income security programs. Or paying employees living wages and providing full-time hours and benefits. All of which means that many have learned to disconnect the problem of hunger from its root source—lack of income.

No one wants to see others go hungry. The idea that anyone in a rich country like Canada would be hungry is almost inconceivable, unbearable to contemplate. And yet, even before COVID-19 struck, over 4.4 million Canadians (12.7 percent of the population), including 1.2 million children, were food-insecure.

In April 2020, the first full month of the public-health shutdown of the economy, the government's cautious best guess was that food insecurity had increased by a third, despite the government's rapid Canada Emergency Response Benefit.[15] The 2020 pandemic only made things harder for many low-income people, with intake data for Toronto's food banks showing that 6,100 people began showing up at food banks in June, compared to just 2,000 in February, before the pandemic.[16]

Food insecurity tightly tracks along the fault line of poverty. The same groups of Canadians who are more likely to be poor are also more likely to be food-insecure.[17] The usual overlaps come into play: Indigenous peoples (28.2 percent); Black Canadians (28.9 percent); new immigrants (17.1 percent); parents with young children (16.2 percent); single mothers (33.1 percent).

Being on social assistance or EI dramatically increases the odds of food insecurity (60.4 percent), but most Canadians who are food-insecure (65 percent) actually have employment income—it's just not enough to alleviate food insecurity. The main group of Canadians protected from food insecurity are the ones who already have a Basic Income: seniors (6.8 percent). Rates of food insecurity among the poorest single adults drop in half once they turn sixty-five and are eligible for the Old Age Security pension and the Guaranteed Income Supplement.[18]

Food insecurity is associated with major health problems in adults, from diabetes and heart disease to depression. Food-insecure people are more likely to die prematurely from almost all causes, especially accidental injuries and suicides.[19] For children and youth, living in a food-insecure household increases the likelihood of having asthma, poor overall health, developmental and behavioural problems and higher rates of depression. And children who grow up in food-insecure households are more likely to think about and attempt suicide. Not surprisingly, food insecurity is tightly linked to health care costs as well.[20]

Food banks are so inadequate to deal with the scale and scope of poverty that the vast majority of those who live in food-insecure households never go there. And even if they do, they are still food-insecure. Only one thing has been demonstrated to improve household food insecurity status: additional income.

PRECARIOUS WORK

Soon after Lance Dingman started to receive a higher income as part of the Basic Income Pilot, researchers based at Hamilton's McMaster University published (in collaboration with Toronto's United Way) the latest in a series of groundbreaking studies. Their investigation of growing inequality focused on the new labour landscape—which has been marked by a catastrophic decline in working-class power and the rise of humiliatingly precarious labour.

The research had taken place over a decade, and the data were conclusive. On the basis of more than ten thousand surveys and a hundred interviews over the course of seven years, the researchers shone a light on the alarming emergence of polarized income during a period of sustained growth. A split-level labour market had fractured Canada's industrial economic heartland.

The Poverty and Employment Precarity in Southern Ontario (PEPSO) studies started soon after the global meltdown of 2008. During the gradual recovery that followed, the social scientists abandoned their usually cautious tone, describing how the "shocking portrait" and "stark picture" of the regional labour market had become clear. Only half of working adults reported being in classic "full employment"—the secure, full-time jobs with benefits that so many white working-class men had been able to secure in the postwar era that was now clearly over.

The reports were chockablock with data, the evidence reflected in their titles:

- *Losing Ground*
- *It's More than Poverty: Employment Precarity and Household Well-Being*
- *The Precarity Penalty: The Impact of Employment Precarity on Individuals, Households and Communities and What to Do About it*
- *The Generation Effect: Millennials, Employment Precarity and the 21st Century Workplace*

The data showed young people struggling with the brave new world of work as well as longstanding discrimination against women—particularly racialized women. PEPSO found that, among those who managed to get thirty to forty hours of weekly work, women were paid 88 percent of men's annual wages. Racialized women earned 67 percent of men's wages. This was especially important in the Toronto-Hamilton Area, where half the residents had been born outside Canada and 43 percent were racialized.[21]

A new era had arrived. The days (roughly from 1945 to 1980) of secure employment that two generations of working-class men in labour union towns like Hamilton came to take for granted are now encountered only in museum exhibits. At the Workers Arts and Heritage Centre (Hamilton's union museum, an underfunded yet vital part of the city's cultural fabric), one labour history panel features a wistful recollection from steelworker Reg Gardiner, the words superimposed in an arc over a photo of a mass rally during the monumental strike victory of 1946: "I feel it yet, the feeling of freedom that we all felt by breaking the hold that Stelco had." In the decade preceding 2014, Ontario lost three hundred thousand manufacturing jobs.

"People's wellbeing hasn't improved with the growing economy," the PEPSO researchers explained in the 2018 report *Getting Left Behind*. That report showed that a third of all workers reported poorer mental health in 2017, with rates of anxiety related to employment remaining largely unchanged from earlier studies. Some 40 percent of workers said that employment anxiety was interfering with their personal and family lives.[22]

The PEPSO researchers were careful to point out that the so-called long boom by no means translated into uniform mass prosperity. Indeed, it was becoming ever clearer that the lengthy postwar boom period during which workers did pretty well in comparison to earlier periods was a historical hiccup:

- Women, racialized workers, and recent immigrants did not share equally.
- What labour market scholars call "union density" had been declining for two generations.
- Productivity continued to rise after 1980, but "labour's share of income began to fall."
- The share of national income tilted in the direction of the rich, whose take nearly doubled after the 1980s.
- Over time, secure pensions had ceased to be the order of the day. Insecurity grew, along with inequality.

The PEPSO authors described a "personal responsibility crusade." It could also be named, after a toy whose origins stretch back to ancient

Greece, a "yo-yo" era; *You're-on-your-own*. This is the ideological dimension of the growing insecurity the researchers had documented—"the power of ideas to shape economic outcomes." The particular idea shaping these particular outcomes: If it's to be, it's up to me.[23]

This old idea marked a return to *market fundamentalism*, a faith in free-market capitalism's ability to determine social outcomes. It is fundamentalism because "the term conveys the quasi-religious certainty expressed by contemporary advocates (perhaps apostles is more appropriate) of market self-regulation."[24] It has much more commonly come to be described as *neoliberalism*, the prefix *neo* suggesting the resurgence of nineteenth-century let-the-market-decide individualism. In the Anglosphere, unfettered capitalism had enjoyed a free run during a century of ideological hegemony until the disaster of the Great Depression in the 1930s.

The yo-yo era. Neoliberalism. A personal responsibility crusade. It all adds up to a recipe for insecurity with familiar ingredients: declining union power, robotics, footloose factories, downsized offices, a privatized public sector. The whole picture was summed up by Canada's then Finance Minister Bill Morneau in 2016. Describing that continuing revolution of falling expectations, he said that Canadians had to face facts and get used to the idea that "people aren't going to have the same pension benefits" as in generations past. Morneau further suggested that we should get used to "job churn"—a kind of constant agitation, the endless shakeup of employment insecurity, short-term employment and a constant cycle of career changes in one's life.

Morneau, a Bay Street Liberal, noted that many would soon be seeing their jobs disappear. As with so many others, he identified truck drivers as likely victims of the arrival of so-called "smart" vehicles.[25] All of which was giving rise to the creeping angst consistently described by PEPSO as a hallmark of precarity and a new class—the precariat.

The PEPSO coordinators repeatedly showed that the workers being churned are also being paid less, widening the inequality gap in Canada's split-level economy. Wayne Lewchuk and Stephanie Procyk also note that women in precarious work are less likely to be eligible for maternity benefits through the Employment Insurance system. Indeed, fewer than half of Canadian workers now get EI benefits, even though they are obliged by law to pay EI premiums.

Their suggestions for improving the grim state of affairs ranged broadly. These included:

- Better public child care (parents who do precarious work being more likely to be forced to use unlicensed day care)
- Stronger unions
- Living wage campaigns, and
- Much improved and better enforced employment standards.

"A more radical solution to the increased uncertainty of those in precarious employment is a guaranteed annual income scheme that would provide a base standard of living, unrelated to participation in the labour market."[26] This separation of work from labour and labour from income is a central point of Basic Income projects, but it represents a dramatic departure from the current and historical ideology about work and income.

A CHANGING HAMILTON

Lance Dingman lives in the modest, low-rise 1970s building known as the Taylor Apartments. The Locke Street building is run by Good Shepherd Non-Profit Homes, a Catholic outfit whose basic aim is "providing *hope* and restoring *dignity* to the most vulnerable" (emphasis in original).[27]

Hamilton has been transformed since Dingman moved there in the 1980s, its famous steel mills now employing a tiny fraction of the people who worked there during the mills' heyday. A hedge fund sold Stelco to U.S. Steel in 2007, and the years following were marked by a toxic brew of corporate greed and incompetence. Research and development were neglected, and the American firm stripped production from the Hamilton plant. U.S. Steel acquired Stelco "for one reason," said Warren Smith, former president of the waterfront complex's once-powerful United Steelworkers local 1005. "That was to capture a customer base and the order list." By 2015, U.S. Steel had walked away from Hamilton altogether.

Even the Conservative federal Industry Minister Tony Clement, a paragon of right-wing politics who had been a senior Ontario cabinet minister under Mike Harris, was moved to describe U.S. Steel as "a predatory organization."[28] An organized working class that had parlayed the bitter struggles of the early postwar years into stable, well-paid—though still dangerous—jobs with solid benefits was gradually turning into the precariat described by the McMaster researchers in *Getting Left Behind*.

Deindustrialization has transformed Hamilton, making it an example of the "rust belt" creeping north from hardscrabble cities in the former industrial heartland of the United States. Pittsburgh and its unionized workers were the wellspring of U.S. Steel's original prosperity, and the United Steelworkers are still headquartered there. Like Pittsburgh, Hamilton has been remaking itself into a centre whose principal industries include health care and education. Many Torontonians living close to The Hammer—the evocative name locals adopted for their city—are less likely to know it as "Steeltown" than as a place with myriad interesting new restaurants, expanded offerings through McMaster University and Mohawk College, and a monthly "Art Crawl," ramped up every September into "Super Crawl"—a four-day festival of music and art that draws tens of thousands.

On the other side of Hamilton's struggling downtown from the old Stelco plant, Locke Street has come to symbolize Hamilton's transformation. Its increasingly upmarket retail strip is nestled between the gritty downtown and leafy Westdale, a planned neighbourhood beside the McMaster University campus and Children's Hospital.

Hamilton tenants have been hammered by sharp rent increases and "renovictions" as landlords squeeze them out, ostensibly to conduct repairs, and then hike the rent. Rents in Hamilton were rising faster than average in a province already facing a crisis in affordable housing. Between 2015 and 2018, rents jumped 21 percent, far above the rate of inflation. According to Hamilton's Social Planning and Research Council, spiralling rents were due to the financialization of rental housing and the commodification of housing in general, accompanied by the "pernicious use of money laundering in real estate."[29] Realtors and developers revelled in the upward price pressures generated in part by people fleeing Toronto's out-of-control housing market.

The view from Lance Dingman's apartment symbolizes the growing divide between the rich and the rest in the once solidly union town. Developer Spallacci Homes built a flashy new condo project directly across the street from Dingman's rent-geared-to-income building, and the upmarket luxury units quickly sold out. It is a luxurious address in "the heart of the Locke Street district," according to the company hype. "At the corner of Locke and your life. . . . Steps to the city's most celebrated culture, fashion, and culinary landmarks."

Spallacci's marketing consultants were appealing to people who they believed would be intrigued by the notion of buying into an apartment building that represented "a state of mind" and offered "rich lifestyle amenities." Lest potential customers be wary of the neighbourhood, the firm assured them that the place with the lofty, marble-lined lobby was "only for the privileged few," illustrated by an image of an attractive fiftysomething white couple with good teeth.[30]

All of which surely helped stoke the ire of Hamilton's militant action faction. In 2017, anti-gentrification activists sprayed sour milk at Toronto developers on a "Try Hamilton" real estate bus tour. An upmarket realtor's west-end office had its locks glued shut, and graffiti appeared on a renovated co-working space: "Hamilton Is Not Your Blank Canvas!" Things heated up further in 2018 just as an Anarchist Book Fair was winding down in town. On a Saturday night, a group of masked anarchists marched down the middle of Locke Street toting a banner that read "We Are the Ungovernables"; some smashed store windows. Damage costs were pegged at $100,000.

The attacks generated national attention, and the next day an explanatory post appeared. "Locke St. was downtown's first gentrified street," said the anonymous writer. "The surrounding neighbourhoods [have been] the first to see the rent hikes that have since come to dominate so many of our lives. . . . Saturday night helped me to shake off some of the fear and frustration that build up when you're trapped in a hopeless situation."[31]

While the attacks may have been therapeutic for some, the political message was cloudy. An independent doughnut shop striving to buy local products and pay its twenty-five workers a living wage was vandalized, while a nearby Tim Hortons—by this time owned by a Brazilian multinational and the target of labour activists focused on minimum wages and poor working conditions—remained untouched.

McMaster geographer Richard Harris, a lifetime student of housing policy, called the Locke Street attacks "profoundly misguided." But he added that they were a symptom of "desperation and anger" that "says much more about our times than it does specifically about gentrification."[32] Shannon Franssen agreed. She co-ordinates Solidarité Saint-Henri, a coalition of twenty-seven community groups fighting poverty in a traditional Montreal working-class district. Storefronts have been smashed and Audis and BMWs burned by anarchists. "Very, very, very few people are resorting to violence, but many, many people are feeling angry," said Franssen. "That's the real story."[33]

A WELCOME BUT TEMPORARY BOOST

Lance Dingman may not be angry, but he is unfailingly determined. And cheerfully so, working his way over and around the seemingly endless hurdles he and so many others face as they seek to get by on incomes far below the poverty line. Dingman's small unit in the Taylor Apartments building costs an affordable $139 a month, down from $559 that he paid when he was on Basic Income. His time on the Basic Income Pilot offered him a welcome, albeit temporary, boost.

Basic Income advocates consistently argue, and Dingman's experience seems to confirm, that while a program guaranteeing people something close to a livable income is necessary, it is nowhere near enough to live in dignity—particularly in the face of stratospheric rents common in Canada's big cities. Simply put, Basic Income is no silver bullet. Absent a comprehensive, publicly funded program to build modest Taylor-Apartment-style projects across Canada, a stand-alone Basic Income would be insufficient. That is because, left to the private sector, housing will always be a prime example of market failure.

The market succeeds for those at the top. In 2020, a tiny one-bedroom unit the same size as Dingman's, in the new Spallacci development right across the street from the Taylor Apartments, was selling for $519,000.[34] Of course, buyers could be assured they were moving into "an award-winning project and neighbourhood." It was unclear what awards had been tendered. What was clear was that deregulated capitalism was failing to meet the needs of people with modest incomes.

Against a background of public policy to address income security and housing affordability, as well as affordable child care and pharmacare, some Basic Income advocates believe that the project is about more than money. It is about freedom, and Basic Income constitutes an instrument of freedom. Just as Reg Gardiner explained that the 1946 Stelco struggle meant freedom from the claw of the boss, Dingman said that getting a Basic Income in 2017 translated into freedom to live with some dignity. And well before the Basic Income pilot came along, Dingman was holding fast to the belief that he had to be free from charity, rejecting the food bank—and not just because the charity offerings almost always failed to meet his complex dietary needs.

It is not uncommon to be wary of charity. Many first-time food bank users never return, preferring to leave the food for those who "really" need it. Many, like Dingman, hold proudly to the prevailing ethic of self-sufficiency. It is welded firmly to the value of the work, both volunteer and paid, that he undertakes with unalloyed zeal. Clearly, our identities and moral worth continue to be bound up with work.[35]

EMPATHY AND HOPE

Dingman's work ethic tells the world something important. He is not a victim. He is an autonomous person, in charge of his own life. The cancellation of the Basic Income pilot that was helping him out was a blow, yet he was undeterred. *If I study, if I work hard at my volunteer work, if I work hard getting back to more school, I could get a decent, decent job with some decent, decent hours.* It reminded him of the time when he was a young man and the doctors told him he should not have children because of his multiple medications. He just kept going, his reserves of empathy helping to sustain him as well as those around him.

Along with a busload of some twenty-five others from the Hamilton Roundtable for Poverty Reduction, Dingman travelled to the Ontario Legislature in 2018 to protest the government's Basic Income cancellation. Not being a political animal, Dingman remained hopeful as the group arrived at Queen's Park. "I knew that if it was going to be cancelled, it would just change so much of my life."

Within days of killing the Pilot, Premier Doug Ford—a right-wing populist in office for only a few weeks—announced with great fanfare the headline-friendly "Buck-A-Beer" program, designed to cut the price of beer. As the visit unfolded and it became clear that the government was not going to continue with Basic Income, Dingman grappled with the disappointment. That emotion shifted when Premier Ford started to boast about the new program his government was introducing: "He started to go on about buck a beer. I thought that was just so insulting."

The mood on the bus back to Hamilton was sour, verging on bitter. Dingman, however, was not focused only on his own situation, the injustice of it all, the broken election promises, and the callous disregard for marginalized people. He was concerned about Tom Cooper, who had done so much to convince him and many others to apply for the pilot program. He knew that the Poverty Roundtable organizer had taken "a big blow" because he hadn't always supported Basic Income.

"I've known Tom for years," he recalled. "He's got nothing but a good heart. He does what he does because he wants to help people."

Dingman's years of group therapy work had left him with a keen appreciation of the shifting moods of others—and the impulse to offer whatever support he could. "He felt bad. You could see it in him. He was taking a little bit more on himself that he should."

Dingman paused with a thoughtful sigh: "But he'll be all right."

CHAPTER 6

HAMILTON II
Thinking Further Down the Road

I wasn't working. I was looking after my children.
—Jodi Dean, OBIP participant

The unpaid care work done by women is estimated at $10.8 trillion a year—three times the size of the tech industry.
—Oxfam

JODI DEAN: PAPERWORK AND PERSISTENCE

Jodi Dean has lived in a modest detached brick house in Hamilton's east-end Crown Point district for much of her life. She grew up there, left for a time, and now lives in the small place once again. It is a dozen blocks and two sets of train tracks south of the sprawling Dofasco steel complex where her father worked. The house has been in the Dean family for nearly a hundred years.

Dean's high school sweetheart lived three blocks away. After they married and he started work as a mechanic, the couple moved to a moderately more upscale neighbourhood closer to the foot of the Niagara Escarpment, known to people in The Hammer as The Mountain. They had three children together—Tory, Jacob, and Madisen. "We owned our own home," Dean recalled, a trifle wistfully. "We had two vehicles. We had a trailer for the summer. And we made the choice for me to stay at home with the kids."[1]

Madi Dean was not yet a year old when her parents separated. Jodi's ex moved out of town, leaving her with the kids, a mortgage, and one of those sometimes tricky to enforce child-support agreements. Like many women running on a treadmill with someone else controlling the speed, she began a prolonged scramble to keep up. Dean sold her car. Most of her jewellery went, along with unnecessary appliances. When she and her husband separated, they had been putting in a basement bathroom; a toilet and pedestal sink, still in their shipping boxes, were easy to offload: "I sold anything that was not a necessity."

Jodi Dean had entered a world familiar to many single mothers. Some 1.4 million Canadian children—18.6 percent of Canadians under 18—live with the corrosive effects of poverty.[2] Statistics Canada's 2016 census calculations showed that nearly two in five children in lone-parent families lived in a low-income household, three and a half times the proportion for children in two-parent families.

The overwhelming majority of children living in single-parent families live with their mothers, and poverty rates for them (42.0 percent) are much higher than for children who live with their fathers (25.5 percent). The federal government's Canada Child Benefit has illustrated how public policy can change this by giving people money. In 2017–18, the new program kept 278,000 children above the poverty line. The CCB helped 37 percent of lone-parent families whose income would have been below the poverty line stay above it; 80 percent of these families were led by women.[3]

As soon as Dean found herself on her own with three kids, she applied for Ontario Works, the province's welfare program—which leaves recipients far below that poverty line, offering even less support than the disability payments for which Lance Dingman qualifies. Nevertheless, Dean was disqualified because the court-ordered support she was supposed to be getting from her ex was more than she would have received from Ontario Works. Describing herself as "a very big advocate," Dean began her long march across the tricky terrain that constitutes "the system." In the years that followed, she became an expert in paperwork and persistence. When she was accepted into the Basic Income pilot, Dean found the forms pretty simple.

"Paperwork is part of our day," she shrugs. Dean has learned that the system certainly has its helpful people, including the first welfare case officer she met: "When I got turned down, the worker was wonderful. She actually cried. And she said, 'I'm sorry. I just can't help. My hands are tied.'" The system's shopworn rules-are-rules strictures can be hard on those charged with enforcement; social service workers make up the system's shock absorbers, with many quickly burning out. The social service staffer told Dean that there might be help with utility bills. A hundred-dollar cheque arrived along with a list of food banks.

"I used to *work* at one of them," she said ruefully, hinting at her sense of pride. "When I sold our home, . . . the foreclosure sign was on the door. I took it down so my children never saw it." Dean and the children found themselves as tenants in a ramshackle townhouse, watching as housing costs escalated. Middle-class refugees from Toronto's overheated housing market had begun to arrive in Hamilton.

The signs of gentrification even started appearing in Hamilton's working-class east end, far from Dingman's place on Locke Street. Dean noted that Ottawa Street was becoming upmarket, featuring "expensive, exclusive places." By 2020, Barefoot Babies was offering cloth diapers and Simply Zen featured vegan protein powders and truffle-infused olive oil. Yoga studios and massage therapists proliferated, popping up near the mouldering remains of the old Avon Theatre, a classic seven-hundred-seat movie palace where locals used to catch a double bill before heading across the street to Ward's restaurant for an ice cream float.

Slipping into poverty while surrounded by signs of rising prosperity came as a shock. It was, however, a world with which she was familiar. Dean had volunteered at St. Matthew's House, an Anglican Church outreach agency that runs a food bank and child-care centre while offering services to isolated seniors in need of meals and a comfy space to gather.

I worked with kids at St. Matthew's who taught me a lot. I never saw a cockroach until I worked there. Every time I saw one, I'd scream, and they'd make fun of me. Two of the kids that I worked with lived upstairs in the building we used for the after-school program. They just laughed at me. "Oh Jodi, why are you screaming? They don't hurt you. When we lie on the floor watching TV, they run right over us."

Dean soon figured out that poverty is not just about food insecurity and the gnawing anxiety related to end-of-month bills. It also imposes a weighty emotional burden. It can "completely strip you down to feeling nothing but shame, especially when you've never been that person to need help. Being on that opposite side is really difficult."

The family trailer had been one of the casualties of Dean's separation, so Gage Park became a welcoming sanctuary during Hamilton's withering summers. The huge leafy public space offered shade and gardens, a splash pad, and play structures. "Our whole summer, all we did was walk," Dean explained. "We'd walk to the park. The kids would play at the splash pad. What else are you going to do in the summer?"

There is a sprawling McDonald's outlet directly across busy Main Street from the park, and Dean knew she had to be ready for the predictable requests. She recalled the time that she figured out a way to turn fast-food temptation into a life lesson for her son Jacob, then a young teenager: "I said to him, 'Look, kid. We have fifteen dollars. I don't have any more money coming in until tomorrow. Can you figure out how to treat us to McDonald's *and* buy dinner? You've gotta feed everybody, because that's how it works.'"

Dean beams at the recollection. Luckily, her children are fond of pasta. They headed to the nearby supermarket, where she handed over all her money to Jacob. He grabbed the weekly flyer and proceeded to canvass the aisles, doing the anxious comparative-shopping math so familiar to people with shallow pockets. The four then proceeded to McDonald's to share fries and a Dollar-Day drink. It wasn't that much, but it meant a lot. Jacob was happy to get a modest, if rare, treat—but even happier that he had figured it all out.

Dean's kids were used to opening the fridge for a snack, only to have their mom tell them that the contents were earmarked for that week's school lunches. She struggled to maintain as much a sense of normality as she could, explaining to her children yet again that they need one another—along with friends and relatives—to get by. The alternative was stark. The streets of Hamilton's lower city abound with ragged people whose lives have been hollowed out by destitution.

"The kids understand that without having outside support, we could have easily been those people on the street. So, I've tried to teach them a lot of empathy." Indeed, the phrase *people on the street* creeps routinely into the story of just managing to get by. She insists in a practical, matter-of-fact manner, projecting the idea that "surviving's totally different than living."

LIFE GETS EVEN MORE COMPLICATED

Jodi Dean's daughter Madisen was born in 2007. In the aftermath of a difficult separation, her mother began to sense that something was wrong. The child had been complaining of backache shortly after learning to speak. She would fall out of bed, adding to what seemed like chronic distress. "I had a three-year-old with heat packs on her back, lying on the couch, taking Tylenol every four hours. It wasn't normal."

Nor were the seizures. In 2010, doctors diagnosed Madi with epilepsy, a condition that would alarm any parent, but conventional treatments did not seem to be having the predictable effects. Two years later, her mother took her to a neurologist for a regular checkup. Madi, a cheery child in spite of it all, had even managed a kindergarten "skip-a-thon." When the specialist asked how she was doing, "she said, 'My back *hurts*.' And the doctor looked at me and went, 'Mom?' I'm, like, 'Well, I've taken her to the doctor three times. I'm not a bad mom.'"

Years later Dean chuckles at the recollection, but it hardly seemed funny at the time. Her customary self-confidence was fast being eroded by Madi's distress and her own inability to fix things. She told the physician about the skip-a-thon, and he said that it was time for a full-body scan. The MRI showed that Madi had compressed vertebrae from the base of her neck all the way down her thoracic spine (the longest section of the back) to her lumbar spine. Each of the twelve vertebrae was compromised: "Obviously, at that point, everybody was, like, 'Oh crap. We dropped the ball. A bit of a backache!'"

Dean is not the sort of person to look for someone to blame. It was, once more, a matter of carrying on and managing. If the Deans had any good fortune, it was that they lived in a city with one of Canada's most sophisticated health care systems. Indeed, education and health care (including McMaster medical school and associated hospitals) had taken over from manufacturing as the city's principal source of jobs. Once Madi was diagnosed with idiopathic juvenile osteogenesis imperfecta, years of appointments, advice, and physiotherapy followed.

As explained in an article in the prominent medical journal *The Lancet* in 2016, osteogenesis imperfecta (OP) is a rare bone disease for which there is no cure: "The combination of fragile bones, weak muscle, and cycles of fracture and disuse creates substantial challenges for a patient to attain and maintain gross motor skills, especially walking."[4] Cycles of fracture mean that people with the condition often break bones—a lot of them. Hence the common name for OP—brittle bone disease. The principal treatment focuses on preventing and controlling the symptoms—those "substantial challenges" referred to in *The Lancet*.

Madi has had ten physicians, along with regular and intense physical and occupational therapy sessions. She became familiar with bracing and seating arrangements, passing many of her waking hours in a specialized wheelchair. The family travels regularly to Montreal's Shriners' Hospital for specialized orthopedic care for complex disorders like OP. At any moment—and for pretty well any reason—she can break a bone.

Over the years as a single mother looking after a daughter with a severe disability, Dean had become used to making hard, often apparently impossible choices. These are not choices between wants and needs, she explained, but between needs and needs. One event in particular stands out. Madi broke her leg at home, and her mom had no money for a cab to get to the hospital. The child was in excruciating pain; the forty-five-minute bus ride was out of the question. And so Dean drove—in the full knowledge that she could not pay the exorbitant cost of hospital parking. She was close to panic at the prospect of being ticketed or, even worse, having her recently acquired, well-used vehicle towed.

"I crossed my fingers and I started texting everybody I knew, saying, 'I need you to bail me out of the hospital. Can you bring me twenty-five bucks?'" Although a friend soon came through, the feeling she had of being in jail wouldn't go away. "It's almost shame that you can't take care of your own child," she recalled. "Living in poverty brings shame. They go hand in hand."

As the years passed, Dean managed the juggling act of combining whatever paid jobs she could cobble together with looking after Madi, all the while also taking care of her older children. She tried to keep things stable and predictable, hoping that her efforts would rub off on her kids. The reality of juggling precarious contract work became ever clearer. One of Madi's particularly severe seizures meant that Jodi had to drop one of her contracts to buy some precious time between jobs. Soon after she started her next contract, her daughter was hospitalized, so Dean needed two days off each week. As Madi's illness developed, Dean found herself relying on friends and family to handle her daughter's complex care.

"I couldn't afford babysitters. I couldn't afford to leave her with just anybody," she said. "So, it became a huge struggle to try to work and take care of her needs. And I don't blame employers for not wanting to hire me or keep me on. I'm technically unreliable to them." Dean recalls, "I wasn't working. I was looking after my children." Which says something about dominant cultural assumptions about work, and which in turn is why some feminist thinkers regard the Basic Income movement as critically important. The American scholar Kathi Weeks explains it this way:

> The political movement for a basic income can be advanced as a way to open conversations about what counts as work, about the value of different kinds of work, and also about what else besides work we might want to do with our time—what other models of care, creativity, and cooperation we might want to build.[5]

SPEAKING UP AND SPEAKING OUT

In 2014, following a twelve-week training phase, the Hamilton Roundtable for Poverty Reduction launched its Speak Now program in the sumptuous Tanenbaum Pavilion at the Art Gallery of Hamilton. At the launch, Joscelyn Bottos described the day she went to school so hungry that she fainted in front of her Grade Seven classmates.

The program's goal is to "empower individuals by giving voice to their lived experience with poverty and social exclusion." Program participants are available "for speaking engagements to promote acceptance of community diversity and enhance awareness of local poverty issues through the telling of their personal stories."[6] Aware of the narrative power of the storyteller's art, the Hamilton Roundtable for Poverty Reduction organizers had set out to change the way people see the world inhabited by so many of their neighbours.

The Speak Now initiative originated in the Roundtable's Shifting Attitudes working group and reflected the Roundtable's commitment to offering a public voice to Hamilton's poor. The hope was that Speak Now would help to undermine the deep-seated prejudice that feeds negative and corrosive but commonly held stereotypes about poverty.

Many of the remarkable stories that emerged reflect the rising tide of precarious work. Fifty-two-year-old Isabella Daley told of her culinary arts diploma and her twenty-five years of kitchen work that came to an end when she was injured. Her separation from her husband had left her in debt, struggling to care for her children. Despite two college diplomas, she noted that "I've never had a job that wasn't minimum wage and permanent part-time."

Daley was forever conscious of the exact amount she needed to feed her family. If one of her kids surprised her by bringing a friend home for dinner, she went without. It took its toll. "I use the term financially induced anorexia," she quipped. Things bottomed out when Daley's twenty-two-year-old son Dylan died and she didn't have money to bury him. "Not being able to put him in the ground was the lowest moment of my life," she said.[7]

Jodi Dean joined Speak Now soon after it started, becoming active with the Roundtable. The group had come together after a 2005 report by City Council showed that fully a quarter of Hamilton children were growing up in low-income households—households like her own. She was especially inspired by Lance Dingman, whose story of what it is like to live with schizophrenia moved her to tears: "He explained it so I could feel it." Dean became an energetic Poverty Roundtable activist. Tom Cooper, the Roundtable's Director, was amazed. "I think Jodi may be the most resilient person I've ever met. It must be so incredibly stressful, yet Jodi always finds time for volunteer activities, supporting her friends or family while helping to highlight the issues that need addressing."[8]

DESPERATE MEASURES

Dean explains that mental health issues are "one of my big advocacies." There's a commonplace saying that some things "just make me crazy." It is a kind of throwaway line to describe one of life's garden-variety frustrations. Dean understands that for people enduring the crunch of poverty, it has an entirely different meaning. The system seems designed to supercharge stress in ways that leave people vulnerable to poor mental health.

For example, in 2018, a single person was getting under $1,200 per month in Ontario Disability Support Program benefits—certainly not enough to live on. Not surprisingly, this takes a further toll on people already dealing with chronic disabilities and stressed out by their inability to afford basic shelter and diet.

Desperate people are moved to desperate measures. The streets of downtown Hamilton, together with depressed parts of other Canadian cities, feature payday loan storefronts that critics claim are little better than loan sharks. "You've got predators like payday loan people," said Dean. "I know somebody on ODSP who got a payday loan and got wrapped in the cycle. Every single month, nine hundred dollars, [most of] her cheque, was being paid back."

Disadvantaged people across North America are routinely victimized by payday loan operators, whose numbers have exploded in lockstep with precarious work, poverty, and inequality; one U.S. study as early as 2006 revealed that there were more of these operations than all the McDonald's and Starbucks outlets combined.[9] Their presence in Hamilton's lower-city neighbourhoods like Dean's grew as banks pulled out of areas where profits were no longer promising. The heyday of the big banks that once dotted so many streets was over, the solid corner buildings often repurposed as upmarket coffee shops. Between 2006 and 2016, there was a 19 percent decline in bank branches in the lower city and a 32 percent jump in payday loan storefronts. The lower city has the highest poverty rates in Hamilton. One study by British Columbia credit union Vancity revealed that consumers believe a $23 fee on a two-week $100 loan means a 23 percent interest rate, which would be comparable to already usurious credit card rates. In fact, the rate—or "vig" in loan-shark lexicon—is really 598 percent.[10]

As it turned out, it was not just those on social assistance who were being fleeced by the predators. People like Dean who worked on temporary contracts or at insecure low-wage jobs were also vulnerable—and their numbers were rising. A 2016 report on predatory lending by Hamilton's Social Planning and Research Council pointed to an eight-thousand-person survey that revealed that nearly a third of Hamilton workers were precariously employed. "Payday loan users were much more likely to not receive benefits at work, including not being paid if they miss work for illness or other reasons."

These already vulnerable workers had generally exhausted their savings, with 40 percent having to work more as they struggled with bills. Some 60 percent were using credit cards to pay their bills: "This indicates that payday loans may often be added to a person's other debts, making it even more difficult to pay the high interest rates." The title of the SPRC report asked, "Is the payday loan industry cashing in on Hamilton's rise in precarious employment?"[11] The answer seemed obvious.

In 2016, Dean addressed Hamilton's City Council to tell another story. It happened to be her own. Dean recounted how she had taken out a three-hundred-dollar loan in December of 2014, when her child support payment failed to arrive. She got some help for rent and food from friends and family but could not abide the prospect of not being able to give her children Christmas gifts. The three-hundred-dollar loan ended up costing her fifteen hundred dollars *in interest alone*. Dean's presentation was instrumental in persuading City Council to restrict the number of payday loan operators in each district—the first Ontario city to do so.

"We call them predatory because that's what they are," she said. "The proliferation of payday loans in our city preys on the working poor and those on fixed incomes."[12]

AN ANALYSIS FROM LIVED EXPERIENCE

The North American Basic Income Guarantee (NABIG) congress convened in Winnipeg in 2016, attracting two hundred BI supporters. The theme for the Congress, held at the University of Manitoba, reflected the movement's ambitious nature: "Basic Income: A Meeting Place for Equality, Rights, and Justice." Many of the speakers were professors and policy wonks. Presentations included the cost of child rearing on Basic Income, Bitcoin, and the feminist case for Basic Income.

John Mills, a member of the Hamilton Roundtable for Poverty Reduction, also spoke. He offered an overarching analysis, stressing the importance of Basic Income to any meaningful attack on poverty, his straightforward title reflecting the thinking of so many Basic Income advocates: "Where Capitalism Fails and How Basic Income Will Help."

At sixty-four, the lanky, craggy-faced Mills had struggled for decades with regular bouts of debilitating depression. In an understated manner, he immediately established his identity as someone with "lived experience" of poverty, introducing himself as a member of the Roundtable's Speak Now group and President of MoodMenders, a Hamilton peer-support service for people with depression, anxiety, and PTSD: "I want to apologize for any difficulty in speaking I may have. My timing for getting dentures didn't quite mesh with reality. This is one of the many issues surrounding attempting to live on suicidal assistance."[13]

Mills was on *social* assistance at the time, so the reference was freighted with irony; few trying to subsist on $8,160 a year would have questioned the deliberate misnomer. He acknowledged that a Basic Income would obviously benefit him personally, but went on to explain that society at large pays a high, often hidden, price for poverty. For example, he pointed out that in Canada's multibillion-dollar prison system, "the majority of incarcerated people come from lower socio-economic conditions."

Mills underlined what many in the audience knew: Evelyn Forget had already uncovered the results of Manitoba's 1970s Mincome project, clearly demonstrating the positive effects of Basic Income: "We saw an increase in high school completion; we saw a reduction in hospitalizations, specifically for accidents and injuries and mental health; and an improvement in mental health in terms of access to family doctors." Mills also underlined another advantage that feminist BI supporters were highlighting. "One of the problems of living in poverty is the increased stress that generates anger and frustration. Relationships often break down."

The mental health activist offered a perspective on liberty and freedom that differed from the market-based notions peddled by Milton Friedman: "Basic Income would allow everyone autonomy. It would allow an abused person to leave a bad situation and not become destitute by doing so." When someone faces a "bad situation" in the workplace, Basic Income would likewise allow that person to say no to a bad boss.

Mills focused principally on the austerity mindset that had for so long colonized the political class—relentless reductions in public programs; rampant individualism; the world of self. More than a few Basic Income supporters in the audience realized that Mills, soon to be receiving a guaranteed basic income for which all Canadians are eligible at age sixty-five, was summarizing why Basic Income needed to be pitched well beyond people living with disabilities. It could offer freedom and autonomy for everyone feeling the effects of the yo-yo (you're-on-your-own) mantra: "This period of austerity is not being financed by increased taxes on industry, which increasingly works to *not* pay any taxes. It is being financed by a slow dismantling of the social safety net."

Canada's recently elected government had ridden to victory a few months previously on a platform featuring an endless emphasis on the "middle class." The Trudeau Liberals' polling and focus-group analysis revealed that low unemployment numbers masked a prevailing sense of insecurity abroad in the land. For more and more Canadians, unease and insecurity had become stark facts of life. "The middle class is shrinking and middle-class jobs are turning into contract and part-time positions," said Mills. "All in all, the situation for workers is becoming increasingly precarious."

Mills had personally watched as the balance of power in Hamilton had tilted in favour of the boss at the expense of the organized working class. He stated:

Along with a decreasing number of full-time jobs, industry has made certain that wages have not kept pace with production improvements, and unions have lost their influence. Real wages have remained stagnant and, in many cases, regressed over the last several decades, while profits have been directed to the top of the economic pyramid and moved offshore to tax havens.

The Hamilton Roundtable for Poverty Reduction had launched its Speakers' Bureau to demolish the ugly stereotypes of people living in poverty. It was all about amplifying the voices of the unheard. John Mills's fleeting reference to his mental illness before outlining his understanding of the way labour market trends meshed with shifts in political power may not have been exactly what the Roundtable had in mind for service clubs, church groups, and schools—but it was supremely appropriate for a gathering of people interested in understanding and promoting Basic Income. A longtime advocate for raising social assistance rates, he had concluded that merely tinkering with a broken system was hardly worth the trouble. As Tom Cooper put it, Mills was "kind of a visionary."[14]

MEASURING HEALTH BY POSTAL CODE

There is a street in Hamilton called Upper Paradise Road. It forms one of the boundaries of a West Mountain neighbourhood and, while the name is surely a bit of hyperbole, it is genuinely a realtor's delight.[15] At the other end of the spectrum is a North End neighbourhood bounded on the west by Wellington Street North. One apartment on that street was listed in 2019 on the Rent-It-Or-Not rating site as faring poorly on the Cockroach Meter, with one tenant posting a graphic first-hand account of cohabiting with the undesirable creatures.[16]

Hamilton seems like it was designed by a sociologist to prove a theory, its class divisions sharply delineated. Anyone inclined to scepticism could turn to the local paper's Code Red series. It began in 2010 when *Hamilton Spectator* investigative journalist Steve Buist launched a remarkably lengthy and insightful investigation into how health and illness can be measured not simply in individual terms but on a broad social scale, underlining the impact of poverty by postal code.

"There's no clearer measure of health than whether you're dead or alive," Buist wrote in the first of dozens of stories that the "*Spec*" published in its initial Code Red series. In the West Mountain neighbourhood bounded by Upper Paradise Road (L9C 5B7), life expectancy was 86.3 years. Down around Wellington Street North (L8R 1M9), hard by the waterfront, the average was 65.5 years, just ahead of Pakistan but worse than India or Turkmenistan.

The analysis relied on some four hundred thousand hospital and death data points, with Buist enlisting help from Neil Johnston, an epidemiologist specializing in respiratory disease at McMaster's Department of Medicine. They found that Hamilton's best-performing areas outperformed its worst by factors of ten, twenty, and even thirty when it came to psychiatric emergencies, cardiovascular incidents, emergency room visits, and respiratory problems, among others. Johnston described the disparities as "staggering."[17]

Buist's reporting generated National Newspaper Awards while feeding a growing recognition that the city's social fabric had been ripped apart. In the central Hamilton neighbourhood where the cockroaches were running rampant, 74 percent of children were living below the poverty line.

Basic Income advocates have long been frustrated by widespread ignorance of one single, irrefutable fact: poverty and inequality are staggeringly expensive on a broad, societal level. These costs are usually overshadowed by narratives of neoliberal individualism. Most obvious is the staggering toll on the health system, a central Code Red message. The cost of hospital use at the neighbourhood level provides the evidence. In well-heeled suburban Flamborough, the per capita cost was $138. Down in the lower city around Wellington Street, hospital use came to $2,060 per person.

Over the postwar period, many workers who had lived in Hamilton's lower city decamped to greener, car-dependent suburbs farther from toxic factory emissions. Pollution had long been trapped by the Mountain as prevailing winds from Lake Ontario blew across the old industrial zone around Burlington Street. Though cancer can strike anywhere, seemingly at random, cancer and environmental degradation are inseparable. Cancer "clusters" are common—both within factory populations and in communities adjacent to concentrated heavy industry. In 2019, the Canadian Labour Congress marked Black History Month by targeting "environmental racism," highlighting racialized communities exposed to carcinogens and other toxins: Africville in Halifax, Grassy Narrows in northwestern Ontario, Hogan's Alley in British Columbia. The list is long.[18]

By 2013, the *Spec*'s data revealed that breast cancer rates in what had once been a cradle of Canadian industrialization were 16 percent higher than the national average. A downtown area just south of the tracks had a rate of 52.8 new cases per 1,000 between 2000 and 2009—80 percent higher than the Canadian rate. Meanwhile, a neighbourhood up on the Mountain, not far from Upper Paradise, had the lowest rate in the city at 15.4 new cases per 1,000. Two Mountain neighbourhoods had *no* breast cancer deaths between 2000 and 2009. Stated simply, women in poor areas were disproportionately dying of breast cancer.

The Code Red series also reported extensively on education and the impact it has on employment and financial well-being. During the city's industrial heyday, the cliché had it that a young man with a high school education—or often without one—could quit a job in the morning and get hired at another plant the same afternoon. By the early twenty-first century, the jobs landscape had changed dramatically.

International Harvester made agricultural implements and employed 2,900 workers in 1958. Two generations later, all those jobs were gone. Firestone had 1,000 workers making tires in 1964, and after the turn of the century those, too, were gone. In the early 1980s, Stelco's Hilton Works still had 13,000 workers, and a generation later a mere handful remained.

Education was no longer about the class ladder. It was becoming a prerequisite for even a half-decent job. The education sector became a major employer in a city where making things was increasingly a thing of the past. In the Westdale district, hard by McMaster University, two of three adults aged twenty-five to sixty-four have university degrees. People living in a neighbourhood near the Centre Mall downtown, repurposed as a "power centre" big box mall, included 1,375 employed adults when Code Red reported in 2010; ten had university degrees. In another poor east-end neighbourhood, over 40 percent lacked a high school education.

WIDENING THE LENS: SOCIAL DETERMINANTS OF HEALTH

The Code Red project's sharp focus on health subjected Hamilton's class structure to what amounted to an intense MRI scan. It applied the insights of the social determinants of health (SDOH) to Hamilton. Scrutinizing the city through this SDOH lens revealed that health, like wealth, is unevenly distributed—and they are connected.

Over two thousand years ago, the founders of the Western medical tradition, Hippocrates and Galen, observed inequities in health related to social circumstances. Some groups of people in ancient Greece had higher rates of sickness and died earlier than other groups.

This observation held true as industrial capitalism took hold in the nineteenth century. The German philosopher Friedrich Engels produced a book called *Conditions of the Working Class in England, 1844,* that connected the exploitation of workers and their gruesome living and working conditions to their high rates of disease and shortened life spans.

Working-class people lived in overcrowded, dilapidated housing, suffered from inadequate diets featuring contaminated food, drank alcohol to avoid contaminated water, lacked sanitation, worked horrendously long hours in dangerous factories, and had neither medical care nor access to education. Infectious diseases like cholera and typhus were rampant. Citing official reports, Engels wrote that the average working-class life span in Liverpool was only fifteen years, less than half that of the upper class. He accused the rich and powerful of "social murder" for ignoring the dangerous and unhealthy conditions in the fast-growing industrial cities that were the source of their fortunes. "I have never seen a class so incurably debased by selfishness, so corroded within, so incapable of progress, as the English bourgeoisie."[19]

Prominent Toronto physician Dr. Danielle Martin is among many who have explained how income relates to health. More money means people can get what they need to thrive—decent food and adequate shelter for a start. "Income affects health indirectly, through its effect on social participation and the ability to control life circumstances," she wrote in her 2016 book *Better Now: Six Big Ideas to Improve Health for All Canadians.* "Put another way, the biggest disease that needs to be cured in Canada is the disease of poverty, and part of the cure is to implement a big idea: A Basic Income Guarantee for all Canadians."[20]

Interest in SDOH started to grow in the 1980s, just as neoliberal common sense was taking hold. By 2005, there was enough solid evidence about the social determinants that the World Health Organization (WHO) appointed a special international study group, the Commission on the Social Determinants of Health, not just to examine global health inequities but to come up with recommendations to improve them.

The commissioners included Canada's Monique Bégin, twice Minister of Health and Welfare, one of the first Quebec women elected to the House of Commons and the midwife of the *Canada Health Act,* adopted in 1984. The WHO Commission report concluded that "social injustice is killing people on a grand scale" and that "bad policies, economics and politics" are responsible for global health inequities.

What was true for Hamilton in the twenty-first century was true elsewhere. The SDOHs, not biology, are responsible for children born in the poorest part of Glasgow, Scotland, living on average twenty-eight years less than those living only thirteen kilometres away. The inequity is, not surprisingly, reflected between countries as well. Girls born in Lesotho were living on average forty-two years less than those born in

Japan. Afghan women had a one in eight chance of dying in childbirth compared to a one in 17,400 chance in Sweden. The WHO insisted that the inequitable distribution of power and money generated those circumstances within and between countries. Governments need to understand this, taking action and measuring the resulting effects.[21]

While there have been many public policy initiatives that led to improved health outcomes, general awareness of this connection has been much slower to develop. Governments built clean drinking water and sewage disposal systems. Child labour was eliminated and the foundations of workplace health and safety regulation established.[22] For much of the twentieth century, Canadians took such health improvements for granted, paying scant heed to how social organization affects health. The rise of modern Western medicine during the twentieth century, coupled with the increased power and status of physicians, meant that the medical model of illness care got credit for the increase in life spans. Access to physicians and hospital care came to be seen as the most important determinant of health, a canard that persisted even though health inequities persisted long after medicare came to Canada.[23]

I'M MADISEN

Madisen Dean has long red hair, a round face and a near constant smile. She also has her mother's determined self-confidence. "You want not to be defined by your disability," she insists. "I'm *Madisen!*"[24]

Madi's brittle bone condition has meant that she has broken her hip, leg, elbow, and several bones in her feet. In 2019, she blacked out on the stairs at home and fell, breaking her knee. "We were lucky it was only her knee," says her mother Jodi.

Sitting in her wheelchair, Madi wears a thoracic-lumbar-sacral orthosis, a corset-style brace that resembles a piece of medieval armour called a cuirass. Unlike the cuirass, it is not for warding off arrows and swords; rather, it is designed to restrict movement as part of the treatment for conditions like compression fractures. "There are enough long words in our lives," Jodi Dean says wryly. She was diagnosed in 2016 with systemic lupus erythematosus, usually known simply as "lupus."

Outside the Dean house, a caution sign, its stylized image showing someone in a wheelchair, warns drivers to slow down. Inside, it's a busy place. Dean has made time for intimate touches like a homemade kitchen wall-hanging with photos of family friends who have passed on. It hangs beside a sign saying "Friends gather here." Still in her forties, Dean has held hands as three contemporaries, close friends, died before their time.

Yet she and her younger daughter remain remarkably upbeat. They have been instrumental in organizing an all-inclusive choir to accommodate people with disabilities, and Jodi helped establish a lacrosse league for children with disabilities. "I've always wanted to help other children who have anxiety about things," says the twelve-year-old. "Or they just *want* to vent out to somebody, but they feel like they have to hold it in because they have to be strong. Which is not always the answer."[25]

Dean beams as she predicts confidently that one day Madi will land a hospital job doing work that "will make lots of changes to little lives. I really do think that will happen."

Madi became the 2019 Ontario Easter Seals Ambassador. She has a hospital bed for her bedroom, courtesy of the organization that aids children with disabilities. The campaign has also funded a stair lift, prompting her mother to insist that, in spite of it all, the family has really been lucky. "Many nights we've stressed and many nights I've cried," Dean says, her voice breaking. "Because I feel like I can't give her everything she needs."

LIKE WINNING THE LOTTERY

Dean was of two minds when the news arrived that the Ontario Basic Income Pilot would be looking for participants in Hamilton and nearby

Brantford. She had learned not to trust government social assistance systems that had denied her support after her separation, forcing her to sell off so much of what she owned. She also feared that getting involved would usher her into an institutional maze with no promise of a positive outcome.

On the other hand, what did she have to lose? She had helped people she had met through the Roundtable with the weeds of fear that can paralyze vulnerable people confronted by intimidating bureaucracy. Tom Cooper was urging her to give the Basic Income Pilot a try. The government had assured him that the Pilot program was "the real deal," guaranteed to last for the three full years that the consultants said they needed to generate meaningful data about Basic Income's effectiveness.[26]

"I have a special needs kid. Paperwork is normal," she recalled. "I went down, and I thought, 'This is it? This is all we have to do? Okay.' Boom! We were done. In and out of there in forty-five minutes." Then she forgot about it, getting on with her life. She was surprised when she got the news.

"We were like, 'Are you kidding me? We actually qualified?'" she laughs. "When we got the first cheque, I even said to my husband Stephen [she had remarried in 2018], 'It just doesn't feel real.' Ontario Works turns you down, you're not going to expect that Basic Income is going to help you at all."

The extra three hundred and forty-five dollars per month meant Dean could suddenly afford those hospital parking passes, leaving three hundred dollars to put towards household needs. There were also little extras for Madi after she had worked "her little buns off" at physiotherapy. Her daughter could now buy little treats for herself during one of her many hospital visits when wait times could stretch on for hours. A smoothie. A juice: "Those seem like such minuscule things to most people. They're a big deal to her. And it was a big deal to me to be able to give them to her. I didn't have to worry. To me, Basic Income was like winning the lottery."

In the months following the start of Ontario's Basic Income pilot, Jodi Dean became a Hamilton poster person, living proof that Basic Income was working. Her interview with Britain's *Independent* was picked up all over, from the Dubuque (Iowa) *Telegraph Herald* to the Namibia Press Agency. The Hamilton poverty reduction Roundtable had a keen sense of how particular issues catch the interest of editors.

The Roundtable volunteers who had direct, lived experience of poverty had by this time come up with a new, rather catchy name for the group. It started with Tim Button, who had been living in poverty for years. His last job was low-wage roofing, work that exposes men to harsh weather and perilous conditions, but he hadn't been able to work for some twenty years after falling from a roof. Unable to qualify for workers' compensation, he subsisted on Ontario Works and its starvation-level welfare payments. Button looked to Out of the Cold programs for food and the companionship he needed to tamp down the scourges of mental illness.

Basic Income transformed his life. He used to talk so fast it was hard to step away from a conversation with him. But after he received Basic Income, he calmed. It's as though a weight had been lifted. Featured in an Associated Press story, Button became something of a Hamilton celebrity, his photo appearing in papers across the United States—including on Fox News.

Button even joined Tom Cooper to make a United Way presentation outside London, something he would not likely have been able to pull off before Basic Income. He told the crowd he had been able to visit his family in Timmins for the first time in years, proudly emailing Cooper that he had been shovelling his sister's driveway. He had a sudden sense of purpose and pride. Back in Hamilton, he got up at a Roundtable meeting to confidently proclaim that "I'm living proof that Basic Income works." The name stuck. The Roundtable's Speakers' Bureau became "Living Proof."

In March 2018, Tom Cooper got a call from PBS *Newshour,* the American public broadcaster's flagship TV evening news broadcast.

The economics reporter came to Hamilton to interview Dean and Alana Baltzar. Both women were part of the Roundtable's Living Proof speakers' bureau, their stories showing the way Basic Income was working. "When the reporter was done," Cooper said, "he accused me of 'stacking the deck' with the most compelling participants I could find. He wasn't completely wrong."[27]

THE IMPACT OF SCARCITY

In 2018, an American social work professor with an interest in how stringent eligibility barriers affect social assistance began examining the Ontario Pilot. Leah Hamilton noticed that "coming from a place of economic privilege," it is easy to forget how a few hundred extra dollars could change things. Citing the 2013 book *Scarcity: The New Science of Having Less and How It Defines Our Lives,* Hamilton and Canadian social policy specialist Jim Mulvale noted that living in poverty generates psychological stress, together with "a myopic focus on everyday survival." This makes it very difficult to make long-term financial plans.[28]

The authors of *Scarcity,* Princeton behavioural psychologist Eldar Shafir and University of Chicago behavioural economist Sendhil Mullainathan, showed that reducing stress about money allowed people to think more clearly. They tested their hypothesis in a New Jersey mall and in villages in rural India. The emotional impact of financial stress—even imagined stress as in the New Jersey experiment—was similar to the impact of doing without a whole night's sleep.

"The key to our story," they wrote, is showing that the same people perform differently in different circumstances, with IQ points actually declining in the face of scarcity. "Poverty *itself* taxes the mind . . . not because [poor people] are less capable but rather because part of their mind is captured by scarcity." Shafir and Mullainathan know the value of metaphor, comparing the stress brought on by scarcity to the way an older computer seems to slow down. Overloaded by programs, the browser crawls tediously from page to page. The user assumes the machine is inherently slow rather than realizing it is overburdened with other tasks. "Similarly, it is easy to confuse a mind loaded by scarcity [with] one that is inherently less capable," wrote Shafir and Mullainathan. They explain that they are "emphatically not saying that poor people have less bandwidth." Indeed, they are showing quite the opposite. "We are saying that all people, if they were poor, would have less effective bandwidth."[29]

Annie Lowery, who had studied the Kenyan Basic Income pilot, also noted that poverty acts "as a kind of tax on mental bandwidth," trapping people's minds in the present, making planning for tomorrow so difficult. Endless worry about immediate needs such as whether there will be enough food for the family or how to pay for hospital parking makes thinking about the future or abstract planning almost impossible.[30]

In the months after Tom Cooper had convinced her to sign up for Basic Income, Jodi Dean had come to believe in the program. She was able to resume her social work studies at Mohawk College. Like many other BI recipients, she started to notice that she could now do some planning: "Before Basic Income, it was just 'live for today'... get through today—tomorrow at the most. But thinking about what would happen further down the road just didn't happen."

The reduction in financial stress liberated Dean. She gained a sense of possibility that had long been missing when things were insecure and unpredictable:

> Now it's more like, "I have a need to have a three-year plan." I need to know that, at the end of this, I'm going to be able to do something to continue moving forward and not staying stagnant or going back to the positions we were in. I don't want to ever be there again.

Her work as a speaker for Living Proof gave Dean the opportunity to explain to Hamilton audiences how the Basic Income pilot was working for her family. And how it would work beyond individual households to government balance sheets and the country at large. The proof was ready to hand. The malaise was clear at King and James streets in downtown Hamilton:

> We are a rich society which has people living on the street. We have people begging on corners. And we can afford this. This is not going to be any more expensive. . . . In mental health alone [we're] going to save a ton of money with something like Basic Income.

The day after Dean pointed this out, the Ontario government terminated the Basic Income Pilot. But it couldn't terminate Dean's uncanny yet wry self-awareness: "If positive thinking could make me rich, I'd be a millionaire."

CHAPTER 7

HAMILTON III
New Choices

Only somebody who performs some useful work for the public at large, whether by hand or brain, can be entitled to receive from society the means for satisfying his needs.

—Rosa Luxemburg

Take this job and shove it.

—sung by Johnny Paycheck

JAMES COLLURA: THE JOB PERFORMANCE PARADOX

"The first month I was out of school, I went to a job interview at Scotiabank," recalled Hamilton millennial James Collura, noting rue-fully, "I ended up getting it. I was pretty lucky." Then he added, his voice tinged with irony as he raised both hands in the familiar, four-finger gesture, "Air quotes, lucky."

There was a time when banks designed their buildings to impress clients. What was once known as the Bank of Nova Scotia built its main downtown branch opposite Gore Park in downtown Hamilton with that in mind. As with medieval cathedrals, the idea was straight-forward: Powerful institutions like to convey a particular image. Solid. Trustworthy. Permanent. The pillars of high finance lavished money on monumental spaces, soaring ceilings, and polished marble.

Not anymore. Although "Bank of Nova Scotia" is still, literally, carved in stone far above the sidewalk, the eye is instead drawn to the shiny red plastic Scotiabank logo atop the wide glass doors. In the twenty-first century, it's all about the flash and grab of marketing.

Collura, a tall, well-spoken Hamilton native with a stubble-style beard, arrived for his Scotiabank job, undergraduate degree from McMaster University in hand. He assumed that it would be a first step on the financial sector's career ladder. His father had worked his way up to be CEO of the credit union that handles the mortgages and savings of Hamilton municipal and hospital workers.

James Collura, however, was to take a very different path. First, he came to what he regarded as his first real job with an iconoclastic understanding of the world of finance. He had been impressed by a book that mainstream economists would surely regard as quirky—*Sacred Economics* by the American writer Charles Eisenstein. Influential in the Occupy Movement of 2011, Eisenstein is emphatic: "Money seems to be the enemy of our better instincts; [it] seems to be destroying the earth, as we pillage the oceans, the forests, the soil, and every species to feed a greed that knows no end."[1]

During his five years working as a bank teller, Collura made just over the minimum wage. "I was getting paid about the same as the guy flipping burgers," he says, though he did qualify for benefits. His job was not full-time; he clocked fewer than thirty hours a week—typical in today's precarious job market. Not as marginalized as many other millennials perhaps, but nothing like the days of standardized, full-time work—nothing like his father's experience.

Other aspects of the job had been changing and were continuing to change. Of course, automated teller machines had been displacing human tellers for decades, and many customers used the ATMs located just inside the front door. By the time Collura started at the bank, electronic banking and smartphone apps had also arrived. He watched as the lineups for his teller services shortened and his employer gradually shut down more wickets.

It quickly became apparent that he was meant to spur this trend along. A key performance gauge was something called "digital conversion rates," meaning that a significant part of Collura's job was actually to persuade customers *not* to use his services. Collura referred to this as a "job performance paradox"—where the indicator of a job well done involved rendering one's own job more insecure. "The better we performed, the less relevant we were. . . . It was like the only metric they measured for a successful teller at the time I was there was digital conversion rates."[2]

There were, of course, still senior citizens who had never bothered with flip phones, let alone iPhones and Android contraptions. Older folk can be hard to keep out of bank branches because, for many, a visit to the bank performs an important social function. The daily list of errands holds out the promise of personal contact that the ATM, much less a hand-held app, can hardly offer.

THE VIEW FROM THE BANK TELLER'S WINDOW

The sharp edges of poverty in his home town also became clear to Collura during his years at the bank. The product of a suburban upbringing, he had read about poverty and inequality at McMaster, but here he was, face-to-face with it every day. He now truly understood that many people were living from one paltry paycheque to the next—or worse. Collura would later recall, "As I counted the coins emptied from the hats and cups of homeless customers onto the bank's imported Italian marble countertops, I had plenty of time to think about how we as a society could better provide for the mentally ill, sick, poor, and the precariously or under employed."[3]

The lower city's ragged people trooped into the bank with handfuls of coins gleaned from panhandling, their common plight stemming from a range of possible causes. They were:

- Struggling to afford shelter, displaced as upwardly mobile people moved into neighbourhoods where rents were once low

- Deinstitutionalized psychiatric patients
- Women who had fled domestic violence and become homeless, and/or
- Caught up in the opioid crisis, perhaps using the powerful pain-killers to dull the edge of poverty (17,602 Canadians died from opioid-related causes between January 2016 and June 2020).[4]

Hamilton Medical Officer of Health Dr. Elizabeth Richardson explained that an alarming 31 percent of Hamilton's senior kindergarten children are vulnerable in at least one area of their social, physical, cognitive, communications and emotional maturity. "In some areas of our city, that rate is more like 47 percent."[5]

Hamilton has also been hit by a serious housing crisis. Between 2010 and 2016, the city witnessed a 95 percent increase in landlord applications to evict tenants. According to the Hamilton Social Planning and Research Council, "landlords use tenant turnover as a strategy to increase rental prices and profits." Newcomers to Canada—and Hamilton has emerged as an immigration magnet—are vulnerable when they are unaware of the rights and responsibilities of tenants.

This sort of displacement, sometimes called "renoviction," had become commonplace in a deregulated environment. Hamilton rents were skyrocketing; meanwhile, social assistance rates had been shrinking in real-dollar terms for twenty-five years. Of course, the crisis is not restricted to Hamilton or even Ontario; it's evident to varying degrees across the country.

This crisis in housing affordability constitutes a classic market failure, given that markets treat shelter as a commodity instead of a social need. With the growing financialization of rental housing, it is no longer a matter of small or even large landlords being key players in the rental housing market. Financialization is about massive global firms, such as Blackstone Group Inc., a "leading global investment business" with $176 billion USD in global real estate holdings,[6] amassing apartments worldwide.

This practice has been condemned by the United Nations Special Rapporteur on the Right to Adequate Housing.[7] In the face of it, the Hamilton Social Planning and Research Council's report on skyrocketing housing costs reached an important conclusion: "The dominance of large corporations in Ontario's rental sector makes it all the more urgent to improve tenant protection policies, as the concentration of corporate power against individual tenants and small tenant associations and advocacy groups has created an unfair rental housing market."[8]

Collura was coming to realize that, since his job involved putting himself out of a job, housing was not the only sector that was out of control. The labour market was also wildly volatile. Given to self-reflection, Collura wondered about his work: "Are they going to let us go? Am I going to be laid off? Is a robot going to replace me?"

Collura also asked himself about human nature. Do too many believe that people are basically selfish? His economics studies had taught him neoclassical theory, which assumed people are essentially self-maximizing social atoms. He couldn't agree, believing that compassion and connection are central to the human spirit. He was fond of quoting the African-American poet, memoirist, and civil rights activist Maya Angelou: "If it is true that a chain is only as strong as its weakest link, isn't it also true that a society is only as healthy as its sickest citizen and only as wealthy as its most deprived?"[9]

A DIP IN INCOME, A BOOST IN FULFILMENT

When the Ontario Basic Income Pilot landed in Hamilton in 2017, Collura attended a town-hall-style information meeting about it. He joined others in thinking about filling out the forms.

Collura was not on social assistance. He had no disability. He was not a single parent struggling to make ends meet. He was simply a young man frustrated with dull, dead-end labour that he figured had little or no social value. However, because he was between eighteen and sixty-four, making less than $30,000 annually, he met the OBIP criteria. Collura was pleasantly surprised when he got a letter indicating that he had been accepted as part of the research project. Convinced that his bank job would soon be eliminated by online banking anyway, he quit.

He quickly caught on at a float therapy business. Zee Float was in a downtown building where meditation and psychotherapy were on offer alongside a yoga centre and a cartooning studio. Zee Float featured salt-water flotation tanks more buoyant than the Dead Sea—"no gravity, no touch, no sight, no sound, just pure nothing. . . . Your body gets to rest, de-stress, and heal."[10]

Collura's career shift led to a slight dip in income, the loss of his benefit package, and a big boost in his sense of fulfilment and social engagement. It wasn't long before *Lindsay Advocate* publisher Roderick Benns published an interview with Collura. It featured a photo of him painting a Super Mario likeness on a wall, explaining his hopes about the way things might be.

"I'm a big believer in the sharing, giving, and trading economy," Collura said, echoing the freedom dividend concept that Basic Income promoters had long held out as a positive possibility. He continued,

> Since I've received basic income, I've embodied that philosophy. I work in a building full of entrepreneurs and use my skills to help with event planning, posters, marketing, and social media. I've even painted the logos of three different businesses on the walls in their office spaces. I've done all of it for free. Zero dollars.[11]

WHY AIN'T YOU WORKING?

The Lindsay interview caught the attention of a Toronto *Sun* columnist, Brian Lilley, and apparently drove him into a spasm of rage. For Lilley, formerly of the far-right Rebel Media, Basic Income exemplified everything he hated. Lilley acknowledged that one of his ideological soulmates had supported Basic Income. "Yes, I know that prominent economists, such as the late Milton Friedman, have supported the idea," he wrote. "So what? It's still stupid."[12]

Voices like Brian Lilley scorned Basic Income as a sop to deadbeats wanting a free ride on the backs of hardworking taxpayers. His denunciation of James Collura was steeped in blind resentment of the young man's "taxpayer funded degree in economics" and how he had quit his job and enrolled in the Pilot—not mentioning that Collura had immediately found another part-time job or that by 2020, the Ontario government's funding of postsecondary education had plunged to only about a quarter of university revenues.[13]

It was an appeal to populist sentiments that trade on working-class insecurity in the face of the continuing evaporation of reliable, secure, decent-paying jobs: "Justin Trudeau is telling blue-collar workers that he'll pay them to stay home. He's also telling people like James Collura that it is OK to quit your job and do your art for free, the government will take care of you."[14] (In fact, Ottawa's Liberal government had demonstrated little or no interest in Basic Income.)

This take on government help is hardly new. Before the Great War, Marion Crerar, a middle-class member of several Hamilton charitable boards, helped to deploy platoons of "lady visitors" to inspect the lives of the poor. Crerar claimed to know of families "where people simply lived on charity. The whole family at ease while the eldest daughter played the piano at her leisure." As early as 1926, the *Hamilton Spectator* offered that "to adopt a policy of giving relief to all who ask for it would be to put a premium on shiftlessness and invite an epidemic of malingering." In 1929, Hamilton businessman R. I. Smith, first president of the Central Bureau of Family Welfare, proclaimed the need to weed out a "mendicant class" of people who were "gradually becoming habitual seekers of aid [and] could move about from one organization to another."[15]

Such attitudes persisted even into the Depression years of the 1930s. One unemployed steelworker lined up all night for municipal city relief "only to be confronted with open allegations and insults. 'Why the hell ain't you working?' the staff wanted to know." Hamilton's welfare commissioner maintained a rigorous policy, insisting that the unemployed had to mortgage their houses and use up all their loans before they could get municipal relief. Although that term would soon give way to "assistance," the dominant ideology of suspicion and mistrust remained, accompanied by strict surveillance. Divorced, unmarried, or deserted mothers were particularly suspect. In the 1930s, a family on assistance could expect to receive a visit at home every ten days. They might well be lectured on how to shop economically. Hamilton employed forty-two full-time municipal relief investigators, half of whom were women.[16]

During a bitter Depression-era controversy over the advisability of public pensions, the prominent social worker Charlotte Whitton denounced the idea of a mothers' pension, refusing to call it that. She preferred "mothers' aid" to pension. Whatever it was called, Whitton stood resolutely opposed. A stalwart supporter of traditional private charity and moral vigilance, Whitton—later Ottawa's mayor—was for many years the influential head of the Canadian Council on Child and Family Welfare. She had headed up an inquiry into a British Columbia pension proposal and had a foreboding warning:

> There is a grave danger of the development . . . of a general tendency to reliance on social aid that [our] inquiry regards with grave disquiet as destructive of personal effort, and self-dependence, and so destructive of the very basis of initiative, enterprise, and strength of character that must be the greatest resource of any people.[17]

Of course, not all women regarded mutual aid as dangerous and destructive. Another tradition long predates Whitton's stern, hard-faced individualism. Indigenous wisdom about the common good was poignantly explained by Gramma Geraldine Shingoose, a Sauteaux woman from Manitoba's Tootinaowaziibeeng First Nation. "Our ancestors . . . always took care of the little ones, we took care of our families, and we took care of the community. And we always did that through the generations, even up to now. That's always our priority."[18] Settler society's understanding owed more to policing than caring.

One review of the Ontario Mothers' Allowance, one of Canada's oldest social assistance programs, had a title that eloquently summed up dominant attitudes towards people in need—*No Car, No Radio, No Liquor Permit*. This was what the "investigators" hired to conduct home visits to assess a woman's worthiness often wrote at the top of applications to indicate that the woman did not have any of these ostensible luxuries and was thus considered worthy of support.

The system of scrutiny in most "wet" provinces was so intrusive that liquor permits (booklets in which each booze purchase was recorded by provincial liquor clerks, *de facto* social workers) could be revoked by either police or welfare authorities. In 1932 alone, Ontario conducted over 59,000 special investigations into people on relief. If a Mothers' Allowance applicant had had a liquor permit, turning it in was a prerequisite for getting help. A radio? Clearly frowned upon. A car? Definitely a sign of profligacy.[19]

Low-income people, according to prevailing attitudes (then and apparently now as well), should not be permitted to enjoy the things available to others. Particularly leisure. Particularly if they do not hold jobs. Putting aside the fact that millions of poor Canadians hold jobs— often two or three—the stubborn insistence that some are deserving while others are not persists as part of a commonplace objection to Basic Income.

CRAZIES AND LAZIES

Basic Income, done right, would be a modest step to the democratization of prosperity at a time when inequality is on the rise. It might allow us to see leisure as the fruit of economic progress. Hardly a free pass for freeloaders.

Putting aside Bertrand Russell's observation that "the idea that the poor should have leisure has always been shocking to the rich," the logic of free riding can be extended to the injustice of paying poverty-level wages (or no wages at all) to people, mainly women, who get irregular hours doing undervalued but essential work, such as child rearing, elder care, and cleaning. The free riders here are actually those who enjoy the benefits of having racialized newcomers look after their parents and grandparents. Care labour is toil that many, particularly men, consider beneath them. "Women's work."

There is a dichotomy between those who find separating labour from income offensive because they are attracted to the prestige associated with work and regard wage labour as a moral imperative, on the one hand, and those who are attracted by the idea of freedom *from* labour and want to maximize leisure, on the other. Basic Income scholars Philippe Van Parijs and Yannick Vanderborght, their tongues only partly in cheek, describe these two sides as the Crazies and the Lazies.[20] They would count themselves among the Lazies—although their Basic Income book, *Basic Income: A Radical Proposal for a Free Society and a Sane Economy*, with its cascade of references and massive bibliography, would seem to belie sloth. They emphasize distributive justice, asking if attending a rich aunt's tedious tea party so you'll be remembered in her will entitles you "ethically speaking" to a fat chunk of money just because you, unlike everyone else, happen to be related to her. (As noted, Canada stands out among rich countries in not taxing inheritance at all.)

Building a Basic Income floor simply "helps equalize what people are given" and more roughly "what they might achieve with what they are given." And as far as getting free stuff in the form of Basic Income— abhorrent to the Crazies, attractive to the Lazies—is concerned, the Belgian thinkers argue that everyone benefits "very unequally from what was freely given us by nature, technological progress, capital accumulation, social organization, civility rules and so on."[21]

The particular Basic Income controversy involving Brian Lilley (clearly a "Crazy") and James Collura (definitely a "Lazy") shed light on two things. First, it revealed Collura's generosity of spirit, bound up as it was with his hopes for a future free of drudgery and insecurity. No matter how the Basic Income debate eventually played out, Collura wanted to be sure that not only would he be "safe and secure and fed and healthy and well," but other people like him would be as well.[22] Second, the little dustup pointed to something that some Basic Income promoters like to highlight: its potential for being an instrument of freedom. Implemented thoughtfully, it offers the promise of liberation—freedom not just from material deprivation but also from mindless, purposeless labour.

Freedom from poverty was highlighted by Franklin Roosevelt in his famous 1941 Four Freedoms address. The American President linked traditional liberal freedoms—freedom of speech and freedom of worship—to more expansive notions of human security: freedom from want and freedom from fear. Basic Income promises to address the last two by providing everyone with security of food, shelter, and the other necessities of life. Basic Income also offers the opportunity, taken up by James Collura, to say "Thanks, but no thanks" to a bad boss. Moreover, Collura was pondering whether it would be possible to bid adieu not just to a particular job but to alienated labour itself. He was worried about automation and underemployment being driven by digital transformation. Millennials like himself were becoming ever more stressed about their uncertain future.

Collura's unease echoed George Orwell's critique of modernity and that gnawing anxiety that "you'll never get anything unless you grab it from somebody else."[23] Yet his anxiety was tinged with optimism and hope, based on the idea of Basic Income acting as a freedom dividend:

> Consider what those human beings might otherwise do with their lives if they weren't compelled to work in repetitive, mundane, robotic jobs for the sake of putting an over-priced roof over their heads? Perhaps, with Basic Income, they could do something they truly wanted to do, and enthusiastically enjoy doing![24]

According to the iconoclastic thinker David Graeber, author of the 2018 bestseller *Bullshit Jobs: A Theory*, there are two kinds of jobs: shit jobs and bullshit jobs. Shit jobs are undertaken by a huge swath of workers who, in the wake of the Great Plague of 2020–21, were suddenly being recognized by the official opinion makers as essential and even heroic. Their work is "not at all bullshit," wrote Graeber. "They typically involve work that needs to be done and is clearly of benefit to society; it's just that the workers who do them are paid and treated badly."[25] These often precarious workers are forced to take shifts at two or more workplaces every day. Among them are the personal support workers—mostly women, many newcomers to Canada—who struggled to help senior citizens being sickened and killed by COVID-19. Their jobs are, quite literally, shit jobs. They had been doing this work before the pandemic and would continue in its wake.

Bullshit jobs are much different. They sometimes pay very well and come with good benefit packages. They are almost always salaried—for example, a "strategic network manager" in a large firm; people doing telemarketing, consulting, and brand marketing research. Graeber explains further:

> Bullshit jobs are not just jobs that are useless or pernicious; typically, there has to be some degree of pretense or fraud involved as well. The jobholder must feel obliged to pretend that there is, in fact, a good reason why her job exists, even if, privately, she finds such claims ridiculous.[26]

Graeber ended his book with a caution, explaining his wariness of policy solutions. He noted that as an anarchist he is reluctant to look to government and corporations to solve problems. Despite his stated reluctance to make recommendations, however, Graeber felt compelled to put forward the position that Basic Income has the potential to "become a stepping stone" to true human liberation—as it would "unlatch work from livelihood."[27]

THE IDEAS DYNAMIC

"Angels fly from a vision of a better world," wrote three Canadians at the height of the 2020 pandemic, "and this is what we need to allow ourselves to imagine." Their concern was with arts and culture, a sector that had shed 85,000 jobs by April of that year. These thinkers imagined a twenty-first-century Canadian version of the 1930s Works Progress Administration under which the U.S. government under Franklin Roosevelt poured public subsidies into arts education and theatre, visual art, and folklore documentation.

What if Canada made a bold effort to establish a huge digital platform to showcase Canadian actors, dancers, musicians, and artists? How about direct support to immigrant and Indigenous artists, a focus on cultural activity outside big cities, and the promotion of stories from newcomer communities, documented for future generations?[28] The idea was that the culture sector provides a different sort of infrastructure: stories told and songs sung, plays staged and poems written, not just "shovels in the ground."

Ideas are important in nurturing political projects. Milton Friedman once offered the savvy insight that "only a crisis, actual or perceived, produces real change. When that crisis occurs, the actions that are taken depend on the ideas that are lying around." The trick, he continued, is to keep your ideas alive "until the politically impossible becomes the politically inevitable."[29]

Certainly, making it easy for Canadians to collect $2,000 every month at a cost of tens of billions under the CERB would have been regarded as politically impossible a few weeks before it actually happened. Similarly, public health care was not in the cards in Canada for nearly a century after Confederation. Once upon a time, slavery was widely regarded as normal. Only men who owned property could vote, and votes for women were deemed laughable. Social movements—together with the ideas that animate them—change things.

How then does this "ideas dynamic" affect proposals for a Basic Income—an idea that had been lying around for decades if not centuries? Certainly, many have long viewed the idea as nothing short of utopian, but the 2020 pandemic ripped the shroud off the prevailing market thinking. Contradictions abounded: inequality festered; precarious work proliferated in a split-level labour market; manufacturing jobs shrank as a result of both technological change and migration to the Global South. The same factors had started to erode service sector work as well. Full employment—paid labour for everyone at "regular" hours—was clearly no longer achievable, if indeed it ever was. Promoters of the full-employment/jobs-for-all-vision suddenly seemed like historical relics, war reenactors dreaming of past glories.

Other outmoded ideas? How about an economy of endless expansion? In an article promoting Basic Income, novelist John Lanchester pointed out that the current approach is hardly promising. "Will we be fine with the rich taking a bigger and bigger share of total income, until the end of time, as the world drowns and burns and starves?"[30]

In the months leading up to the pandemic, the world had witnessed unprecedented mass demonstrations, "climate strikes" demanding action to curtail global heating. Many were led by youth. "People are suffering. People are dying. Entire ecosystems are collapsing," Greta Thunberg famously told the United Nations. "We are in the beginning of a mass extinction. And all you can talk about is money and fairy tales of eternal economic growth. How dare you!"[31]

A few months into the pandemic, another police murder of a Black American prompted a similar global outpouring of protest, calling attention to the ways that racism is embedded not just into policing but into virtually every sector of our society—leading to the situation outlined in Chapter 1 in which communities of colour intersect with people who perform undervalued but important jobs, intersect with people managing on low incomes, intersect with those who suffer disproportionately from the ravages of climate change—and, by the way, from the pandemic.

Basic Income would not, of course, solve these staggering problems. But it remains a key part of any comprehensive program challenging market fundamentalism. That's because of its potential for wide appeal—an idea embodying the type of cooperative, sharing ethic that underpins other similarly necessary programs of public provision. Basic income provides the freedom from want that is essential for the freedom to imagine and create a different way of living together on the planet.

OVERCOMING ENTRENCHED IDEAS

Before the idea of Basic Income can be widely accepted, however, we need to contend with some other very old, very persistent, and very well-entrenched ideas. For example, the work ethic that serves capitalism so well has formidable cultural power. The idea stretches back to biblical times, as evidenced by the apostle Paul's admonition that "anyone unwilling to work should not eat."[32] Another sticky one: the belief that if you are poor and have little or no paid work, you have no one to blame but yourself. Although this runs contrary to the innate human sharing and caring ethic that underpins many faith traditions, for many it is common sense.

Even the early-twentieth-century German revolutionary Rosa Luxemburg insisted on "a universal duty to work for all those able to work."[33] Luxemburg's avowal of the work ethic might have puzzled radicals from the previous century, who imagined freedom from "wage slavery" as part of the world beyond capitalism. But by Luxemburg's time, even socialists and the labour movement more generally had accepted wage labour as the most effective way to distribute income. Writing in the venerable socialist magazine *Canadian Dimension*, long-time Canadian author and journalist Richard Swift noted, "It is a central irony of the history of the Left that it so frequently comes to defend the very exploitive and unjust institutions that were its sworn enemies from the outset."[34]

We have seen the misery that results from a failed market-oriented approach in various sectors—from labour to housing to health—and noted how the 2020 pandemic finally exposed these failures for all to see. An unconditional Basic Income floor could offer protection from increasing inequality and insecurity, thus challenging the moral vacuity of market thinking. When the World Bank addressed Basic Income in a landmark 2020 report, the notion of "social protection" appeared as a unifying theme[35]—protection, one could only assume, from the ravages of the market.

The fullest application of Basic Income strikes at the heart of another apparently common-sense idea: our understanding of labour as a commodity. Class power comes into play as well. Are workers forced to take any job? Or are they free to say no to a bad boss? If it is widely accepted that the labour market involves survival of the fittest, then achieving that fullest Basic Income becomes all the more difficult, arguably impossible.

If a different common-sense notion prevails, however—one in which paid labour is "desacralized"—an emancipatory Basic Income is more likely to prevail, "freeing people to work rather than forcing them to work."[36] James Collura took this approach when he quit his job at the bank.

Basic Income boosters have often talked of desacralizing paid labour. In a 2018 reflection on Basic Income and work, Canadian labour economist Jim Stanford suggested that Basic Income, set at a livable level, could shift on-the-job power relationships. "Employers well understand that if workers have the capacity to de-commodify their lives (that is, live decently without selling their labour), the power of employers to hire workers and extract labour will be considerably diminished." Stanford, a prominent public intellectual, cut to the heart of the matter, underlining the importance to employers of the revolution of falling expectations:

> They want to get as close as possible to the pure logic of "work or starve" as possible. We should be aware of the fundamental challenge [Basic Income] poses to the very concept of wage labour—and be prepared to confront the fierce resistance that the idea will spark among employers.[37]

Shortly before the Liberal Throne Speech of 2020, the United Steelworkers came out for a Guaranteed Livable Basic Income, supporting a private member's bill introduced by rookie MP Leah Gazan (NDP—Winnipeg Centre) to convert the CERB to a permanent Basic Income. It was the first major Canadian union to take such a stand, citing "disgraceful levels of income inequality" and the need for living wages and a just labour market.[38] Ideas seemed to be shifting.

PROMOTING BASIC INCOME, DEFENDING PUBLIC SERVICES

The politics of Basic Income are complex. When the new Ontario government of Doug Ford killed the Basic Income Pilot in 2018, the move was part of a long government hit list that included freezing the minimum wage, cutting planned social assistance increases, terminating an expert panel on violence against women, and cutting $300 million from postsecondary education. Unions and left-wing activists, having seen this movie before, prepared to fight back. Tim Ellis, the Leadnow organizer who spoke in Lindsay when the Basic Income pilot started up the previous autumn, was approached to speak at a rally at the provincial legislature.

In addition to his day job at Leadnow, Ellis invested a lot of volunteer time in the Basic Income Canada Network. He felt that Basic Income was part of a broader struggle for a living minimum wage and for offering "the freedom to pursue those kinds of work that people do value but profit-seeking entities do not." He spoke to the crowd both in defence of public services and in favour of Basic Income:

> When we talk about defending public services, Basic Income is part of that. . . . You're talking about things that are universally accessible, that are universally supported. And Basic Income gets at the root cause of that. That doesn't mean that we're going to then eliminate all the other public services, which is the common fear and an understandable fear.[39]

Indeed, the fear was reasonable. The left has been back on its heels for decades. The you're-on-your-own ethic, privileging all that is private, persuaded many that the politics of opposition (to market fundamentalism) was the only way to go. This had cast doubt on the politics of proposition represented by Basic Income.

Social protection campaigns to raise minimum wages, promote living wages, and defend and extend public services remain necessary. But twentieth-century demands are insufficient for twenty-first-century conditions. The weakened state of the union movement—indeed, the catastrophic decline in worker power—has challenged both labour and Basic Income activists to embrace visionary thinking that marries traditional bargaining table demands for worker protection with a radical proposition: Basic Income as central to putting an end to winner-take-all capitalism.

In a fascinating paradox, in 2020 the Canadian Chamber of Commerce—that venerable voice for business—voted in favour of Basic Income, or at least another pilot. The Hamilton and Thunder Bay Chambers of Commerce (both cities involved in the aborted Ontario Basic Income Pilot) brought a resolution to the Canadian Chamber's virtual convention. The national body accepted the motion, calling on the federal government to create a new Basic Income pilot and use the ensuing data to "assess the potential costs, benefits, pitfalls, challenges, and outcomes of a nationwide basic income social assistance program."[40]

FROM CONSUMPTION TO SUFFICIENCY

The old union demand for shorter hours for the same pay virtually vanished as more people worked at part-time jobs, precarious jobs, non-union jobs. The boss holds the whip hand with respect to hours, with the possibility of losing shifts an ever-present threat, stated or unstated. In the case of so-called independent workers offered tenuous, short-term contracts by the likes of Uber and Taskrabbit, contracts may simply not be renewed.

The notion of trading time for money is relatively new—and it makes the struggles for Basic Income more complex than many of its advocates recognize. The time-money exchange concept took hold along with the rise of the consumer society, through which many have come to see consumerism as part of their identity.

The prominent American economist Juliet Schor has made the trade-off her life's work, examining the commercialization of childhood in *Born to Buy*, along with other aspects of the phenomenon in *The Overspent American* and *The Overworked American*. Noting that struggles for shorter hours waned over time, Schor wrote as early as 1991 that "business was explicit in its hostility to increases in free time, preferring consumption as the *alternative* to taking economic progress in the form of leisure."[41]

Consumption now comprises 58 percent of the Canadian economy.[42] Indeed, a key indicator of economic buoyancy is something called "consumer confidence." To be sure, some have sharply criticized this odd turn in human consciousness as the market generated an astonishing array of superfluous commodities, from selfie sticks to battery-driven spaghetti twirling forks and, of course, bottled water.

Basic Income advocates must take into account the way the culture of overwork and consumerism interacts with alternative policies of time and workplace power politics. Reflecting the utopian socialist tradition that imagines emancipation from labour freeing up time for leisure, the iconoclastic left libertarian André Gorz wondered about a reimagined future:

What would happen to the ethics of speed and punctuality, of "we're not here for fun"—an ethic inculcated into children at school ever since the invention of manufactures? What would happen to the glorification of effort, speed and performance which is the basis of all industrial societies, capitalist and socialist? And if the ethic of performance collapsed, what would become of the social and industrial hierarchy? On what values and imperatives would those in command base their authority?[43]

A livable Basic Income, done right as part of a full-blown system of public provision, would require a profound transformation of the economy and way of life in high-consumption countries. It would challenge prevailing understandings and values and would require new thinking—transformation of a magnitude approaching what is urgently needed to achieve net-zero carbon emissions by 2050. The planetary alternative—fire, drought, Siberian heatwaves, melting polar ice caps, mass migration, famine—would make the 2020–21 pandemic look like a picnic in the park.

Among the doubts about Basic Income—and there are many—two important points of scepticism stand out. Sceptics on the environmental side worry that a generous Basic Income (often supported by Green parties, as it happens) would be growth-friendly. Giving people money would just stimulate consumption, thereby simply reinforcing our already out-of-control productivist and consumerist mindset. Therefore, Basic Income would hardly help combat the frying of the planet.

The counter to this would be that a new form of basic security available to all—along with creation of new forms of meaningful activity beyond wage labour—could eliminate a powerful driving force that generates environmentally destructive forms of growth. Unfortunately, such unabashedly hopeful visions run up against the hard reality of inequality, both globally and within high-consumption countries like Canada.

It is clear that rich people—and many middle- and working-class people in rich countries—burn up energy at a rate far exceeding their numbers. Julia Steinberger, professor of ecological economics at the University of Leeds in England and leader of the Living Well Within Limits project, published an analysis with her colleagues in the journal

Nature Energy in 2020 demonstrating this dynamic. Using World Bank and European Union household budget surveys to analyze 374 population segments in 86 countries, they showed that as income inequality rises, the inequality of energy footprint rises even faster.

Transportation-related consumption patterns are among the most unequal. Without massive changes in the vastly unequal distribution of global energy consumption and a move towards radical changes in demand towards *sufficiency*, the basic material needs of billions of people will remain unmet while the planet continues to fry.

Steinberger, lead author of a chapter of the 2022 Intergovernmental Panel on Climate Change Report, explained that the need for an economy of sufficiency will require sacrifice by some. Otherwise, the result will be escalating climate breakdown: extreme weather events like monster storms ravaging areas never before affected, massive flooding accompanied by water shortages, land lost to rising seas, crop-yield loss leading to famine for millions, disease spread, permanent ecosystem and biodiversity losses. It is no surprise that the venerable medical journal *The Lancet* has declared climate change the biggest global health threat of the twenty-first century.[44] Steinberger points out,

> Human needs are satiable. There exist levels of consumption which are *sufficient*, and beyond which we do not benefit in terms of our fundamental well-being. . . . Human wants are not infinite (as mainstream economics would have us believe) but rather are products of advertising and hyperactive capitalist production. [emphasis added][45]

The notion of "sufficiency" runs directly counter to the free-market imperative of endless growth and the belief that there is no such thing as enough. Resource depletion. Capital accumulation. Sales. Infinite growth on a finite planet. With respect to Basic Income, this raises an important question: Is there any point in providing low-income people with enough money for a decent life if little else changes?

Just as Basic Income advocates realize the importance of forging coalitions with trade union and feminist activists open to visionary thinking, they need to make common cause with greens. A transformational Basic Income vision suggests a postmaterialist worldview shared by many environmentalists. But they must also grapple with the paradox that Basic Income can be seen as growth-friendly.

Clearly, we need a new cultural "story" about economics, sufficiency, and what a good life really means. With civilizations currently based on inequality, growth appears promising to people who are striving to have more. Some day they will no longer be "underprivileged," so the limitation of growth feels like a threat. This deep-seated pattern of thought is hard to uproot, particularly in societies where inequality is on the rise.

"How do you change a worldview, an unquestioned ideology?" asked Naomi Klein in *This Changes Everything.* With respect to green transition, she suggests that the push for a minimal carbon tax "might do a lot less good than, for instance, forming a grand coalition to demand a guaranteed minimum income." Klein argues that Basic Income offers workers the option of saying no to dirty energy jobs—or for that matter, all dirty, low-paying, and insecure jobs: "The very process of arguing for a universal social safety net opens up a space for a full-throated debate about values—what we owe one another based on our shared humanity, and what it is that we collectively value more than economic growth and corporate profits."[46]

GETTING READY FOR THE ROBOTS

"Humans! You must prepare!"

A few days before the 2020 pandemic hit in March, a humanoid creature rolled onto the stage of the Ontario Liberal leadership convention, bug eyes flashing blue, robotic arms gesticulating emphatically. "Tech," the anthropomorphized robot with a female voice, sounded ominous: "We came for your manufacturing jobs; we came for your administrative jobs. Also, your bank tellers. And now we're taking your warehouse, retail, and finance jobs. Next, we'll be coming for your truck drivers, call centre workers, accountants, lawyers, doctors, and bankers—jobs with high and low incomes."

The creature was a creation of the Basic Income advocacy group UBI Works and its founder, the tech entrepreneur Floyd Marinescu. He had launched a successful international firm, C4Media, organizing virtual software development conferences. Appearing at the Liberal meeting in support of leadership hopeful and Basic Income booster Alvin Tedjo offered Marinescu the chance to sell the idea to a receptive audience. He told the delegates about his father and uncles who had lost their auto-sector jobs in the early 2000s as their employers automated, adding that when displaced workers did manage to secure new jobs, they earned 18 to 35 percent less than they had previously.

The catchy presentation featured a back-and-forth between Marinescu and the robot. Tech explained that not only didn't she need to be paid, neither did she need sleep or benefits. No family to support, no mortgage to pay. But, she added perkily, there is a bright spot: "Basic Income is how we make sure that technology leads to prosperity, not poverty."

Marinescu, who got behind Basic Income when the Ford government summarily scrubbed the Ontario Pilot, insisted that the time for pilot projects was past. It is clear that people are working harder and longer but not getting ahead. The prospects for millennials (like James Collura) are not rosy. Technology, Marinescu argued, shouldn't push people into low-income work. It should be "freeing people up" to pursue their potential. "A Basic Income is how we turn things around."[47]

Marinescu had attracted media attention in 2018–19 with his CEOs for Basic Income campaign. An avid organizer, he had garnered support from some 114 business operators in a letter asking the Ford government to reconsider the OBIP cancellation. Most were based in Ontario, with average annual revenues of $19 million per company. Another fifty small businesses signed on.[48] The government ignored them.

In 2013, economist Carl Frey and professor of machine learning Michael Osborne, both at Oxford, published a landmark study revealing that 47 percent of American jobs are at risk because of automation. They examined 702 detailed occupations, deploying seven thousand citations. They had a keen eye for social and industrial history, looking back to the sixteenth century and William Lee's 1589 submission of his new stocking frame knitting machine to Queen Elizabeth. "Thou aimest high, Master Lee," replied Good Queen Bess. "Consider thou what the invention could do to my poor subjects. It would assuredly bring to them ruin by depriving them of employment, thus making them beggars."

A little over two centuries later, class power had shifted, the property-owning class becoming dominant. In the face of the so often misunderstood Luddite movement, the Crown dispatched a massive army to put down the domestic revolt. It was larger than the force Wellington had recently taken to fight Napoleon in the Peninsular War.[49]

Today's massive shift in technology and class power has often been called a "second industrial revolution." Historian of technology and its power politics David Noble pointed out, when comparing the displacement of agricultural workers forced into work in the famously dark and satanic mills to the corrosive effects of late-twentieth-century technologies, "The analogy commonly made between the present transformation and that of the early nineteenth century remains only half complete: the catastrophe has been left out."[50]

Official opinion remains divided with respect to what might come next. One 2019 OECD employment outlook report cited survey research showing that, in rich countries, nearly three of every four people say they want their governments to more actively protect their social and economic security. The report concluded that the future of work will "largely depend on policy decisions countries make." The report makes but one passing reference to Basic Income, rejecting it for being either too expensive or hurting the poor. By contrast, in 2020, the World Bank devoted a detailed report to Basic Income, explaining that the cascade of interest in the "seemingly utopian and radical proposal" was "surely symptomatic of larger societal discomforts."[51]

The proposal's profile was raised even further, before the 2020 pandemic vaulted it to a top-of-mind issue in many countries, with dark-horse candidate Andrew Yang's campaign for the Democratic presidential nomination in the United States. The political unknown surprised many with his fundraising and debate success. He tied his modest-to-say-the-least "Freedom Dividend" ($1,000 monthly) to job displacement due to robotization, with the *New York Times* calling him "the internet's favourite candidate." Yang is not a member of the billionaire tech start-up crowd, nor easy to pin down politically with his "Not left, not right, forward" slogan. The "Yang Gang" weren't bothered as their candidate explained that he had become a Basic Income devotee after reading a futurist book about robotization and a jobless future.

Maybe the world is being turned utterly upside down by a digitalized economy. Maybe the robots will simply result in a new wave of jobs in some other sector, with things turning out just fine as some new sector opens up. One thing, however, is undeniable. Uncertainty and anxiety are on the rise.

Floyd Marinescu understood the allure of linking freedom to Basic Income. He also knew from personal experience that freedom can mean more than being liberated from anxiety about machines coming for jobs. Not long before he accompanied Tech the robot to the 2020 Liberal convention, he made a presentation at a TEDx event in Windsor, a city that had been hit hard by automotive sector downsizing. But he didn't start off with anecdotes about Fiat Chrysler and Ford, Lakeside Plastics and Syncreon. Windsor people knew those stories.

Instead, Marinescu described his upbringing, growing up in a home fraught with domestic violence. "Sometimes we didn't know from day to day if our mother was going to live or die. If my birth mother or my stepmother afterwards had had money, they could have left and taken me with them." His father had lost secure work in the southern Ontario auto sector. For Marinescu, Basic Income was about more than workplace security. It was about freedom and security for his mother and stepmother.

"It would have been known . . . that they had the freedom, the options to leave. Freedom is what we'll buy ourselves, as a society," he told the TEDx Windsor audience. It was all about an unconditional Basic Income available to all. "Do we really have freedom if we don't have options to choose?"[52]

TAKING THAT RISK

James Collura quit his Scotiabank job, disenchanted with the ethic of speed and performance. He did not share the financial sector's priorities, let alone the conventional values that emphasized newfangled, speedy ways of doing business by getting "appified." While his laid-back style did not lend itself to telling the boss to take the job and shove it (in the words of Johnny Paycheck's 1977 hit country song[53]), he was able to get up the nerve to say, "thanks, but no thanks." Ontario's brief flirtation with Basic Income offered a helping hand.

"I felt safe to take that leap, take that risk. I think it is being able to take risks as we move into the future in this uncertain economy," he said. "Take a leap and do something a little bit unconventional rather than relying on external institutions and jobs because as we know they may not be there in the future."

His university economics studies had taught him that his personal experience was anecdotal. He mentioned that qualifier regularly. In the wake of the OBIP cancellation, however, a McMaster University research group produced a 2020 study of Hamilton OBIP participants that was both qualitative—anecdotal, if you will—and quantitative. The report explained that, with the unilateral cancellation, valuable research results risked being abandoned and lost.

The research was based on a seventy-question survey of 217 participants as well as forty in-depth interviews. The word that jumped out of the report was that the OBIP was "*transformational.*" Many people who got the Basic Income reported improvements in physical and mental health, labour market participation, food security, housing stability, financial status, and social relationships. People who had been working got better jobs. In addition to more stability and security, some were like Collura: "A basic income meant they could take chances on a new job or career."

As with the 1970s Mincome research in Manitoba, Hamilton recipients cut their visits to emergency rooms and doctors' offices. This "noticeable impact" bolstered traditional Basic Income arguments that the policy would yield substantial payoffs in health care savings. In the end, the report concluded that the evidence "strongly suggests that the Ontario Basic Income Pilot made life better for those receiving it and potentially made life better for all who live in the Hamilton-Brantford region."[54]

For Collura, leaving the bank meant trying a more enjoyable and fulfilling job. It was about more than a simple change of workplace. It was about newfound freedom. Not simply personal freedom, though that was important. Basic Income represented freedom to no longer play things safe but to take a risk, responding creatively to a rapidly changing world.

"Basic Income gave me time to take a deep breath," said Collura, adding that he was no longer doing monotonous and mundane labour, though many had advised him against leaving Scotiabank. He learned more about himself: "It gave me a freedom to explore where I really wanted to be. . . . It was a sense of freedom and ability to make new choices that I didn't have before."[55]

CHAPTER 8

A PROVOCATION TO FREEDOM

Our ancestors . . . always took care of the little ones, we took care of our families, and we took care of the community. And we always did that through the generations, even up to now. That's always our priority.

—Gramma Geraldine Shingoose

CARING ABOUT CARE WORK

As COVID-19 ravaged long-term care homes and mothers suddenly had to juggle their paid jobs with their unpaid work as parents, the virus cast a harsh light on invisible, neglected care work—the paid and unpaid work that nurtures us all. Suddenly, everyone could see the crucial nature of care work and our reliance on it. COVID-19 also highlighted the ways in which our devaluation of care work has contributed to social, economic, gender, and racial inequities.[1] The United Nations projected that the COVID-19 global recession "will result in a prolonged dip in women's incomes and labour force participation, with compounded impacts for women already living in poverty"[2]—who are disproportionately racialized.

Presenting care data in 2020, Ito Peng, University of Toronto scholar and prominent expert on the work of care, stressed "the need to change our mindset [and] really understand the work of care as really skilled work—extremely nuanced, requiring interpersonal, physical, and emotional skill."[3] COVID-19 has helped us recognize that unpaid, taken-for-granted care work—more often performed by women than men[4]—is essential to the functioning of the economy. In pre-pandemic Canada, unpaid care work was estimated to account for about a quarter of GDP.[5] Salary.com, a self-described leader in assessing fair compensation packages, has calculated that if you accounted for all the jobs a stay-at-home mother does, her median salary would have been about $235,000 CAD in 2019.[6]

COVID-19 asks us to reconsider what counts as work—and to keep in mind that traditional income security programs, however scanty, are tilted towards men.[7] Trying to calculate the value of caring labour can be tricky. In making the feminist case for Basic Income, Ailsa McKay and Jo Vanevery argue that the demand amounts to "an implicit recognition that all citizens contribute to society in a variety of ways . . . that may or may not have monetary value or even be measurable."[8]

Another feminist thinker who has recognized the importance of caring work and possible ways of placing it on the public agenda is the American scholar Kathi Weeks. Her support for Basic Income was inspired by the 1970s Wages for Housework campaign. These Marxist feminist activists advocated for a "social wage" to be paid to women for their unpaid, multifaceted, invisible labour that supports and maintains families and communities.

The Wages for Housework advocates argued that women's reproductive labour had long been taken for granted, considered a "natural" product of women's "innate" generosity and loving nature. They aligned with welfare rights' activists, primarily women of colour and Indigenous women, who regarded welfare as state payment for child rearing and demanded better compensation for their work.[9]

Weeks, author of *The Problem with Work,* challenges the notion that waged labour is in and of itself a Good Thing. She notes that when taken as a given, it becomes depoliticized and immune from critique. She considers the demand for Basic Income a *provocation* because it can cast a critical gaze on the status quo—the apparently common-sense way of doing things. From this perspective, Basic Income advocacy becomes a "provocation to freedom." Weeks clarified the concept: "By 'freedom' I mean neither individual self-sovereignty nor libertarian license, but rather what the wages for housework tradition envisioned as a condition of collective autonomy; freedom as the time and space for invention . . . an occasion to contemplate the shape of life beyond work." From this perspective, Basic Income is more than a policy proposal. It is a provocation that questions today's assumptions that care is a commodity. Basic Income offers a very different way of regarding care. It is, argues Weeks, "an imagination of a different future."[10]

Despite its provocative demand, the Wages for Housework campaign never caught on with mainstream liberal feminists, who had, at best, an uneasy relationship with mothering and domestic labour. The mainstream women's movement, predominantly white and middle-class, insisted that women's equality depended on women's participation in the labour force, which was dependent on affordable childcare, paid parental leave, and other services to support women in the workplace. While welfare rights feminists argued for recognition of and adequate payment for care work, liberal feminists held out a narrow vision of employability as the solution to the poverty, inequality, and lack of value women faced. Marxist feminist Silvia Federici, a key figure in the Wages for Housework movement, argued that the refusal to recognize women's essential caring labour reflects and reinforces racist and sexist stereotypes attached to people not engaged in the paid labour force.[11]

Senator Kim Pate has devoted her life to working on behalf of some of the most marginalized and despised Canadians—incarcerated women, men, and youth. The long-time Executive Director of the Canadian Association of Elizabeth Fry Societies became a leading voice in support of Basic Income after becoming a senator. For her, Basic Income is about "taking care of people who take care of others."[12]

LASER FOCUS ON JOBS

Like the liberal feminists who rejected the Wages for Housework campaign because of their commitment to employment as liberation, much of the political left continues to promote full employment as the sole route to salvation. In doing so, they are agreeing with Goldy Hyder of the Business Council of Canada that "the best income-support program is a job" and with Lisa MacLeod, the Ontario Minister who terminated the Basic Income Pilot, who argued that "the best social program is a job."[13]

Notwithstanding the need for living wages, labour market regulation, and strong unions, employment is glorified as "a morally upright end in itself no matter its ecological and social impact," no matter how meaningful or socially valuable it is or is not. Job creation trumps all other worthy goals, permanently locking us into the logic of capital, and destroying the planet in the process. An adequate Basic Income would free workers from compulsory wage labour or "wage slavery," and provide space for workers to imagine different forms of work— ones that could be more cooperative and democratic.[14]

Kathi Weeks argued forcefully that simply getting into the waged-labour force does not, in and of itself, settle the bill for unpaid caring labour: "I want to consider a different way to present the bill, with a demand long familiar to the autonomist tradition."[15] That is, of course, the demand for a basic livable income that is sufficient, unconditional, and continuous.

Basic Income is a provocation because it offers the freedom to reject paid work—"take this job and shove it," as Johnny Paycheck sang. The politics of work refusal were reflected in employer handwringing during the 2020 pandemic when the interests represented by the Business Council wrung their collective hands about people suddenly being able to say "no" because of the Canada Emergency Response Benefit program. Workers were suddenly able to say "no" to the idea of getting on a bus for an hour with people who might be sick, to get to work at a low-wage job that might be just a five-hour shift, with little certainty that the same hours would be on offer the next day. CERB and by extension Basic Income offered the provocative suggestion that wage labour could be a choice, not a necessity.

EVELYN FORGET'S EDUCATION IN ECONOMICS

Christmas can be hard for people without much money. Evelyn Forget, Canada's leading Basic Income researcher and promoter (along with Hugh Segal), tells her own story about this. The University of Manitoba economist has a self-effacing way about her that belies her ground-breaking work on Basic Income. She recalls how her world was jolted when her father died of cancer when she was twelve.

Growing up at the height of the baby boom in Scarborough, a rapidly expanding Toronto suburb, Forget was part of a church youth group: "The first Christmas after my father died, a delegation from our church brought us a Christmas hamper. I had a lot of complicated feelings, not least because I'd been part of the youth group that put together hampers for 'the needy.' I hadn't realized I was one of them."[16] She and each of her two younger brothers got a gift, that Christmas of 1969:

> Someone told them I liked to read, so I got a book which was clearly aimed at a much younger child. I know as an adult how hard it is to gauge the reading level of a child, but I still remember being furious that I'd received a baby book. I rather think it wasn't the book that I was angry about; it's hard to receive. It's still hard for me to receive help from other people graciously.

Forget does not look back on her working-class childhood as anything out of the ordinary. She had a stay-at-home mom; her dad Norman was able to leave his job at a paper cup factory for a union job as a school janitor. The family never went without food or decent housing. After she became a widow, Cathy Forget got a job as a "cleaner" at the school board—which paid substantially less that her late husband's work as a janitor. "No doubt it's harder to clean urinals than toilets," her daughter noted wryly.

Forget's early years left her with a particular understanding of money. Even before her father died, she undertook the accounting work for the household. After his death, she "somehow" took over all the banking and budgeting. Consumed with the insecurity of trying to get by on a very limited income, Forget was frustrated because the money only came at the end of the month: "I remember thinking that if I could only get a month's income upfront, I wouldn't have to scramble to figure out which bills to pay in which order, and which ones could be postponed."

She also gained an appreciation of the world of finance: "I learned very quickly that banks are not your friend. Mother's Allowance arrived monthly by cheque. If you cashed a cheque at a bank when your account was overdrawn, the bank would deduct their money first and give you the remainder. I made that mistake once." She took to using a corner grocery store, which would cash the cheque and take a 10 percent cut: "A high premium, but at least I got 90 percent." The store owner had a "no credit" sign, but Forget sent her cute younger brother in—"the kind of holy terror that looks like an angel."

"I wondered for years what would cause my mother to give a twelve-year old so much financial responsibility. I'm embarrassed to say how old I was when I realized it was probably sheer terror." The childhood experiences remained with her in the form of "a lot of money neuroses." She still keeps jars of loonies and toonies and folded-up money in all her coat pockets:

I know if I need cash, I can always find a twenty in my parka. I'm a tenured professor, and I make a decent salary. There is *never* anything unexpected in my income tax, but I'm always afraid that I'll owe thousands of dollars I can't pay. I have so much food stored in my house that we could eat for two years without shopping.

Forget eventually realized her money trauma had been passed on to her daughter, who keeps money stashed all over her house: "It's funny, but it's also a serious reminder that behaviours and attitudes are intergenerational, and what looks very odd from a middle-class perspective sometimes makes perfect emotional sense."

Characteristically, Forget explains that she has been "fortunate" to tell the story of the Mincome experiment from Finland to Korea, Portugal to Norway. In North America, this understated apostle for a new common-sense approach has spoken in church basements and hotel ballrooms, relating the tale of Basic Income's success in the "very ordinary little town" of Dauphin and the "very ordinary people" there. Nothing dramatic: "Things just got a bit easier for ordinary people."

Forget concluded, without drawing attention to what happened in her own family, "When universal health insurance was introduced in Canada, its greatest support came from middle-aged women—people who had lived long enough to know that life doesn't always unfold according to plan."[17]

A USER'S GUIDE TO
The Case for Basic Income

PEOPLE

Tom Cooper Director of the Hamilton Roundtable for Poverty Reduction, Cooper is a tireless advocate for those living on low incomes. The speakers' bureau he helped organize to empower individuals to speak about their lived experience with poverty meant that a roster of media-savvy, well-spoken OBIP recipients were later ready and able to respond to the international media demand for interviews about the program.

Evelyn Forget University of Manitoba health economist Evelyn Forget unearthed 1,800 boxes of raw data from the 1970s Mincome experiment in Manitoba. Her analyses have provided critical evidence to support the benefits of Basic Income in a wealthy country like Canada. She is the author of *Basic Income for Canadians: From the COVID-19 Emergency to Financial Security for All* (2020) and co-author of *Basic Income Experiments: Theory, Practice and Politics* (2021).

Milton Friedman An influential American right-wing economist and free-market ideologue, Friedman argued that true liberty requires freedom from government regulation. Friedman supported a minimalist version of Basic Income that would involve concurrently eliminating most existing public social support programs.

Frances Lankin and Kim Pate Two senators who in April 2020 persuaded a majority of sitting senators to sign an open letter to

Liberal government leaders, supporting the conversion of the Canada Emergency Response Benefit (CERB) to Basic Income, available to all who need it.

Mike Perry A lawyer and former federal civil servant who was instrumental in having Lindsay named as the saturation site for the OBIP.

Deirdre Pike Senior social planner for the Social Planning and Research Council of Hamilton and Social Justice and Outreach Consultant for the Anglican Diocese of Niagara. Also a freelance columnist for the *Hamilton Spectator,* Pike has worked closely with the Hamilton Roundtable for Poverty Reduction.

Thomas Piketty The French economist wrote *Capital in the Twenty-first Century* in 2013, demonstrating that capitalism has always tended to concentrate the gains from economic growth at the very top, perpetuating or increasing inequality.

Sheila Regehr Co-founder and Chair of the Basic Income Canada Network (see below), Regehr was a federal civil servant for twenty-nine years and a Canadian negotiator at United Nations conferences on gender equality and social development. She was executive director of the National Council of Welfare before it was dismantled in 2012.

Hugh Segal "Dean of Canada's Basic Income movement," Segal has promoted the concept for decades. A Conservative but hard to pigeonhole politically, Segal was a key adviser to Ontario Premier Kathleen Wynne about the design of the Ontario Basic Income Pilot. Segal is a former senator and author of the 2019 memoir, *Bootstraps Need Boots: One Tory's Lonely Fight to End Poverty in Canada.*

Guy Standing Economist, professor at SOAS University of London, and world leader in promoting Basic Income, Standing is a founding member and honorary co-president of the Basic Income Earth Network (BIEN). He has written numerous books about precarious labour, capitalism, and Basic Income, including *The Precariat: The New Dangerous Class* (2011), *Basic Income: And How We Can Make it Happen* (2017), and *Battling Eight Giants: Basic Income Now* (2020).

ORGANIZATIONS

Basic Income Canada Network (BICN)   A voluntary, nonprofit, nonpartisan organization that originated in 2008, in affiliation with Basic Income Earth Network at the international level. BICN promotes informed, constructive public dialogue aimed at the adoption of a progressive, unconditional Basic Income guarantee in Canada.

Cooper Institute   A community development and education centre in Charlottetown, P.E.I., founded in 1984, Cooper Institute works for progressive causes, including social and economic justice. Cooper Institute has done public education and political advocacy for Basic Income, successfully convincing all four provincial political parties to support it.

Mincome   A guaranteed annual income experiment that ran in Manitoba from 1975 to 1978 with funding from the federal and provincial governments. During the study, everyone eligible in the town of Dauphin was able to sign up for the Basic Income payments, creating a "town without poverty." Evelyn Forget's analysis of the extensive data collected during the study has helped inform the contemporary Basic Income movement.

National Anti-Poverty Organization (NAPO)   Originating at the 1971 Poor People's Conference held in Toronto, NAPO (now Canada Without Poverty) has been dedicated to the elimination of poverty in Canada. It is governed by people who have lived in poverty themselves.

With its 2009 name change, NAPO adopted a human rights orientation to poverty elimination.

National Council on Welfare (NCW) First established by federal legislation in 1962, the National Council on Welfare was an independent body set up to advise the federal government about the realities of Canadians living on low incomes and ways of combating poverty. In 1976, NCW endorsed a guaranteed annual income. In 2012, Stephen Harper's government cut its entire budget of $1.1 million, effectively shutting NCW down.

Ontario Basic Income Pilot (OBIP) A scientific experiment implemented by the Ontario government in 2017. OBIP was open to adults aged 18 to 64, enrolling 1,000 people in Hamilton, 1,000 in Thunder Bay, and 2,000 in Lindsay. Participants were eligible for an unconditional basic income of $16,989 per year for a single person and $24,027 per year for a couple, plus an annual disability supplement of up to $6,000 for those eligible. OBIP also included a control group of 2,000 people who enrolled but would not receive the monthly payments. All 6,000 participants agreed to have several outcomes measured, including food security, mental health, health care usage, employment, education, and housing stability. Despite promising during the 2018 election campaign to continue the OBIP if elected, Doug Ford's Progressive Conservatives cancelled the Pilot on August 1, 2018, less than two months after taking office. Although baseline data were collected, the Pilot was terminated before any further measurements could be collected on the full group, a loss that was mourned by Basic Income advocates around the world.

PEPSO studies The Poverty and Employment Precarity in Southern Ontario project was a joint university-community research initiative housed at McMaster University and co-led by United Way Toronto & York Region. The exhaustive PEPSO research showed that inexorable precarious employment trends have had particularly harsh effects on women, racialized people, immigrants, and the working class in general.

Royal Commission on Taxation (Carter Commission)

A commission to study the tax system, chaired by Bay Street accountant Kenneth Carter. The Commission submitted its report in 1966, in which it recommended reducing taxes on the bottom half of the population by over 15 percent and increasing taxes on the wealthy and corporations. Its proposals were never implemented.

Royal Commission on the Economic Union and Development Prospects for Canada (Macdonald Commission)

Chaired by Bay Street Liberal and former finance minister Donald Macdonald, the Commission submitted its report in 1984. It recommended (a) free trade with the United States and (b) a limited Basic Income program, in the tradition of a Milton Friedman approach, that it called Universal Income Security (UISC). Free trade was instituted, but the UISC was never established.

Special Senate Committee on Poverty (Croll Committee)

Headed by Senator David Croll, this committee issued its landmark report in 1971, recommending a national Basic Income plan. The senators envisioned that the program, initially income-tested, would eventually be extended to all citizens. It was never implemented.

CONCEPTS

Basic Income   A guaranteed income floor below which no one's income can fall. As proposed by the Basic Income Canada Network, Basic Income would be (a) unconditional (not dependent on labour force participation); (b) universally available to all whose incomes fall below a specified threshold; (c) adequate to meet basic needs; (d) a central pillar of a renewed commitment to social security, complementing other social policies, such as pharmacare, affordable housing, and childcare; (e) provided in a manner that is dignified and respectful, free of stigma and surveillance; (f) funded through progressive taxation; and (g) designed so that no one is worse off as a result.

Canada Emergency Response Benefit (CERB) CERB was a federal income support program announced in April 2020, available to Canadians who lost their jobs during the economic shutdown undertaken as a public health measure to control the spread of the COVID-19 virus. A form of Basic Income, but conditional on workforce attachment, it provided $500 a week to those eligible and was delivered through the tax system. It was replaced in September 2020 by a series of other Recovery Benefits and an expanded Employment Insurance program.

Market failure Market failure occurs when market mechanisms do not provide a socially optimal quantity of goods or services. The lack of economically accessible housing for low-income Canadians is an example of market failure, whereby the demand for nonmarket (or "affordable") housing far outstrips the supply. Market failures are inherent in the structure of unregulated capitalism and require government intervention to overcome them.

Neoliberalism / Market fundamentalism Neoliberalism or market fundamentalism is an ideology (or belief system) that presumes that government provision of goods and services wastes public resources. It also presumes that private interests (profit-seeking corporations) are always more efficient than the state at delivering goods and services. The underlying premise of market fundamentalism is that individuals and their families are best served when they are free to pursue their own self-interested economic ends, free of government regulation or support. Policies that liberate the market are often grouped together as "austerity." This philosophy focuses on individuals; it does not acknowledge a common or collective good or any sense of interdependence.

Occupy movement Started in 2011, following the Great Recession of 2007–09, this movement popularized the slogan "We are the 99 percent!" It identified the overprivileged, overpaid 1 percent of the population, bringing inequality into sharp focus.

Opposition to Basic Income programs Some activists and policy strategists on the left have actively opposed the idea of Basic Income because of its association with market fundamentalism (through promotion of limited versions by high-profile people on the right, such as Milton Freidman). Basic Income is often caricatured as a "trojan horse," ushering in further fraying of the social safety net.

Precarious work Employment that is characterized by low wages; short-term contract and temporary work; unstable and unpredictable working hours; and lack of benefits and protections. Women, young people, racialized groups, and migrant workers are most likely to be employed in precarious work. Precarious work is foundational to the "gig economy."

Social determinants of health (SDOH) Conditions of living and working—income, housing, education—that affect people's chances of living long and healthy lives. The social determinants of health produce unfair and avoidable differences in health and longevity, known as health inequities. Income is recognized as one of the most important social determinants of health, affecting other social determinants such as housing, food, and childhood development.

NOTES

INTRODUCTION

1   Marco Chown Oved, Kenyon Wallace, and Brendan Kennedy, "For-Profit Nursing Homes Have Had Far Worse COVID-19 Outcomes than Public Facilities—and Three of the Largest Paid out $1.5 Billion to Shareholders," *Toronto Star*, May 16, 2020; Jennifer Pagliaro and David Rider, "City-Run Long-Term-Care Homes Have Seen Fewer COVID-19 Deaths. Are Staff Wages the Reason?", *Toronto Star*, May 31, 2020.

2   "Several observational studies suggest that for-profit LTC homes tend to deliver inferior care across a variety of outcome and process measures. These include lower levels and quality of staffing, more complaints from residents and family, higher rates of emergency department visits, more acute care hospital admissions and higher mortality rates" (Nathan M. Stall, Aaron Jones, Kevin A. Brown, Paula A. Rochon, and Andrew P. Costa, "For-Profit Long-Term Care Homes and the Risk of COVID-19 Outbreaks and Resident Deaths," *CMAJ: Canadian Medical Association Journal* 192, no. 33 [August 17, 2020]: E946–55, cmaj.ca/content/192/33/E946).

3   Milton Friedman, *Capitalism and Freedom* (Chicago: University of Chicago Press, 1962), 15.

4   Quoted in Philippe Van Parijs and Yannick Vanderborght, *Basic Income: A Radical Proposal for a Free Society and a Sane Economy* (Cambridge, MA: Harvard University Press, 2017), 71.

5   "Virus Lays Bare the Frailty of the Social Contract," *Financial Times*, April 3, 2020.

6   Laura Armstrong and Katie Daubs, "She Takes Care of Your Mother. He Gets Your Groceries to You. These Are the Unsung Heroes Who Will Get Us through the COVID-19 Pandemic," *Toronto Star*, April 12, 2020.

7   "Virus Lays Bare the Frailty."

8   siennaliving.ca/about-us/our-creed; Karen Howlett, "Sienna Senior Living Care Homes Names New CEO as Executives Depart," *Globe and Mail*, June 12, 2020.

9   Kristen Calis, "Pickering Council Calls for Public Inquiry into Orchard
     Villa Outbreak, Deaths," DurhamRegion.com, July 3, 2020, durhamregion.
     com/news-story/10055764-pickering-council-calls-for-public-inquiry-into-
     orchard-villa-outbreak-deaths/
10   Ontario, *How Ontario is Responding to COVID-19*, ontario.ca/page/how-
     ontario-is-responding-covid-19; publichealthontario.ca/-/media/documents/
     ncov/epi/2020/06/covid-19-epi-ltch-residents.pdf?la=en
11   Laura Stone and Jill Mahoney, "Ontario Long-Term Care Commission
     Still Deciding Whether to Hold Public Hearings, Drawing Concerns,"
     Globe and Mail, September 15, 2020, theglobeandmail.com/canada/
     article-ontario-long-term-care-commission-still-deciding-whether-to-hold/
12   Laura Stone, "Ontario Criticized for Position on Nursing Home Suits," *Globe
     and Mail*, September 2, 2020; Jeremiah Rodriguez, Jason Kirby, and Nick
     Taylor-Vaisey, "Here are All of Doug Ford's Promises in Ontario Election
     2018," *Maclean's*, June 7, 2018.
13   Bertrand Russell, *In Praise of Idleness* (1932), zpub.com/notes/idle.html

CHAPTER I. A GOOD IDEA GOES VIRAL

1   Elements of this chapter appeared in Jamie Swift and Elaine Power with
     Wayne Lewchuk, "A Good Idea Goes Viral: Basic Income 2020," in *Sick of the
     System: Why the Covid-19 Recovery Must be Revolutionary*, ed. Between the
     Lines Editorial Committee (Toronto: Between the Lines, 2020).
2   David Remnick, "Leonard Cohen Makes It Darker," *New Yorker*, October 16,
     2016; Cassie Werber, "'There is a Crack in Everything, That's How the Light
     Gets in': The Story of Leonard Cohen's 'Anthem,'" *Quartz*, November 11,
     2016.
3   City of Toronto, "Toronto Public Health Releases New Socio-
     demographic COVID-19 Data," July 30, 2020, www.toronto.ca/news/
     toronto-public-health-releases-new-socio-demographic-covid-19-data/
4   Kate Allen et al., "Tracing COVID's Grim Path," and Joe Cressy, "Latest
     Stats Show Virus Preys Heavily on Poverty," *Toronto Star*, August 2, 2020;
     Canadian Institute for Health Information, *Pandemic Experience in the Long-
     Term Care Sector: How Does Canada Compare with Other Countries?*, August
     16, 2020, cihi.ca/sites/default/files/document/covid-19-rapid-response-long-
     term-care-snapshot-en.pdf?emktg_lang=en&emktg_order=1; Kelly Grant,
     "81% of COVID-19 Deaths in Canada were in Long-Term Care, Nearly Double
     OECD Average," *Globe and Mail*, June 25, 2020.
5   Kelly Grant and Carly Weeks, "Examining Hot Spots for Community Spread

Across Ontario," *Globe and Mail*, May 29, 2020, theglobeandmail.com/canada/article-examining-hot-spots-for-community-spread-across-ontario/

6   thompsonteam.ca/mylistings.html/listing.c4400010-8-dale-avenue-toronto-m4w1k2.85068633, June 28, 2020.

7   Clare Bambra et al., "The COVID-19 Pandemic and Health Inequalities," *Journal of Epidemiology and Community Health*, June 13, 2020.

8   Bruce report cited in Bryan Palmer and Gaétan Héroux, *Toronto's Poor: A Rebellious History* (Toronto: Between the Lines, 2016), 178–81.

9   Bambra et al., "COVID-19 Pandemic and Health Inequalities."

10   Cindy Wooden, "Same Storm, Different Boats: Vatican Looks at Ways to Help All Survive," *Angelus*, April 30, 2020, angelusnews.com/news/vatican/same-storm-different-boats-vatican-looks-at-ways-to-help-all-survive/

11   André Picard, "Senior Care Facilities are Especially Vulnerable to COVID-19," *Globe and Mail*, March 8, 2020.

12   Government of Canada, *Canada Emergency Response Benefit Statistics*, canada.ca/en/services/benefits/ei/claims-report.html, accessed May 16, 2020.

13   David Macdonald, "1.4 Million Jobless Canadians Getting No Income Support in April," *Behind the Numbers,* Canadian Centre for Policy Alternatives blog, April 23, 2020, behindthenumbers.ca/2020/04/23/1-4-million-jobless-canadians-getting-no-income-support-in-april/

14   Rutger Bregman, *Utopia for Realists: The Case for a Universal Basic Income, Open Borders and a 15-hour Workweek*, trans. Elizabeth Manton (Amsterdam: The Correspondent, 2016), 197, 199–200.

15   PBS Newshour, *How the 2008 Financial Crisis Crashed the Economy and Changed the World*, September 13, 2018, pbs.org/newshour/show/how-the-2008-financial-crisis-crashed-the-economy-and-changed-the-world

16   Mattathias Schwartz, "Pre-Occupied: The Origins and Future of Occupy Wall Street," *New Yorker*, November 21, 2011, newyorker.com/magazine/2011/11/28/pre-occupied

17   Bregman, *Utopia for Realists*, 136–37.

18   Facundo Alvaredo et al., *World Inequality Report 2018*, wir2018.wid.world/files/download/wir2018-full-report-english.pdf; "2 Richest Canadians Have More Money than 11 Million Combined," *CBC News*, January 15, 2017, cbc.ca/news/canada/oxfam-davos-report-canadians-wealth-1.3937073

19   theleap.org

20   Interview, October 25, 2018; Ron Fanfair, *Awards Recognize Women who are Making a Difference*, March 15, 2018, ronfanfair.com/home/2018/3/14/awards-recognize-women-who-are-making-a-difference

21   Fanfair, *Awards Recognize Women.*

22   Quoted in Margaret Little, *No Car, No Radio, No Liquor Permit: The Moral Regulation of Single Mothers in Ontario, 1920–1997* (Toronto: Oxford University Press, 1998), 164.

23   Interview, October 25, 2018.

24   Erich Fromm, "The Psychological Aspects of the Guaranteed Income," in *The Guaranteed Income: Next Step in Socioeconomic Evolution*, ed. Robert Theobald, 183–93 (Garden City, NY: Anchor Books, 1967), 184.

25   Interview, October 25, 2018.

26   This and subsequent quotes from the video of the debate, *Basic Income: A Way Forward for the Left?*, April 15, 2017, youtube.com/watch?v=TfAxpc-r_EM

27   Basic Income Canada Network, "New Report Shows How Canada Could Fund $22,000 Basic Income for Adults," January 23, 2020, d3n8a8pro7vhmx.cloudfront.net/bicn/pages/3725/attachments/original/1579728426/Policy_Options_Media_Release_EN_Final.pdf?1579728426

28   David Macdonald, "Transitioning from CERB to EI Could Leave Millions Worse Off," *Behind the Numbers,* Canadian Centre for Policy Alternatives blog, September 15, 2020, behindthenumbers.ca/2020/09/15/transitioning-from-cerb-to-ei-could-leave-millions-worse-off/

29   Employment and Social Development Canada, *Tackling Poverty Together: What it is Like to Live in Poverty in Canada and How the Federal Government Can Help*, canada.ca/en/employment-social-development/programs/poverty-reduction/reports/tackling-poverty-together.html

30   Chandra Pasma and Sheila Regehr, *Basic Income: Some Policy Options for Canada* (Ottawa: Basic Income Canada Network, 2020), d3n8a8pro7vhmx.cloudfront.net/bicn/pages/3725/attachments/original/1579707497/Basic_Income-_Some_Policy_Options_for_Canada2.pdf

31   Personal communication, July 2, 2020.

32   Hugh Segal, *Bootstraps Need Boots: One Tory's Lonely Fight to End Poverty in Canada* (Vancouver: University of British Columbia Press, 2019), 172, 167, 169.

33   Evelyn Forget, *Basic Income for Canadians* (Toronto: Lorimer, 2018), Chapter 2, "Rediscovering Mincome."

34   Comments on Patrick Brethour, "Could the CERB program Lead Canada Toward Offering a Universal Basic Income?", *Globe and Mail*, April 10, 2020.

35   Guy Standing, Speech to National Union of Public and General Employees Convention, Winnipeg, June 22, 2019.

36   Laurie Montsebraaten, "Ottawa is Handing Out $2000 Cheques to Out-of-Work Canadians: Could a Basic Income be Next?", *Toronto Star*, April 5, 2020.

37   Stephen Burgen and Sam Jones, "Poor and Vulnerable Hardest Hit
     by Pandemic in Spain," *Guardian* (U.K.), April 1, 2020; Rodrigo
     Orihuela, "Spanish Government Aims to Roll Out Basic Income 'Soon,'"
     Bloomberg, April 5, 2020, bloomberg.com/news/articles/2020-04-05/
     spanish-government-aims-to-roll-out-basic-income-soon

38   Ratna Omidvar, "Open Letter From Senators to Prime
     Minister, Deputy PM and Finance Minister Calls for
     Minimum Basic Income," April 21, 2020, ratnaomidvar.ca/
     open-letter-from-senators-calls-for-minimum-basic-income/

39   Pearson Centre webinar "Basic Income: Is This the Time?", July 9, 2020.

40   National Inquiry into Missing and Murdered Indigenous Women and
     Girls, *Reclaiming Power and Place: Final Report*, Vol. 1b, mmiwg-ffada.ca/
     wp-content/uploads/2019/06/Final_Report_Vol_1b.pdf

41   *Policy Options*, May 22, 2020, policyoptions.irpp.org/magazines/
     may-2020/a-feminist-approach-to-ending-poverty-after-covid-19/

42   Ken Boessenkool, "In Normal Times, Universal Basic Income is a Bad
     Idea. But it's the Wisest Solution for COVID-19 Economic Strain," *Globe
     and Mail*, March 19, 2020, https://www.theglobeandmail.com/opinion/
     article-in-normal-times-universal-basic-income-is-a-bad-idea-but-its-the/

43   Evelyn L. Forget and Hugh Segal, "CERB is an Unintended Experiment
     in Basic Income," *Globe and Mail*, April 19, 2020, theglobeandmail.com/
     opinion/article-cerb-is-an-unintended-experiment-in-basic-income/

44   Andrew Coyne, "The CERB is Nothing Like a Basic Income, but it Might
     be the Platform we Use to Build One," *Globe and Mail*, May 22, 2020,
     theglobeandmail.com/opinion/article-the-cerb-is-nothing-like-a-basic-
     income-but-it-might-be-the-platform/

45   Chief Public Health Officer of Canada, *From Risk to Resilience: An Equity
     Approach to COVID-19*, canada.ca/en/public-health/corporate/publications/
     chief-public-health-officer-reports-state-public-health-canada/from-risk-
     resilience-equity-approach-covid-19.html

46   Hugh Segal, Evelyn Forget, and Keith Banting, *A Federal Basic Income Within
     the Post COVID-19 Recovery Plan* (Ottawa: Royal Society of Canada, October
     2020), rsc-src.ca/sites/default/files/FBI PB_EN_0.pdf

47   "Everybody Knows" was co-written by Cohen and Sharon Robinson.

CHAPTER 2. A BRIEF HISTORY OF BASIC INCOME IN CANADA

1   Philippe Van Parijs and Yannick Vanderborght, *Basic Income: A Radical*

Proposal for a Free Society and a Sane Economy (Cambridge, MA: Harvard University Press, 2017), 51.

2   Ibid., 246.

3   David R. Elliott, "William Aberhart," *Canadian Encyclopedia*, thecanadian encyclopedia.ca/en/article/william-aberhart; "Aberhart argued for regular cash payments made by the provincial government to all, as a means of economic stimulus and redistribution. But the promise of a "social credit" paid to all citizens proved difficult to implement, in part due to a lack of funds in the provincial treasury and opposition from Ottawa. The plan ultimately ran afoul of judicial insistence that the federal government alone had constitutional control over currency and banking" (Margot Young and James P. Mulvale, *Possibilities and Prospects: The Debate Over a Guaranteed Income* [Vancouver: Canadian Centre for Policy Alternatives, British Columbia Office, 2009], policyalternatives.ca/publications/reports/possibilities-and-prospects).

4   Alvin Finkel, *Social Policy and Practice in Canada: A History* (Waterloo, ON: Wilfrid Laurier University Press, 2006), 132.

5   M. W. Bucovetsky, "The Mining Industry and the Great Tax Reform Debate," in *Pressure Group Behaviour in Canadian Politics*, ed. A. Paul Pross (Toronto: McGraw-Hill Ryerson, 1975), 96.

6   Special Senate Committee on Poverty, *Poverty in Canada* (Ottawa: Information Canada, 1971), vii.

7   Rodney S. Haddow, *Poverty Reform in Canada, 1958–1978: State and Class Influences on Policy Making* (Montreal: McGill-Queen's University Press, 1993).

8   Evelyn Forget, *Basic Income for Canadians* (Toronto: Lorimer, 2018), Chapter 2, "Rediscovering Mincome."

9   Robert M. Sapolsky, *Why Zebras don't Get Ulcers*, 3rd ed. (New York: Henry Holt, 2004).

10   Forget, *Basic Income for Canadians*, 46.

11   Mel Watkins, *Madness and Ruin: Politics and the Economy in the Neoconservative Age* (Toronto: Between the Lines, 1992).

12   Cited in Jamie Swift, *Wheel of Fortune: Work and Life in the Age of Falling Expectations* (Toronto: Between the Lines, 1995), 181–82.

13   Rodney Haddow, "Canadian Organized Labour and the Guaranteed Annual Income," in *Continuities and Discontinuities: The Political Economy of Social Welfare and Labour Market Policy in Canada*, ed. Andrew F. Johnson, Stephen McBride, and Patrick J. Smith (Toronto: University of Toronto Press, 1994), 359.

14   Ibid., 360.

15 Ibid., 357.

16 Cited in Haddow, "Canadian Organized Labour and the Guaranteed Annual Income," 358.

17 Lisa MacLeod, "MACLEOD: The Best Social Program is a Job," *Toronto Sun*, November 23, 2018.

18 Hugh Segal, *Bootstraps Need Boots: One Tory's Lonely Fight to End Poverty in Canada* (Vancouver: University of British Columbia Press, 2019), xiii–xiv; personal communication, July 15, 2020.

19 Canadian Conference of Catholic Bishops, Episcopal Commission for Social Affairs, "Ethical Reflections on the Economic Crisis" (1982), in *Do Justice! The Social Teaching of the Canadian Catholic Bishops (1945–1986)*, ed. E. F. Sheridan S.J., 399–410 (Sherbrooke, QC: Éditions Paulines / Toronto: Jesuit Centre for Social Faith and Justice, 1987).

20 Personal communication, July 14, 2020.

21 Segal, *Bootstraps Need Boots*, 146.

22 Bill Curry, "Senators Urge Ottawa to Target Income-Support Programs on Economic Recovery," *Globe and Mail*, July 14, 2020.

23 Evelyn L. Forget, "The Town with No Poverty: The Health Effects of a Canadian Guaranteed Annual Income Field Experiment," *Canadian Public Policy* 37, no. 3, (2011): 283–305; Jordan Weissmann, "Martin Luther King's Economic Dream: A Guaranteed Income for All Americans," *The Atlantic* August 28, 2013; Forget, *Basic Income for Canadians*, 183.

24 cooperinstitute.ca/Who-We-Are

25 John Deverell and Latin American Working Group, *Falconbridge: Portrait of a Canadian Mining Multinational* (Toronto: Lorimer, 1975).

26 Interview, August 6, 2020.

27 Email communication with Rob Rainer, July 17, 2020.

28 Personal communication, October 14, 2020.

29 Interview with Marie Burge, August 6, 2020.

30 Kerry Campbell, "Basic Income Would Require 'Transformation' of Social Supports, Committee Hears," *CBC News*, September 19, 2019, cbc.ca/news/canada/prince-edward-island/pei-basic-income-poverty-committee-1.5290366

31 Interview with Marie Burge, August 6, 2020.

32 Basic Income Canada Network, *The Basic Income We Want*, April 6, 2016, basicincomecanada.org/the_basic_income_we_want

33 Jeff Rubin, "Why Do Canada's Wealthiest Families Get Huge Tax Breaks?", *Toronto Star*, August 24, 2020

34 Anna Fruttero, Alexandre Ribeiro Leichsenring, and Luis Henrique Paiva, *Social Programs and Formal Employment: Evidence from the Brazilian Bolsa*

Família Program, International Monetary Fund Working Paper, 2020, wpiea2020099-print-pdf.pdf

35   Ibid.; Guy Standing, *Basic Income: And How We Can Make It Happen*, (London: Pelican, 2017), 169; *World Development*, Vol. 59, July 2014.

36   *The Economist*, January 30, 2020.

37   *Making the Difference!: The BIG in Namibia, Basic Income Grant Assessment Report*, April 2009, bignam.org/Publications/BIG_Assessment_report_08b.pdf

38   BIG Coalition Namibia, bignam.org/

39   2020 Korea Basic Income Fair, basicincomefair.gg.go.kr/2020_en/

40   The authors thank Tara Kainer, a Kingston Basic Income supporter and longtime social justice activist, for providing her notes on the 2016 World Social Forum, on which this section is based.

41   Oxfam International, 5 *Shocking Facts about Extreme Global Inequality and How to Even it up*, oxfam.org/en/5-shocking-facts-about-extreme-global-inequality-and-how-even-it

42   Van Parijs and Vanderborght, *Basic Income*, 247.

43   Ibid., 246.

44   Comment on Andrew Coyne, "The CERB is Nothing Like a Basic Income, but it Might be the Platform We Use to Build One," *Globe and Mail*, May 22, 2020.

45   Jurgen De Wispelaere and José Antonio Noguera, "On the Political Feasibility of Basic Income: An Analytical Framework," in *Basic Income Guarantee and Politics: International Experiences and Perspectives on the Viability of Income Guarantee*, ed. Richard K. Caputo, 17–38 (New York: Palgrave Macmillan, 2012).

46   Interview, June 21, 2019.

47   Guy Standing, *The Precariat: The New Dangerous Class* (London: Bloomsbury, 2011), Chapter 1.

48   Guy Standing, Speech to National Union of Public and General Employees Convention, Winnipeg, June 22, 2019.

CHAPTER 3. BASIC INCOME COMES TO ONTARIO—BUT BRIEFLY

1   liunaevents.com/liuna-station/

2   Mike Crawley, "Ontario's Biggest Political Donors Revealed," *CBC News*, April 19, 2016, cbc.ca/news/canada/toronto/ontario-political-party-fundraising-largest-donors-1.3540674

3   See Larry Savage and Nick Ruhloff-Queiruga, "Organized Labour, Campaign

Finance, and the Politics of Strategic Voting in Ontario," *Labour/Le Travail* 80 (Fall 2017): 247–71.

4   "Ontario Basic Income Pilot Project to be Tested in Hamilton, Lindsay, Thunder Bay," *Global News*, April 24, 2017, globalnews.ca/video/3399639/ ontario-basic-income-pilot-project-to-be-tested-in-hamilton-lindsay-thunder-bay#autoplay

5   Government of Ontario, *Ontario's Basic Income Pilot: Studying the Impact of a Basic Income*, files.ontario.ca/170508_bi_brochure_eng_pg_by_pg_proof.pdf

6   Interview, July 22, 2019.

7   Brendan Kennedy, "Twenty-five Years after 'Welfare Diet' Debacle, Social Assistance Still Hasn't Recovered from Mike Harris Cuts," *Toronto Star*, October 19, 2020, thestar.com/news/gta/2020/10/19/25-years-after-welfare-diet-debacle-social-assistance-still-hasnt-recovered-from-mike-harris-cuts.html

8   Interview, November 13, 2018.

9   "Ontario Liberal Leadership Candidate Kathleen Wynne: 'I Want to be the Social Justice Premier,'" *Toronto Star*, January 15, 2013.

10   Evelyn Forget, *Basic Income for Canadians* (Toronto: Lorimer, 2018), 37; Interview, June 26, 2018.

11   Interview, June 26, 2018.

12   Interview, April 16, 2019.

13   "Hamilton Anti-Poverty Group Asks Ontarians to Reveal the Contents of Their Fridge," *Global News*, October 16, 2017.

14   The first Green member, party leader Mike Schreiner, was elected in Guelph in 2018.

15   Interview, November 13, 2018.

16   Hugh D Segal, *Finding a Better Way: A Basic Income Pilot Project for Ontario*, discussion paper, August 31, 2016, ontario.ca/page/finding-better-way-basic-income-pilot-project-ontario

17   Interview, July 22, 2019.

18   Segal, *Finding a Better Way*.

19   Hugh Segal, *Bootstraps Need Boots: One Tory's Lonely Fight to End Poverty in Canada* (Vancouver: University of British Columbia Press, 2019), 160.

20   Joseph Zeballos-Roig, "Finland's Basic-Income Trial Found People were Happier, but Weren't More Likely to Get Jobs," World Economic Forum, May 8, 2020, weforum.org/agenda/2020/05/finlands-basic-income-trial-found-people-were-happier-but-werent-more-likely-to-get-jobs

21   Jimmy O'Donnell, "Why Basic Income Failed in Finland," *Jacobin*, December 1, 2019, jacobinmag.com/2019/12/basic-income-finland-experiment-kela

22 Guy Standing, *Basic Income: And How We Can Make It Happen* (London: Pelican, 2017), 268.

23 Frances Lankin and Munir A. Sheikh (Commission for the Review of Social Services in Ontario), *Brighter Prospects: Transforming Social Services in Ontario* (Toronto: Ministry of Community and Social Services, 2012), mcss. gov.on.ca/documents/en/mcss/social/publications/social_assistance_ review_final_report.pdf

24 Interview, July 22, 2019.

25 Interview, May 28, 2019.

26 The program had a rolling start, with Hamilton beginning to sign people up right after the announcement in April 2017. Lindsay came next, with enrolment starting in November 2017, after local publicity in late August and September. Enrolment was kept open until April 2018, when the government had reached the full complement of participants. Payments started within a month after signing up.

27 Quotes that follow (except when noted) from a recording made by Jamie Swift, November 3, 2017.

28 Theodore M. Brown and Elizabeth Fee, "Rudolf Carl Virchow: Medical Scientist, Social Reformer, Role Model," *American Journal of Public Health*, December 2006, https://doi.org/10.2105/AJPH.2005.078436

29 Personal communication, April 29, 2020.

30 Greg McArthur and Shannon Kari, "Globe Investigation: The Ford Family's History with Drug Dealing," *Globe and Mail*, May 25, 2013, theglobeandmail.com/news/toronto/globe-investigation-the-ford-familys-history-with-drug-dealing/ article12153014/

CHAPTER 4. LINDSAY: THE SATURATION SITE

1 Roderick Benns, "'Norman Rockwell' Town of the North to be Scrutinized as Basic Income Pilot Unfolds," *Lindsay Advocate*, August 22, 2017, lindsayadvocate.ca/norman-rockwell-town-of-the-north-to-be-scrutinized-as-basic-income-Pilot-unfolds/

2 Ron Graham, *Old Man Ontario: Leslie M. Frost* (Toronto: University of Toronto Press, 1990), 30.

3 Interview with Mike Perry, February 18, 2020.

4 Interview with James Janeiro, July 22, 2019.

5 Roderick Benns, "Basic Income Panel Talks about Hope,

Human Rights, and the Choice we Make to Allow Poverty," *Lindsay Advocate*, November 6, 2017, lindsayadvocate.ca/basic-income-panel-talks-hope-human-rights-choice-poverty/

6   Roderick Benns, "Laurie Scott 'Certain' Health will Improve under Basic Income Pilot," *Lindsay Advocate*, September 11, 2017, lindsayadvocate.ca/laurie-scott-certain-health-will-improve-basic-income-Pilot/

7   Roderick Benns, "Police Chief John Hagarty Talks Fentanyl, Building Community, and Basic Income," *Lindsay Advocate*, October 4, 2017, lindsayadvocate.ca/police-chief-john-hagarty-talks-fentanyl-building-community-basic-income/; Roderick Benns, "Lindsay's Police Chief Welcomes Basic Income Pilot," *Lindsay Advocate*, August 22, 2017, lindsayadvocate.ca/lindsays-police-chief-welcomes-basic-income-Pilot/

8   Roderick Benns, "Hope Says Lindsay Residents will 'Rise up and Contribute' with Basic Income," *Lindsay Advocate*, September 19, 2017, lindsayadvocate.ca/hope-says-lindsay-residents-will-rise-contribute-basic-income/

9   Basic Income Canada Network, basicincomecanada.org/endorsements; Mary Riley, "Council Backs Away from 'Conversation' about Basic Income Guarantee," *My Kawartha*, January 27, 2016, mykawartha.com/news-story/6251871-council-backs-away-from-conversation-about-basic-income-guarantee/

10   Interview with Roderick Benns and Joli Scheidler-Benns, August 20, 2019.

11   lindsayadvocate.ca/about/

12   Interview with Tracey Mechefske, February 2, 2020.

13   Vincent J. Felitti et al., "Relationship of Childhood Abuse and Household Dysfunction to Many of the Leading Causes of Death in Adulthood," *American Journal of Preventive Medicine* 14, no. 4 (1998): 245–56, https://doi.org/10.1016/S0749-3797(98)00017-8; see also Centers for Disease Control and Prevention, "About the CDC-Kaiser ACE Study," cdc.gov/violenceprevention/acestudy/about.html

14   Marianne Opaas and Sverre Varvin, "Relationships of Childhood Adverse Experiences With Mental Health and Quality of Life at Treatment Start for Adult Refugees Traumatized by Pre-Flight Experiences of War and Human Rights Violations," *Journal of Nervous and Mental Disease* 203, no. 9 (2015): 684–95, ncbi.nlm.nih.gov/pmc/articles/PMC4554230/

15   Jane Ellen Stevens, "Addiction Doc Says: It's not the Drugs. It's the ACEs . . . Adverse Childhood Experiences," *ACES Too High News*, May 2, 2017, acestoohigh.com/2017/05/02/addiction-doc-says-stop-chasing-the-drug-focus-on-aces-people-can-recover/

16   Ibid.

17   Dr. Gabor Maté, "Beyond Drugs: The Universal Experience of Addiction," April 5, 2017, drgabormate.com/opioids-universal-experience-addiction/

18   Ibid.

19   Jane Stevens, "ACES Science 101 (FAQs)," *ACEs Connection*, October 1, 2019, .acesconnection.com/blog/aces-101-faqs

20   Martha Henriques, "Can the Legacy of Trauma be Passed Down the Generations?", *BBC Future*, March 26, 2019, bbc.com/future/article/20190326-what-is-epigenetics; Andrew Curry, "Parents' Emotional Trauma May Change Their Children's Biology. Studies in Mice Show How," *Science*, July 18, 2019, sciencemag.org/news/2019/07/parents-emotional-trauma-may-change-their-children-s-biology-studies-mice-show-how

21   Karen Fish and Hannah Moffatt, *Let's Talk: Moving Upstream* (Antigonish, NS: St. Francis Xavier University, National Collaborating Centre for Determinants of Health, 2014), http://nccdh.ca/images/uploads/Moving_Upstream_Final_En.pdf

22   Interview with Mike Perry, February 18, 2020.

23   Interview, August 7, 2018.

24   Interview, August 7, 2018.

25   Interview with Luis Segura, August 21, 2019.

26   Interview with Rod Sutherland, August 20, 2019.

27   *Dana Bowman, Grace Marie Doyle Hillion, Susan Lindsay, and Tracey Mechefske, Plaintiffs, v. Her Majesty the Queen in Right of Ontario, Defendant,* Motion to Certify Class Action, Ontario Superior Court of Justice, August 29, 2019, cavalluzzo.com/docs/default-source/default-document-library/vol-1-motion-record-motion-to-certify-4840-0386-9090-v1.pdf?sfvrsn=f22b56d5_0 (Superior Court Judge Stephen T. Bale ruled in favour of the government on November 30, 2020).

28   Ibid.

29   Interview with Luis Segura, August 21, 2019.

30   Los Poetas, wearelospoetas.com

31   Interview, February 2, 2020.

32   Interview with Tracey Mechefske, March 1, 2020.

33   Roderick Benns, "Sit-in at MPP's Office to Renew Tomorrow Morning after no Word on Apology," *Lindsay Advocate*, March 25, 2019, lindsayadvocate.ca/sit-in-at-mpps-office-to-renew-tomorrow-morning-after-no-word-on-apology/

34   Ibid.

35   Roderick Benns, "'Demonstrate that You Truly Have the Concerns of Your Constituents at Heart,'"

Lindsay Advocate, March 27, 2019, lindsayadvocate.ca/
demonstrate-that-you-truly-have-the-concerns-of-your-constituents-at-heart/

36   Material from Lindsay rally recorded by Jamie Swift, August 7, 2018.

CHAPTER 5. HAMILTON I:
THE FREEDOM TO LIVE WITH SOME DIGNITY

1   Interview, July 31, 2018.

2   Steve Buist, "Code Red: Ten Years Later," *Hamilton Spectator*, March 23, 2019.

3   Mowat Centre, "How Ontario Lost 300,000 Manufacturing Jobs (and Why Most Aren't Coming Back)," July 29, 2014, munkschool.utoronto.ca/ mowatcentre/how-ontario-lost-300000-manufacturing-jobs/

4   Quotes from interview, July 30, 2018.

5   Matthew Keegan, "Benefit or Burden? The Cities Trying out Universal Basic Income," *Guardian* (U.K.), June 27, 2018, theguardian.com/cities/2018/ jun/27/benefit-or-burden-the-cities-trying-out-universal-basic-income

6   Interview, July 31, 2018.

7   Valerie Tarasuk, Andrée-Anne Fafard St-Germain, and Rachel Loopstra, "The Relationship Between Food Banks and Food Insecurity: Insights from Canada," *Voluntas* 31 (2020): 841–52, https://doi.org/10.1007/ s11266-019-00092-w).

8   Valerie Tarasuk and Andy Mitchell, *Household Food Insecurity in Canada, 2017–2018* (Toronto: Research to Identify Policy Options to Reduce Food Insecurity [PROOF], 2020), proof.utoronto.ca/

9   Valerie Tarasuk, Joyce Cheng, Claire de Oliveira, Naomi Dachner, Craig Gundersen, and Paul Kurdyak, "Association Between Household Food Insecurity and Annual Health Care Costs," *CMAJ: Canadian Medical Association Journal* 187, no. 14 (2015): E429–36, https://doi.org/10.1503/ cmaj.150234

10 *Everyone Has a Home . . . Home is the Foundation: Hamilton's Housing and Homelessness Action Plan Summary*, October 2013, sprc.hamilton.on.ca/ wp-content/uploads/2014/04/Hamilton-Housing-and-Homelessness-Action-Plan-Summary.pdf; Hamilton, "Point in Time Connection," hamilton. ca/social-services/housing/point-in-time-connection

11 Roderick Benns, "Food Bank Use Swells after Cancellation of Basic Income; Donations Needed," *Lindsay Advocate*, May 1, 2019, lindsayadvocate.ca/ food-bank-use-swells-after-cancellation-of-basic-income-donations-needed

12 Ibid.

13   Daily Bread Food Bank, *Who's Hungry: 2017 Profile of Hunger in Toronto*, dailybread.ca/wp-content/uploads/2018/03/Whos-Hungry-2017-Report.pdf

14   Elaine Power, "Food Banks," in *Sage Encyclopedia of Food Issues*, ed. Ken Albala, 553–59 (Thousand Oaks, CA: Sage, 2015).

15   Valerie Tarasuk, *CanCOVID Speaker Series: Food Insecurity* (video), youtube. com/watch?v=8b2kanuOaK0&feature=youtu.be

16   Osobe Waberi, "Toronto-Based Food Bank Sees Surge in Clients amid Pandemic-Related Food Insecurity," *Global News*, July 29, 2020, globalnews. ca/news/7230807/toronto-food-bank-surge-coronavirus/

17   Tarasuk and Mitchell, A *Household Food Insecurity in Canada, 2017–2018*.

18   Lynn McIntyre, Daniel J. Dutton, Cynthia Kwok, and J. C. Herbert Emery, "Reduction of Food Insecurity among Low-Income Canadian Seniors as a Likely Impact of a Guaranteed Annual Income," *Canadian Public Policy* 42, no. 3 (2016): 274–86, https://doi.org/10.3138/cpp.2015-069

19   Fei Men, Craig Gundersen, Marcelo L. Urquia, and Valerie Tarasuk, "Association Between Household Food Insecurity and Mortality in Canada: A Population-Based Retrospective Cohort Study," *CMAJ: Canadian Medical Association Journal* 192, no. 3 (2020): E53–E60, https://doi.org/10.1503/cmaj.190385

20   Fei Men, Craig Gundersen, Marcelo L. Urquia, and Valerie Tarasuk, "Food Insecurity is Associated with Higher Health Care Use and Costs among Canadian Adults," *Health Affairs* 39, no. 8 (August 2020), 1377–85.

21   "The Pepso Story," Preface to Stephanie Procyk, Wayne Lewchuk, and John Shields, eds., *Precarious Employment: Causes, Consequences and Remedies* (Halifax and Winnipeg: Fernwood, 2017), viii–ix; Wayne Lewchuk and Stephanie Procyk, "Workers' Precarity: What to Do About It?" in *Precarious Employment*, ed. Procyk et al., 155.

22   PEPSO (Poverty and Employment Precarity in Southern Ontario), *Getting Left Behind: Who Gained and who Didn't in an Improving Labour Market* (June 2018), 8.

23   Wayne Lewchuk, Stephanie Procyk, and John Shields, "Origins of Precarity: Families and Communities in Crisis," in *Precarious Employment*, ed. Procyk et al., 3–9.

24   Fred Block and Margaret Somers, *The Power of Market Fundamentalism: Karl Polanyi's Critique* (Cambridge, MA: Harvard University Press, 2014), 3.

25   "Get Used to the 'Job Churn' of Short-Term Employment and Career Changes, Bill Morneau Says," *National Post*, October 22, 2016, nationalpost. com/news/canada/get-used-to-the-job-churn-of-short-term-employment-and-career-changes-bill-morneau-says

26   Lewchuk and Procyk, "Workers' Precarity," 158.

27   goodshepherdcentres.ca/affordable-supportive-housing

28   Paul Weinberg, "Is This the End or the Rebirth for Stelco's Remaining
      Steelworkers?", *CCPA Monitor*, January 1, 2016; Bruce Livesey and Nicole
      Mercury, "Who Killed Stelco?", *Globe and Mail*, September 29, 2016.

29   Social Planning and Research Council of Hamilton, *Hamilton's Rental
      Landscape: Understanding the Rental Housing Crisis and Solutions to End It*,
      sprc.hamilton.on.ca/wp-content/uploads/2019/11/SPRC-Hamilton-Rental-
      Landsape-Intro.pdf

30   101lockecondos.com/

31   Molly Hayes, "Weekend Vandalism in Hamilton was Anti-Gentrification Act,
      Blogger Writes," *Globe and Mail*, March 6, 2018.

32   Ibid.

33   Stephen Smith, "Who is Behind the Anti-Gentrification Violence in Saint-
      Henri?", *CBC News*, July 30, 2017.

34   Strata Hamilton, "101 Locke Condos," strata.ca/hamilton/101-locke-
      condos-101-locke-st-s

35   Zygmunt Bauman, *Work, Consumerism, and the New Poor* (Buckingham, UK:
      Open University Press, 1998).

CHAPTER 6. HAMILTON II: THINKING FURTHER DOWN THE ROAD

1   Quotes from interview, July 30, 2018.

2   Campaign 2000: End Child & Family Poverty, *2020: Setting the Stage for
     a Poverty-Free Canada*, campaign2000.ca/wp-content/uploads/2020/01/
     campaign-2000-report-setting-the-stage-for-a-poverty-free-canada-updated-
     january-24-2020.pdf

3   Statistics Canada, *Census in Brief: Children Living in Low-Income
     Households*, September 13, 2017, www12.statcan.gc.ca/census-
     recensement/2016/as-sa/98-200-x/2016012/98-200-x2016012-eng.cfm;
     Canadian Centre for Economic Analysis, *Economic Contribution of the
     Canada Child Benefit: A Basic Income Guarantee for Canadian Families
     with Children* (Toronto: Author, 2019), https://assets.website-files.
     com/5f07c00c5fce40c46b92df3d/5f15bedac06f696f39c915ab_Economic
     Contribution of the Canada Child Benefit - Final - 20190916.pdf

4   Antonella Forlino and Joan C. Marini, "Osteogenesis Imprefecta,"
     The Lancet 387 (April 16, 2016): 1657–71, https://doi.org/10.1016/
     S0140-6736(15)00728-X

5   Katie Cruz, "A Feminist Case for Basic Income: An Interview with Kathi Weeks,"

Canadian Dimension, August 16, 2016, canadiandimension.com/articles/
view/a-feminist-case-for-basic-income-an-interview-with-kathi-weeks

6   hamiltonpoverty.ca/preview/speakers-bureau/

7   Carmela Fragomeni, "Speak Now: This is What it's Like Living in Poverty,"
     Hamilton Spectator, April 2, 2014.

8   Interview, February 9, 2020.

9   Sendhil Mullainathan and Eldar Shafir, *Scarcity: The New Science of Having
     Less and How it Defines Our Lives* (New York: Henry Holt, 2013), 107.

10   VanCity, *Short-Term Gain, Long-Term Pain: Examining the Growing Payday
     Loan Industry in B.C.,* 2016, cited in Social Planning and Research Council
     of Hamilton, *Money for Nothing, Debt for Free,* 2016, sprc.hamilton.on.ca/
     wp-content/uploads/2016/02/MoneyForNothingPaydayLoanReport_2015.pdf

11   Social Planning and Research Council of Hamilton, *Money for Nothing.*

12   Carmela Fragomeni, "Hamilton Moves to Control Payday Loan Agencies,"
     Hamilton Spectator, February 17, 2016.

13   John Mills, presentation to North American Basic Income Guarantee
     congress, Winnipeg, May 13, 2016.

14   Interview, April 16, 2019.

15   realestate.mitula.ca/houses-upper-paradise-hamilton-ontario

16   rentitornot.com/apartment/8110/125-Wellington-St-N-Hamilton-Ontario

17   Steve Buist, "Worlds Apart," *Hamilton Spectator,* April 10, 2010; also April 12,
     2010; October 28, 2013; November 26, 2011.

18   Canadian Labour Congress, "Why Canada's Unions are Highlighting
     Environmental Racism during Black History Month," February 6, 2019,
     canadianlabour.ca/why-canadas-unions-are-highlighting-environmental-
     racism-during-black-history-month/

19   Friedrich Engels, *Condition of the Working Class in England,* marxists.org/
     archive/marx/works/download/pdf/condition-working-class-england.
     pdf: "The Report on the Sanitary Condition of the Working-Class contains
     information which attests the same fact. In Liverpool, in 1840, the average
     longevity of the upper classes, gentry, professional men, etc., was thirty-five
     years; that of the business men and better-placed handicraftsmen, twenty-
     two years; and that of the operatives, day-labourers, and serviceable class in
     general, but fifteen years."

20   Dr. Danielle Martin, "The One Thing that Could Improve the Health of
     All Canadians," *Chatelaine,* December 14, 2016, chatelaine.com/health/
     poverty-health-basic-income/

21   World Health Organization Commission on the Social Determinants of
     Health, *Closing the Gap in a Generation: Health Equity through Action on the
     Social Determinants of Health* (Geneva: World Health Organization, 2008).

22   Simon Szreter, "Rethinking McKeown: The Relationship Between Public Health and Social Change," *American Journal of Public Health* 92, no. 5 (May 2002): 722–25.

23   Trevor Hancock, "Lalonde and Beyond: Looking Back at 'A New Perspective on the Health of Canadians,'" *Health Promotion International*, 1, no. 1 (May 1986): 93–100, https://doi.org/10.1093/heapro/1.1.93

24   Interview, May 28, 2019.

25   www.easterseals.org/category/ambassadors/

26   Personal communication, February 9, 2020.

27   Ibid.

28   Mullainathan and Shafir, *Scarcity*, cited in Leah Hamilton and James P. Mulvale, "'Human Again': The (Unrealized) Promise of Basic Income in Ontario," *Journal of Poverty* 23, no. 7 (2019), https://doi.org/10.1080/1087554 9.2019.1616242

29   Mullainathan and Shafir, *Scarcity*, 52, 60, 65–66.

30   Annie Lowery, *Give People Money: How a Universal Basic Income Would End Poverty, Revolutionize Work and Remake the World* (New York: Crown, 2018), 85.

CHAPTER 7. HAMILTON III: NEW CHOICES

1   sacred-economics.com/sacred-economics-introduction/

2   Interview, May 27, 2019.

3   James Collura, "My Experience with Ontario's Basic Income Pilot," *Raise the Hammer*, April 9, 2019.

4   Government of Canada, *Opioid- and Stimulant-related Harms in Canada* (December 2020), health-infobase.canada.ca/substance-related-harms/ opioids-stimulants/

5   Dr. Elizabeth Richardson, "We Need a Change: Tackling Poverty and Focusing on Prevention," *Hamilton Spectator*, February 28, 2019.

6   blackstone.com

7   United Nations Human Rights, Office of the High Commissioner, *Financialization of Housing*, ohchr.org/EN/Issues/Housing/Pages/ FinancializationHousing.aspx

8   *Out of Control: Ontario's Acute Rental Crisis: Lessons from Hamilton and Quebec City*, sprc.hamilton.on.ca/wp-content/uploads/2018/05/SPRC-Out-of-Control-rental-housing-report-June-2018-1.pdf

9   Quoted in Collura, "My Experience."

10   zeefloat.com

11 Roderick Benns, "Hamilton Man Uses Basic Income Floor to Stay Active in Community," *Lindsay Advocate*, May 15, 2018, lindsayadvocate.ca/hamilton-man-uses-basic-income-floor-to-stay-active-in-community/

12 Brian Lilley, "You'll be Footing the Bill for Freeloaders with Guaranteed Annual Income," *Toronto Sun*, December 21, 2018.

13 Mariana Valverde, "As Public Postsecondary Funding Stagnates, the University of Toronto Explores 'Alternative Funding Sources,'" *Academic Matters*, Fall 2019, academicmatters.ca/the-university-of-toronto-explores-alternative-funding-sources/

14 Lilley, "You'll be Footing the Bill."

15 Cited in Craig Heron, *Lunch-Bucket Lives: Remaking the Workers' City* (Toronto: Between the Lines, 2015), 185–87.

16 Ibid., 185, 192.

17 Quoted in Dennis Guest, *The Emergence of Social Security in Canada*, 3rd ed. (Vancouver: University of British Columbia Press, 1999), 57.

18 *GLBI—Day of Action* (video), youtube.com/watch?v=fKyGiReG3yU

19 Margaret Little, *No Car, No Radio, No Liquor Permit: The Moral Regulation of Single Mothers in Ontario, 1920–1997* (Toronto: Oxford University Press, 1998); Craig Heron, *Booze: A Distilled History* (Toronto: Between the Lines, 2003), 280.

20 Philippe Van Parijs and Yannick Vanderborght, *Basic Income: A Radical Proposal for a Free Society and a Sane Economy* (Cambridge, MA: Harvard University Press, 2017), 104–05.

21 Ibid., 101, 107, 105.

22 Interview, May 27, 2019.

23 George Orwell, *Coming Up For Air* (London: Folio Society, 2001), 132.

24 Collura, "My Experience."

25 David Graeber, *Bullshit Jobs: A Theory* (New York: Simon & Shuster, 2018), 14.

26 Ibid, 8.

27 Ibid., 240, 281.

28 Daniel Silver, Gail Lord, and Mark S. Fox, "Canada's Arts Sector Needs Transformative Action Similar to Works Progress Administration," *Globe and Mail*, May 25, 2020, theglobeandmail.com/arts/article-canadas-arts-sector-needs-transformative-action-similar-to-works/

29 Milton Friedman, *Capitalism and Freedom* (Chicago: University of Chicago Press, 1982), 7.

30 John Lanchester, "Good New Idea," *London Review of Books*, July 18, 2019.

31 "Transcript: Greta Thunberg's Speech at the U.N. Climate Action

Summit," *NPR*, September 23, 2019, npr.org/2019/09/23/763452863/
transcript-greta-thunbergs-speech-at-the-u-n-climate-action-summit

32   2 Thessalonians 3:10 (New Revised Standard Version).

33   Rosa Luxemburg, "*Die Sozialisierung der Gesellschaft*," quoted in Van Parijs
and Vanderborght, *Basic Income*.

34   Richard Swift, "The Dead End of Wage Labour," *Canadian Dimension*,
September 16, 2016, canadiandimension.com/articles/view/the-dead-
end-of-wage-labour

35   World Bank, *Exploring Universal Basic Income: A Guide to Navigating
Concepts, Evidence, and Practices*, February 4, 2020, worldbank.org/en/
topic/socialprotection/publication/exploring-universal-basic-income-a-
guide-to-navigating-concepts-evidence-and-practices

36   Van Parijs and Vanderborght, *Basic Income*, 27.

37   Jim Stanford, *Work, Technology and Basic Income: Issues to Consider*, August
2018, d3n8a8pro7vhmx.cloudfront.net/theausinstitute/pages/2844/
attachments/original/1535041931/Basic_Income_Symposium_Stanford.pdf

38   Ken Neumann, "United Steelworkers Endorses Motion 46 Guaranteed
Livable Basic Income," September 9, 2020, usw.ca/news/media-centre/
articles/2020/body/USW-Endorsement-Motion-46-1.pdf

39   Interview, November 23, 2018.

40   Brendan Kennedy, "Reviving Basic Income? Canadian Chamber of
Commerce Urges Federal Government to Pick up Ontario's Cancelled Pilot
Project," *Toronto Star*, October 31, 2020, thestar.com/news/gta/2020/10/31/
reviving-basic-income-canadian-chamber-of-commerce-urges-federal-
government-to-pick-up-ontarios-cancelled-pilot-project.html

41   Juliet B. Schor, *The Overworked American: The Unexpected Decline of Leisure*
(New York: Basic Books, 1991), 120.

42   *The Canadian Economy at a Glance*, March 2019, investorsfriend.com/
canadian-GDP-canadian-imports-and-exports/

43   André Gorz, *Farewell to the Working Class: An Essay on Post-industrial
Socialism* (Boston: South End Press, 1982), 136.

44   "Editorial: A Commission on Climate Change," *The Lancet* 373, no.
9676 (May 16, 2009): 1659, thelancet.com/journals/lancet/article/
PIIS0140-6736(09)60922-3/fulltext

45   Julia Steinberger, "On Sacrifice," *Medium*, January 8, 2020, medium.com/@
JKSteinberger/on-sacrifice-1790b1311708

46   Naomi Klein, *This Changes Everything: Capitalism vs the Climate* (Toronto:
Knopf Canada, 2014), 461.

47   *Floyd Marinescu on UBI & Automation at 2020 Ontario Liberal Party
Convention*, youtube.com/watch?v=EhluKyWXyR4&feature=emb_logo

48   ceosforbasicincome.ca/signatories
49   Carl Benedikt Frey and Michael A. Osborne, *The Future of Employment: How Susceptible are Jobs to Computerisation*, September 17, 2013, oxfordmartin. ox.ac.uk/downloads/academic/The_Future_of_Employment.pdf
50   David Noble, *Forces of Production* (New York: Knopf, 1984), 353.
51   OECD, *The Future of Work: OECD Employment Outlook 2019: Highlights*, oecd.org/employment/Employment-Outlook-2019-Highlight-EN.pdf; World Bank, *Exploring Universal Basic Income.*
52   Floyd Marinescu, *Basic Income and the New Golden Age of Capitalism*, TEDxWindsor, ted.com/talks/floyd_marinescu_basic_income_and_the_new_golden_age_of_capitalism/transcript?language=en
53   The song was written by David Allan Coe.
54   Mohammad Ferdosi, Tom McDowell, Wayne Lewchuk, and Stephanie Ross, *Southern Ontario's Basic Income Experience* (Hamilton, ON: McMaster University School of Labour Studies, Hamilton Roundtable for Poverty Reduction, and Hamilton Community Foundation, March 2020), labourstudies.mcmaster.ca/documents/southern-ontarios-basic-income-experience.pdf
55   Collura on Tamarack webinar "Basic Income and Youth," tamarackcommunity.ca/library/basic-income-youth

CHAPTER 8. A PROVOCATION TO FREEDOM

1   Queen's University, *Building Back Better: "Rethinking Social Protection and the Care Economy"* (video), September 8, 2020, youtube.com/watch?v=z_NpHv4RrzY&list=PL57JJtmhwgXnmmYI4668x5RoZNKCLZJ3S&index=5
2   United Nations, *Policy Brief: The Impact of COVID-19 on Women*, April 9, 2020, un.org/sexualviolenceinconflict/wp-content/uploads/2020/06/report/policy-brief-the-impact-of-covid-19-on-women/policy-brief-the-impact-of-covid-19-on-women-en-1.pdf
3   Queen's University, *Building Back Better.*
4   Melissa Moyser and Amanda Burlock, *Time Use: Total Work Burden, Unpaid Work, and Leisure*, cat. no. 89-503-X (Ottawa: Statistics Canada, July 30, 2018), www150.statcan.gc.ca/n1/pub/89-503-x/2015001/article/54931-eng.htm
5   Queen's University, *Building Back Better.*
6   *How Much is a Mother Really Worth?*, salary.com/articles/mother-salary/
7   Brittany Lambert and Kate McInturff, *Making Women Count: The Unequal*

Economics of Women's Work (Ottawa: Canadian Centre for Policy Alternatives and Oxfam Canada, 2016), policyalternatives.ca/sites/default/files/uploads/publications/National Office/2016/03/Making_Women_Count2016.pdf

8   Quoted in Kathi Weeks, *The Problem with Work: Marxism, Antiwork Politics and Postwork Imaginaries* (Durham, NC: Duke University Press, 2011), 143.

9   Louise Toupin, Pluto Press blog, plutobooks.com/blog/wages-housework-campaign-history/

10   Weeks, *Problem with Work,* 145, 147.

11   Sarah Jaffe, "The Factory in the Family: The Radical Vision of Wages for Housework," *The Nation*, March 14, 2018, thenation.com/article/archive/wages-for-houseworks-radical-vision/

12   Kim Pate, Remarks at online Basic Income rally, September 16, 2020.

13   thebusinesscouncil.ca/news/goldy-hyders-statement-on-new-income-support-for-workers/; "'Best Social Program is a Job,' Minister Hopes to Duplicate Windsor Job Centre Service Model," *CBC News*, January 24, 2019, cbc.ca/news/canada/windsor/macleod-uhc-windsor-1.4992041

14   Richard Swift, "The Dead End of Wage Labour," *Canadian Dimension*, September 16, 2016, canadiandimension.com/articles/view/the-dead-end-of-wage-labour

15   Weeks, *Problem with Work,* p.137.

16   Personal communication, September 12, 2020.

17   Evelyn Forget, *Basic Income for Canadians* (Toronto: Lorimer, 2018), 186–87.

INDEX

ABOUT THE AUTHORS

Jamie Swift is the author of a dozen books, including *The Vimy Trap: Or, How We Learned to Stop Worrying and Love the Great War,* with Ian McKay, which was a finalist for the Shaughnessy Cohen Prize for Political Writing and the Canadian Historical Association prize for best work of history. He has lectured at Queen's University's Smith School of Business, produced documentaries for CBC Radio's IDEAS, held the Michener Fellowship for Public Service Journalism, and written widely for newspapers and magazines. In 1995 he joined a weekly social justice vigil at Kingston City Hall, standing for twenty years in solidarity with victims of poor-bashing government. Which led to his interest in Basic Income.

Elaine Power is a professor in the School of Kinesiology & Health Studies and Head of the Department of Gender Studies at Queen's University. She has conducted food insecurity research for almost thirty years and taught the first undergraduate course in the social determinants of health at Queen's. She is a founding member of the Kingston Action Group for a Basic Income Guarantee.